Society: Institutions and Activity

SOCIETY
INSTITUTIONS AND ACTIVITY

Leon Mayhew
University of California, Davis

SCOTT, FORESMAN INTRODUCTION TO MODERN SOCIETY SERIES

Albert J. Reiss, Jr.

Harold L. Wilensky

Editors

Scott, Foresman and Company

Glenview, Illinois   London

Library of Congress Catalog Number: 73-133408

Copyright © 1971 by Scott, Foresman and Company, Glenview
    Illinois 60025.
Philippines Copyright 1971 by Scott, Foresman and Company.
All Rights Reserved.
Printed in the United States of America.

Regional Offices of Scott, Foresman are located in Dallas, Oak-
    land, N.J., Palo Alto, and Tucker, Ga.

"There is no people and no state which is not a part of another society, more or less unlimited, which embraces all the peoples and all the states with which the first comes in contact, either directly or indirectly; there is no national life which is not dominated by a collective life of an international nature. In proportion as we advance in history, these international groups acquire a greater importance and extent."

Emile Durkheim

Elementary Forms of the Religious Life

Preface

This short study represents an expansion of an earlier article. The earlier work, entitled "Society," appeared in the *International Enclyclopedia of the Social Sciences*. It is a short piece, condensed to the point of being rather cryptic. In the present longer format I have been provided an opportunity to expand the central themes of "Society" in more concrete and understandable detail and to deal with several other time honored themes in macrosociology.

Throughout the work my intention has been to keep one thought foremost in the mind of both author and reader: most discussions of the concept of "Society" treat society as a context for the study of less macroscopic subjects rather than as an object in its own right. This is one of the reasons for the extraordinarily ideological character of such discussions. Society is the larger social context which justifies our ideals and programs, either by its constraints or by its inexorable movements. My attempt has been to interpret thought about society in this light. My second task has been to attempt to reformulate a concept of society as object. As an object society becomes rather slippery. The first problem is to define the boundaries of a society and this task proves formidable. Fortunately, the obstacles to conceptualization of the boundaries of society constitute important empirical problems in their own right for it is the overlapping character of the boundaries of our social systems that explains much of the tensions and dynamics of social life.

In any endeavor as broad ranging as this, one must rely heavily on the suggestions and ideas of others. In this case I am especially grateful to my former colleagues at the University of Michigan, most notably Otis Dudley Duncan, Albert J. Reiss, Jr., Beverly Duncan, Thomas Smith, Gayl Ness, Paul Siegel, and Guy E. Swanson. Of course they may not recognize, let alone accept, the forms their contributions have come to assume.

Foreword

Modern societies are complex territorial organizations whose populations are integrated by economic, legal, military, and political institutions and by the media of mass communication. Sociology reflects this complexity. It is often packaged in separate sociologies such as those of work, religion, minorities, politics, and the community.

By looking at modernization as a process and urban-industrial ("modern" "affluent") society as a distinctive social system, this series hopes to avoid fragmentation into separate sociologies at the same time that it provides intensive treatment of major institutional areas (economy, polity, kinship), units of social organization (society, community, complex organization, family), and of processes that cut across all institutional areas (social differentiation and stratification, social control, demographic and technological change). The series is "relevant" in that all authors address themselves to a single question: "What is modern about modern society?" It is comparative in that all authors know that we cannot answer that question unless we compare the different shapes of modern and pre-modern societies and of contemporary nations, totalitarian and pluralist, "capitalist" and "socialist." Our abiding concern is the macroscopic, comparative analysis of social organization, especially its changing social structure.

Each book in this series can stand alone for specialized courses; each can also be used in combination with others as a flexible substitute for conventional textbooks.

Society: Institutions and Activities starts from the premise that most sociological discussion merely assumes a larger society as a context for the study of less macroscopic phenomena. This is why such discussion is so often heavily laden with ideology. Society as context is taken to be justification for all our ideals and programs, either because of its constraints or because of its inexorable movements. Looking at society as an object in its own right, rather than a context for something less global, is a very difficult undertaking. Not the least of the difficulties is encountered in the first problem the analyst encounters. Where are the boundaries of a society? Mayhew attempts to turn this obstacle into an opportunity for analysis.

He argues that men participate in a number of differentiated varieties of organized social systems, some solidary, some cultural, some political, and others economic. These systems have variable and overlapping boundaries. Moreover, men participate in systems of stratification, networks of organizations and associations, morphological structures, and communication networks that crosscut the more differentiated systems of society. The resulting networks of overlapping and crosscutting links are the roots of the tensions and dynamics of society, roots that are easily overlooked in any theory that would define society as a social system with clear external boundaries and well isolated internal subsystems.

In explicating this approach Mayhew first treats morphological, solidary, economic, political, and cultural systems separately and then concentrates on the total complex, emphazing the multiplicity of overlapping patterned ties that define the fabric of society.

Albert J. Reiss, Jr.
Harold L. Wilensky

CONTENTS

Society: Institutions and Activity

1

Introduction:
The Concept of Society

HISTORY OF THE CONCEPT

If a newcomer to the study of sociology were to begin his acquaintance by casually noting the titles of standard texts in the field, he would soon conclude that one principle object of sociological study is something called "society." After diligent study of these works, our neophyte would be surprised to discover that occasionally more attention is given to the concept of society in the book titles than in the materials between their covers. Even if our scholar moved on to the study of the current research and writing by professional sociologists, he might be hard-pressed if he were asked by another fledgling student to define "society."

Our student will have seen the word "society" used in two rather loose ways. First, it is used as a convenient shorthand label for the fabric of social life in general. Used this way, the things that fascinate sociologists — social relations, social networks, the interdependencies between persons, groups, or institutions — are all loosely designated "society."

The second major use of the term is to label the larger social context of some particular social phenomenon. Thus, a student of race relations may insist that interracial behavior can only be understood against the background of the "larger society" in which it occurs. By implication, we are meant to understand that society is an encompassing network of social relationships and that interracial behavior is only a part of this larger web. Since interracial behavior is a part of a larger whole and is presumably affected by its inclusion in the whole, the social analyst must always be aware of the larger social context of his study materials. Yet even those who readily insist on the significance of the larger social context often fail to provide any analytic conception of the larger inclusive unit so casually termed a "society."

The focus of the present book is not on society as *context* but on society as *object*. We seek to define and depict societies as units of study and to outline their organization and operation.

In recent years, the study of society as object has been heavily in debt to the concept of a "social system." Those who have sought to deal directly and analytically with the concept of society have viewed society as a special sort of social system, characterized by a relatively high degree of independence and self-containment. Roughly speaking, a social system is a highly interdependent set of social roles, groups, and institutions, held together by subtle processes of adjustment, and stabilized by common ideas of meaning and value among its members.

This perspective deserves great respect from sociologists, for it has increased our appreciation of the complex interdependence between the varied institutions of society. Further, the "social-system" approach, as used by some talented analysts, has increased our sensitivity to the subtle functions and consequences of intellectual ideas in social life. At the same time, accounts of society as a social system often seem strangely abstracted from the historic role of such crucial and obvious forces as war, domestic disruption, international trade, and the movements of peoples. Such realistic matters are not ignored in social-system theory, but neither are they incorporated into its basic framework. Rather, they are treated historically, on an *ad hoc* basis, as explanations of particular events or institutions.[1]

This book presents a different concept of society, a concept designed to incorporate some of the more important ideas of the theory of the social system, and yet retain a flexible theoretical perspective on the realistic movements of human history.

---

[1] There are notable exceptions, particularly Neil Smelser, *Theory of Collective Behavior* (New York: The Free Press, 1963).

The Development of the Concept of Society: Constraint and Ideology

The concept of society developed directly from attempts to specify the character of encompassing social relations. From the very beginning of the development of the concept to the present day, social theorists have found in "society" a convenient foundation for relating their specific problems to a larger context. For example, a student of bureaucracy may seek to show that bureaucracies are embedded in larger networks of social relations that influence the emergence of a bureaucracy and the forms it assumes, and which constrain purposive attempts to shape bureaucratic development.

If society is conceived as a set of external and constraining social forces, it is natural that the concept should be put to ideological use. He who would assert that some social institution ought to change or ought to be protected from change may point to the external and constraining forces of the larger society and claim to find in such forces both an evaluative standard and realistic justification for that standard. Ancient and medieval social thought often used this device, but the emergence of modern analytical concepts of society has been especially strongly tied to the development of political ideologies of this sociological form.

The argument that society is a source of ethical standards can be used by the adherents of a variety of political persuasions. The flexibility, indeed ambiguity, of the argument is manifest in the diverse interpretations that can be given to the ideas of some of those who have used it. For example, Rousseau's *Social Contract*, one of the key works in this sociological tradition of political thought, has been regarded as a fountainhead of both democratic and totalitarian ideology. In arguing for the absolute sovereignty of the "general will," and in claiming that this general will is specifically collective, not the mere sum of the interests of individuals, Rousseau insisted upon social criteria for political values. But who is the agent of the general will and what are its directives? In the variety of answers to these questions lies the diversity of sociologically grounded political theories.

The Concept of Society in the Eighteenth and Nineteenth Centuries

As the philosophers of the Enlightenment sought secular foundations for the critical analysis of existing political institu-

tions, they came to posit the existence of a social order outside of
the state. The social contract theory was one of the first battle-
grounds of the theory of society. The conservative philosopher
Hobbes had sought to establish the inseparable unity of the social
contract, the law of nature, and civil society.[2] Such a conception fails to give society any separate analytical independence;
order and the state are identical. In opposition, Locke distinguished a layer of natural order outside of and prior to the
state.[3] The state is a mere utilitarian device, created by the social
contract and intended to implement and stabilize the natural
order. Since it is merely a utilitarian device, the state is subject
to criticism, indeed revolution, if it fails in its socially derived
purposes. Thus, in the process of creating foundations for liberal
thought, Western thinkers came to assert the analytical separate-
ness of society.

The foundations were not very firm. Locke and the philosophers of the Enlightenment failed to give a satisfactory account
of the assumed larger society beyond the civil society. To be
sure, the state is a dependent sector of a larger social order. But
what is the source of that order? Committed as they were to faith
in reason and in the method of reason, the Enlightened philosophers attempted to derive social order from the faculty of reason
in the individual. As Parsons has shown, Locke and his followers were unable to explain how separate, isolated individuals
could construct a social order from their individual reason and
were forced to introduce arbitrary metaphysical concepts such as
"the natural identity of interests," "natural rights," or "the spirit
of sociability."[4]

In the latter part of the eighteenth century, and especially in
the aftermath of the French Revolution, many social theorists
became disillusioned with individual reason. A conservative
theory of society developed around the idea of the unity of the
integrated whole. Society came to be viewed as an organic
growth, embodying the practical and profound wisdom of con-
vention and tradition. Again, we see the concept of society as a
larger whole which contains within it the standards by which

---

[2] Thomas Hobbes, *Leviathan, or the Matter, Form, and Power of a Commonwealth, Eccle-
siastical and Civil* (London: Crooke, 1651).

[3] John Locke, *Two Treatises of Government* (London: Churchill, 1690). See the second trea-
tise.

[4] Talcott Parsons, *The Structure of Social Action* (New York: McGraw-Hill Book Company,
1937).

particular phenomena are to be judged, but in this instance the stress on natural growth, complex interdependence, and organic unity effectively refutes demands for arbitrary or rapid changes in social institutions.

The organismic conception sharpened the concept (already implicit in Enlightened philosophy) of society as a set of interdependent functions. At the same time, a new element, cultural tradition, was recognized as a necessary part of a society. In the early nineteenth century, Comte, as a synthesizer of warring traditions, incorporated into his sociological system elements of both liberal and organismic thought.[5] He accepted the liberal idea that there is a natural level of order arising from man's natural economic interdependence, and he saw the state as a dependent sector of a larger social order. At the same time, he refused to believe that society derives from a mere concurrence of interests. Drawing upon the conservative tradition, Comte insisted that the specifically collective factor in society is consensus, that is, a system of common opinions about man and society. Armed with this assumption, Comte advocated a vast program of social reconstruction based upon his hope for universal acceptance of scientific sociology as the new ultimate foundation for the social order. Again, the ideological use of the concept of society is apparent, but in Comte's thought the concept did undergo some elaboration. For Comte, bare consensus is not a sufficient condition for organized collective life; consensus must be embodied in a complex of religious, familial, educational, and political institutions which symbolizes, teaches, enforces, and implements moral ideas and rules.

The belief that society is an institutional order that embodies a fundamental set of cultural ideas was also stressed in Idealism. Especially prominent in nineteenth-century German thought, idealism stresses the cultural distinctiveness of each society. According to Hegel, an important figure in the Idealist tradition, every society or civilization reflects a peculiar *Geist*, or spirit, manifest in its distinctive traditions and institutions as they progressively unfold in history. For the Idealist Hegel, as well as for Marx, his materialist successor, society undergoes continuous transformation according to an imminent and inexorable logic of development.[6] Again, the ideological implications

[5] Auguste Comte, The Positive Philosophy of Auguste Comte, trans. and condensed Harriet Martineau (London: Chapman, 1868).
[6] Georg W. F. Hegel, Philosophy of History, trans. J. Sibree (New York: Collier, 1861).

are clear; human endeavor is to be judged by its correspondence to the inner forces of ever-changing society.

Marx insisted that these forces are entirely material.[7] A *Geist* or spirit cannot be an explanation of the collective; it is a mere term of art used by an analyst to summarize the main features of a given society.[8] The real foundations of the collective lie in the fact that men must always organize their labor if they are to wrest a living from nature. The economic structures that men develop as they enter into relations of production are the foundation of society. Economic structures are variable, but they generally involve two crucial phenomena—the division of men into classes and the exploitation of one class by another. Stratification and exploitation make the continuing stability of economic structures precarious, and, for this reason, whole complexes of compulsive apparatus develop to support the economic order. The state, law, religion, and ideology function to bring temporary stability into inherently unstable situations. Since economic structure is more basic, it can be termed the substructure of society, and the supporting institutions may be termed the superstructure; they are derivative in the sense that they are responses to the problems of economic relations. In the theory of substructure and superstructure, we see one of the first and most comprehensive theories of society as an institutional order.

The Marxian concept of society is an example of a classic "conflict theory."[9] The premise of conflict theory is that men, because they are organisms, must compete for access to the resources of life. The struggle for existence is not between isolated individuals; it is a struggle between groups—families, bands, classes, nations, or races. As conflict between groups becomes stabilized, organized, and regulated, we may speak of the emergence of a structured society. Society is a device for relating populations of organisms to an environment. By adopting what we may broadly term an *ecological* perspective, social analysts were able to use the concept of society to relate social life to natural forces. In consequence, they were able to develop a more naturalistic account of society than had been produced by either Enlightened or Romantic philosophers.

---

[7] Karl Marx, *Manifesto of the Communists* (New York: Schaerr and Frantz, 1883), and *Capital*, two vols., trans. E. and C. Paul (London: Dent, 1930).

[8] Karl Marx and Friedrich Engels, *The German Ideology* (New York: International Publishers, 1931), pp. 42–43.

[9] Don Martindale, *The Nature and Types of Sociological Theory* (Boston: Houghton Mifflin Company, 1960), Part 3.

The ecological perspective does not necessarily renounce interest in cultural and normative phenomena. Custom, mores, conventions, laws, and institutions are viewed as emergent phenomena, serving to organize and regulate competition and conflict. The perspective remains naturalistic in insisting that normative complexes develop gradually and naturally as a response to the environment and to the problem of obtaining the resources of life. They do not emanate from cultural spirits, nor are they created *de novo* from a social contract.

Conflict theory has been put to a variety of ideological uses. In some forms, it becomes a racial or nationalistic ideology, as in the pseudo-Darwinian appeals to racial purity of Arthur de Gobineau and H. S. Chamberlain. On the other hand, it was used in the post-Darwinian era in an attempt to rework classic liberal doctrine into a naturalistic mold.[10] According to evolutionary versions of conflict theory, the course of social development is best described as a movement toward the development of larger, more inclusive, and more complex societies. Processes of consolidation, conquest, and incorporation increase the scale of human society; in consequence, relations with other societies become more stable and regulated. The basic problem of day-to-day existence ceases to have overriding importance. Consequently, internal development and elaboration becomes the route to progress; social organization can be founded on free discussion, free exchange, and the pursuit of individual interests. The stability provided by custom and military organization is no longer adaptive because of its inflexibility; only a looser organization, an organization founded on individual rationality and freedom, can improve the adaptation of society to the environment by unleashing the forces of creativity and innovation. The utilitarian society that eighteenth-century liberals contemplated became for the evolutionary theorist not a mere political ideal but the actual culmination of the processes of natural evolution. According to this theory, rational men should not attempt to interfere with the benign logic of societal development.

Not all of the social analysts of the late nineteenth century could view the emergence of the utilitarian society with equanimity. The breakdown of old forms of organization seemed to entail the loss of what had once provided society with integra-

---

[10] See Walter Bagehot, *Physics and Politics* (New York: Alfred A. Knopf, Inc., 1948); Herbert Spencer, *Social Statics* (New York: D. Appleton and Co., 1864); Spencer, *Principles of Sociology* (New York: D. Appleton and Company, 1899), Vol. 2.

tion, coherence, and meaning. The utilitarian society, founded upon the Industrial Revolution, the capitalist system, and the market mentality, fails to provide for either an ethical standard outside of the individual or a viable source of social cohesion. Nevertheless, critic and apologist alike seemed to believe that an atomized, individualistic, and rationalistic world was emerging. Toennies,[11] who obviously worried that the old natural ties of communal feeling would be replaced by artificial ties of calculating self-interest, and Spencer, obviously elated by the same prospect, agree that modern society is a mere collection of wills.

As sociology came to be institutionalized as an academic discipline, more and more thinkers began to insist that society, including modern rational society, is not a collection of individual wills. Sociologists sought to establish the independence of their field from economics, political science, and psychology by treating society as a set of external and constraining forces, more inclusive than the economic order, outside the state, and more than the sum of its individual members. Emile Durkheim, the French sociologist, took the most unequivocal position on this issue. Attacking both Spencer and Toennies, he insisted that modern society, though it is founded on the division of labor rather than on direct participation in a group mind, is no less collective than more primitive groups.[12] He adopted the strategy of stressing the independent reality of such social facts as vital rates, currents of opinion, and established conventions.[13] Persons who are drawn together in a web of interdependency interact as moral beings. They create a body of what Durkheim called "collective representations" of the world and regulative rules, a body external to the utilitarian economic order and external to the actions of individuals, a body which requires explanation in its own right and in its own terms.

Other analysts of the era found other techniques for identifying the reality of the social. Thus, Georg Simmel recognized in the mutual influence which interacting persons have upon each other a specifically social level of reality.[14] Mutual influence

[11] Ferdinand Toennies, *Fundamental Concepts of Sociology*, trans. and supplemented by C. P. Loomis (New York: American Book Company, 1940).

[12] Emile Durkheim, *On the Division of Labor in Society*, trans. and ed. George Simpson (New York: The Macmillan Company, 1933).

[13] Emile Durkheim, *The Rules of the Sociological Method*, 8th ed., trans. Sarah Solovay and John H. Mueller (Glencoe, Ill.: The Free Press, 1950).

[14] Georg Simmel, *The Sociology of Georg Simmel*, trans. and ed. Kurt Wolff (Glencoe, Ill.: The Free Press, 1950).

comes to have coherent forms, and thus, as people interact, they create society. Even Max Weber, the great German sociologist, who insisted on relatively nominalistic definitions of collective entities, developed a perspective on the social order that gave to social processes a somewhat independent reality.[15] As persons orient themselves toward each other, social relationships form; complexes of social relationships comprise a social order. A social order is not a mere collection of wills or economic interests; it is ordered by administrative organization, shared orientations to systems of status, and shared beliefs in the legitimacy of the order.

In American academic circles, a social-psychological approach developed around the concept of symbolic interaction. Cooley,[16] Mead,[17] and others developed a novel conceptualization of society as a symbolically regulated process, and through this device produced an integrated treatment of society and the social person. The human being comes to acquire a social personality as he learns to communicate symbolically. As he learns to adopt the perspectives of others toward himself, he also learns to regulate symbolically his own activity, for he comes to define and evaluate himself and his activities in appropriate ways. It is by participating in the differentiated and interrelated roles and activities we call society that we develop our distinctively human capacities and identities; thus, "self" and "society" are intimately connected by such concepts as "role" and "symbol." Further, we may make the transition in either direction: We may stress the social formation of the individual, or, because men have the capacity for both symbolic control over their action and sympathetic understanding of the conduct of others, we can study men as they act, appreciate others' action, and incorporate activity into complex symbolically-regulated networks. In short, we can watch men construct society.

The developments during the decades when sociology emerged as a discipline can be summarized in the assertion that the most sophisticated analysts converged on the idea that society is an organized process, sometimes tentative and sometimes relatively stable, but always ongoing. If society is more than the

[15] Max Weber, *The Theory of Social and Economic Organization*, trans. Talcott Parsons (Glencoe, Ill.: The Free Press, 1947).
[16] Charles Horton Cooley, *Human Nature and the Social Order* (New York: Scribner's, 1902).
[17] George Herbert Mead, *Mind, Self, and Society*, ed. Charles Morris (Chicago: University of Chicago Press, 1934).

sum of its individual participants, its reality must lie in the organized relations which emerge as men interact. The atomic units of these relations are not people but social activities. Even Durkheim, with his insistence on the independent reality of social structure, stressed that the coherence of society rests on the interdependence of activities and the moral regulation which emerges from human interaction.

The new emphasis on process did not eliminate the ideological uses of the concept of society. Society remained, to a greater or lesser extent, a source of standards for evaluating the acts and programs of individuals and institutions. In some cases, the ideological functions of the sociological method were clear, as in the case of the "sociological jurists," who insisted that the spontaneous moral order which develops in the associations of society as men live and work cooperatively is a "living law."[18] The living law is a yardstick for measuring how well the positive or official law responds to pressing social interests and problems. In other cases, the ideological affinities of the concept of "society as process" are more subtle but nonetheless real. For example, the popularity of the social-psychological approach in America was due to its capacity to provide a sociological foundation for modern liberalism. Twentieth-century liberalism, unlike its eighteenth-century *laissez-faire* counterpart, envisages individual freedom in a context of social regulation. The concept of society as an emergent regulative process founded on the responsible actions of individual social persons, permitting innovation but, at the same time, regulating and incorporating it, helps transcend the apparent paradox of the program of the modern liberal.

Societies as Social Systems

Despite the developments of the turn of the century, relatively little progress was made in defining the concept of *a society*. "Society" remained a term for designating an emergent and constraining level of reality, and most students were preoccupied with establishing the nature of social reality and its modes of constraint, and were relatively uninterested in examining the units and boundaries of concrete societies as entities.

---

[18] Eugen Erlich, *Fundamental Principles of the Sociology of Law*, trans. W. L. Moll (Cambridge, Mass.: Harvard University Press, 1936).

The major technical device used in recent years to attack the latter problem has been the concept of a "social system." This concept has been defined and used in a number of ways. Many versions of the theory of the social system converge upon the idea that a social system is an interdependent set of roles, groups, and institutions that is stabilized by common ideas of meaning and value among its members. A social system is stable because its organization includes mechanisms for maintaining an equilibrium, or some other constancy, in the relations between the units. Such mechanisms include the punishment of deviance or the inculcation of traditional ways of life and can be called "boundary maintaining mechanisms." Systems can be isolated as separate entities only if they maintain some constancies in the face of environmental change, or some boundaries vis-á-vis the environment. If every event within a system were a direct consequence of some event outside the system, it would be impossible to draw a boundary for the system. The so-called "system" would be, in effect, a mere unit in a larger complex. Since the concept of a social system contains within it the crucial concepts of "unit" and "boundary," it would seem well suited to the analytical problem of defining a society. To define society as a special sort of social system automatically prepares the way for identification of its units and boundaries.

The idea of a social system was used by earlier thinkers, notably Spencer[19] and Pareto,[20] but it has been formulated in greater detail and applied to the present problem by the modern school of structure-functionalism. An important paper by Aberle and a group of collaborators provides a good illustration of this approach.[21] According to these analysts, "a society is a group of human beings sharing a self-sufficient system of action which is capable of existing longer than the life span of an individual; the group being recruited at least in part by the sexual reproduction of the members."[22] Four conditions could terminate the existence of a society: biological extinction or dispersion of the members, apathy, the war of all against all, or the absorption of the society into another society. The authors attempt to enumerate

---

[19] Herbert Spencer, A System of Synthetic Philosophy, ten vols. (London: Appleton, 1862–1896). See especially vol. 1, "First Principles," and vols. 6–8, "Principles of Sociology."
[20] Vilfredo Pareto, The Mind and Society, trans. A. Bongiorno and A. Livingston, four vols. (New York: Harcourt Co., 1935).
[21] D. F. Aberle, et al., "The Functional Prerequisites of a Society," Ethics, 9 (January 1950), pp. 100–111.
[22] Ibid., p. 101.

the functional mechanisms which permit a society to avoid extinction: there must be provision for sexual recruitment, adequate relations with the environment, role differentiation and the assignment of members to roles, communication, shared definitions of the world and of the goals of the society, normative regulation of means and emotional expression, socialization, and the control of disruptive behavior. By this route, the authors have defined the meaning of the phrase "self-sufficient system of action," the core concept in their definition of society. A self-sufficient system of action is so organized as to meet all the functional requisites for the survival of the system as a continuous recognizable entity.

This approach resembles a definition of society proposed by Parsons: "A social system . . . which meets all the essential functional prerequisites of long-term persistence from within its own resources will be called a society."[23]

The key concept in these definitions is self-sufficiency. By definition, all social systems are self-sufficient to some degree. If there are no mechanisms for self-maintenance, the entity cannot qualify as a system; it is a totally dependent part of a larger whole. The isolation of total societies involves the search for global complexes with the highest degree of self-maintenance and the least reliance on other social systems. Local communities, administrative units, institutional sectors, and bureaucratic groups all qualify as social systems, but all are relatively dependent parts of a larger whole. Total societies are dependent only on other types of systems—personalities, cultural traditions, and a physical environment. They may carry on relations with other societies, but they are not dependent communities within other societies.

The Unity of Societies

The approach of the social-system theorist is reminiscent of Aristotle's definition of the *polis*.[24] The *polis*, or city-state, is for Aristotle that human association which has reached self-sufficiency, the final end or goal of association. The household and the village are relatively dependent parts of a larger whole; the larger whole is more self-sufficient, and since this is the main

[23] Talcott Parsons, *The Social System* (Glencoe, Ill., The Free Press, 1951), p. 19.
[24] Aristotle, *Politics*, trans. T. A. Sinclair (Baltimore, Md.: Penguin Books, 1962), pp. 25–28.

distinguishing feature of the larger community, we should accept self-sufficiency as the purpose of the growth of wider and more extensive forms of association. It is not that concrete city-states really are self-sufficient; rather, we should define the *polis* as we would any other phenomenon—by reference to its apparent end or final state.

The Parsonian concept of society also seems to make use of ideas about the culmination of historic processes, this time clothed in new evolutionary garb. The social system-society would comprise a group that contained within itself a set of functional systems to provide for all of its needs. Such a system would be integrated; its various parts would mutually facilitate each other and contribute to the unity and coherence of the whole. By implication, all of these functional systems have definite boundaries, and these boundaries are uniform. For example, a self-sufficient social system would not contain some members who participate in one political system and other members whose political requirements are met by participation in the political system of another society. We do know that concrete large-scale collectivities are not really self-contained systems with uniform boundaries. For example, even the casual observer of Central European history must note a confused array of overlapping national groups, cultural groups, and states. On the other hand, we can note certain pressures and trends in social development. With the rise of the territorial state, we see strong pressures toward the congruence of the boundaries of societies and political systems. Parsons argues that we can state on theoretical grounds that "the boundaries of integrated societal systems have a strong tendency to coincide with the territorial jurisdictions of their political systems."[25] Given such pressures and trends, we may construct a model of the integrated, well-developed societal social system as our theoretical definition of society.

Other students have insisted upon a more realistic and inductive account of society and have consequently rejected the theoretical model of a self-contained society with uniform boundaries. The Polish sociologist Florian Znaniecki (himself a participant in the confused Central European political arena) has been the most outspoken advocate of approaching the study of

---

[25] Talcott Parsons, "The Principle Structures of Community," in *Structure and Process in Modern Society*, ed. Talcott Parsons (Glencoe, Ill.: The Free Press, 1960), p. 262.

society with full recognition and acceptance of the overlapping and disjointed character of societal boundaries.[26]

According to Znaniecki, the confusion in the concept of society derives from the fact that most definitions attempt to fuse two incompatible traditions. On the one hand, there is a naturalistic tradition wherein society is an identifiable concrete population. In the naturalistic tradition, the units of society are concrete organisms, and every society occupies a given territorial area. In the cultural tradition, however, society is an ordered community, integrated by possession of common functional institutions and a common culture. When a single definition of society includes both naturalistic and cultural criteria, that definition defines a nonexistent thing, for concrete territorial communities are never unified in their total cultural life. The total cultural life of any human community is too rich and chaotic; it contains too many heterogeneous cultural systems which influence each other in variable and changing ways. The inhabitants of any given territorial area participate in a large number of distinct cultural systems of various sizes with varied and overlapping boundaries. Each of these cultural systems is based upon organized cooperation, but we may not assume that they combine to form an overarching integrated society. Znaniecki did not deny that various cultural systems may unite into more global systematic units, but he insisted on making the degree of such large-scale development problematic. He contended that we must work inductively, starting with elemental social relations. We then should ask whether identifiable social relations are organized into roles, roles into groups, groups into social systems, and social systems into societies. We will make little progress if we merely *assume* the cultural integration of natural communities.[27]

Another sociologist of slavic origins has made a similar point in his critique of the work of cultural historians. According to Pitirim Sorokin, such cultural historians as Toynbee, Spengler, and Danilesky have erred in assuming the integration of complex civilizations as units.[28] Sorokin stated that the "civilizations" of Toynbee are not global systems; they are mere congeries of systems. Since they have no organic unity, it is quite

---

[26] Florian Znaniecki, *The Method of Sociology* (New York: Farrar and Rinehart, Inc., 1934), and *Social Relations and Social Roles* (San Francisco: Chandler Publishing Co., 1965).

[27] Znaniecki, *Method of Sociology*, Chapter 3.

[28] Pitirim A. Sorokin, *Social Philosophies in an Age of Crisis* (Boston: The Beacon Press, 1950). See also *Social and Cultural Dynamics*, four vols. (New York: American Book Company, 1937–1941), esp. vol. 4, "Basic Problems, Principles, and Methods."

inappropriate to speak of the "growth" and "decay" of civilizations. This is not to say that human beings do not unite in groups
with real systematic unity founded on causal and meaningful
ties between their elements. Sorokin's point is that any given
population is differentiated into a number of such groups with
variable membership.[29] The boundaries of organized groups or
social systems do not correspond to the boundaries of vast historic civilizations. Indeed, the organization and way of life of
any group consists in a multitude of large and small systems,
both in and out of harmony with each other. Again, the implication is that the sociologist must inductively isolate social systems and consider the integration of these social systems into
larger-scale social systems as problematic. Sociologists and anthropologists who have been particularly interested in concrete
historical studies have also been very critical of the concept of
society as a social system. Wolfram Eberhard, in introducing a
work on Chinese history, argues that the social system concept
always implicitly assumes that societies have clear territorial
boundaries. But throughout the history of the pre-modern Far East,
there were no borders, only frontiers. Further, the various subgroups within Far Eastern society were variably integrated into
larger systems of variable extent.[30] When the Dutch first came
into contact with Japan, many ordinary Japanese were unaware
that the shogun was not the emperor. Yet there were aristocratic
classes with organized networks of affiliation throughout Japan.
The social-system concept, with its assumptions of uniform and
clear system boundaries, seems out of line with the facts of
traditional Far Eastern social organization.

The historical inaccuracy of the idea of clear boundaries
may cause serious problems in incorporating inconvenient facts
into our accounts of society. The social-system assumptions tend
to color our whole theory of historical development in that they
cause us to look for imminent internal dynamics of development
and to overlook the role of intersocietal and extrasocietal contacts and systems. For example, when Parsons discusses the initial development of differentiation within societies, he stresses
(as do other evolutionists before him) the strengthening of particular kinship lineages within the society and the growth in the

[29] Pitirim A. Sorokin, Society, Culture, and Personality (New York: Harper and Brothers, 1947), pp. 145–310.
[30] Wolfram Eberhard, Conquerors and Rulers: Social Forces in Medieval China (Leiden: E. J. Brill, 1965), pp. 1–14.

power of the central leaders who come to coordinate social activity on a larger scale.[31]

In contrast, the social anthropologist Alexander Lesser has suggested that the initial development of civilization is brought about by shifting relationships *between* peoples and cultures. Technological progress brings about a division of labor between neighboring groups and this is the true origin of surplus production. Group specialization and a regional division of labor took place within a "field" of economic relations extending beyond any single isolated primitive group, and this development profoundly altered the internal organization of the group. Accordingly, Lesser recommends that we conceive of human societies "not as isolated, separated by some kind of wall, from others, but as inextricably involved with other aggregates, near and far, in weblike, net-like connections."[32] From this perspective, each group member is seen as participating not in a single unified society, but in a set of diversified overlapping "social fields." The differentiation, expansion, consolidation, and interchanges of these fields are the stuff of the history of human society.

These points appear so obvious that we are tempted to wonder how social-system theory could ever have overlooked them. We are tempted to consider the idea of a self-contained, self-sufficient society as intrinsically absurd. After all, do not all societies engage in intersocietal trade and cultural exchange? Does experience not tell us that no society is really self-sufficient? Such an argument somewhat misconstrues the concept of self-sufficiency, for self-sufficiency does not imply isolation. It only implies that the social system contains within it sufficient cultural materials and organizational resources to carry on controlled relations with an environment.[33] For example, all societies cannot protect themselves from the superior force of other societies, but they are organized in various ways to try to do so anyway. The social-system theorists are making the powerful theoretical point that only societies with some degree of self-sufficiency in this sense can maintain any cultural identity over time.

The truth or falsehood of alternative approaches to society is

[31] Talcott Parsons, *Societies: Comparative and Evolutionary Perspectives* (Englewood Cliffs, N.J.: Prentice-Hall, Inc., 1966), pp. 42–50.
[32] Alexander Lesser, "Social Fields and the Evolution of Society," *Southwestern Journal of Anthropology* 17 (1961), p. 42.
[33] Parsons, *Societies*, p. 10.

not at issue here. Rather, we are contrasting alternative strategies of approach to the problems of societal analysis. The use of the concept of a self-contained social system does not utterly prevent analysis of a range of problems because of intrinsic logical difficulties. It merely fails to make several important phenomena immediately problematic.

The two strategies are defined by the two poles of Znaniecki's dilemma. On the one hand, the cultural approach, as illustrated by Parsonian societal system theory, starts with defining the boundaries of consensus on a set of ultimate social values. Those who share those values and who participate in a self-sufficient social system based upon those values constitute the members of a society. In this approach the sociocultural system is identified first; then this system is used as a kind of cookie cutter to stamp out the territorial and populational boundaries of the society. The problematic features of society are the processes by which social values come to be embodied in social institutions so as to produce a self-regulated and ordered societal system. In practice, the incorporation of societal communities into national states often provides a convenient societal-level unit for social-system analysis.

The "naturalistic" alternative is to start with the concept of a "population." The theorist then makes problematic the degree to which the activities of this population are organized into systems, the units and boundaries of these systems, and their forms of interdependence. The emergence of a bounded, unified social system is no longer assumed but becomes an object of study.

THE APPROACH OF THIS VOLUME

Societies as Overlapping Process Systems

In this book we will adopt the second or naturalistic approach. We will start with the concept of a population and then examine the characteristics of the various systems in which the members of the population participate. Society, from this perspective, is a set of overlapping process systems. We may abstract from the concrete interaction of concrete social persons a number of types of interaction systems. Economic, religious, political, educational, and other types of activities come to cohere in partially independent systems with units and boundaries of their own. The membership of these systems will overlap, and, when a broad range of such systems come to have a common center of gravity, we may speak of a society. We shall not assume, however, that this society will be self-contained, that it will not overlap with other societies, or that its boundaries will be uniform across its constituent systems.

The treatment of society as a set of overlapping process systems permits a flexible treatment of several problems of societal analysis and draws our attention to a number of important social phenomena. Societal analysis requires the solution of three fundamental problems: What are the boundaries of societies? What are the units within society? What are the mechanisms that bring coherence to society?

The boundaries of societies are usually drawn at the outer limits of the interdependencies and commonalities which order society. Some choose a particular criterion such as political jurisdiction. If we wish nation-states to be our societal-level units, we may say that state-societies are bounded by the limits of their political systems, and that these limits are in turn defined by the limits of territorial jurisdiction. Such an approach asserts the primacy of one type of ordering commonality. On the other hand, we know that the citizens of any given state participate in a number of social systems that transcend political boundaries. If we start from an exclusively political perspective, such social systems must be treated as intersocietal systems without a home in any society. Further, we must treat them as such no matter how closely knit and unified the transcending or cross-cutting system. If, on the other hand, we view society as a complex of overlapping process systems, it becomes natural to recognize the irregular character of societal boundaries, and we are immediately led to consider the sources and consequences of the involvement of national states in international colonial development.

Another single-criterion approach is to adopt the social system's own normatively defined concept of membership.[34] Again, the members of a societal population, so defined, may be involved in well-organized social systems that cross-cut these boundaries. The common solution to this problem is to say that the basic unit of society is not the whole person, but the "person-in-role." Behavior in boundary-crossing roles is then considered *external* to the society, and the analyst then seeks to

[34] Ibid., pp. 16–18.

identify the mechanisms for segregating roles and for regulating members who cross societal boundaries. Again, the focus is on how such regulation is accomplished, not the conditions of its emergence or the consequences of its absence.

To define society as a set of overlapping process systems also permits flexibility in the analysis of the units of society. From the perspective of common sense, the individual is the unit of society; but at least since Comte, sociologists have seen the utility of beginning with more socially relevant units. Comte insisted that the family was the unit of society, and others have continued this tradition in their treatment of the communal aspects of society. With the development of the idea of society as process, segments of the activity of social persons came to be used as units of analysis. Thus, Parsons has spoken of the units of social systems as "actors in roles."[35]

Our emphasis on society as process seems to imply that while the social act is the ultimate atomic unit of society, the intermediate or molecular units of society may be many and varied. Social acts may accumulate into larger meaningful units in a variety of ways. The constituent systems of society have units of different types, and the differences between them may be of considerable interest. For example, many of the strains in modern societies derive from the fact that families are the units of modern status systems, but rational market and bureaucratic systems are predicated on the evaluation of specific performance in roles. In consequence, competing bases of evaluation are present in society.

The links between units may also vary from system to system. Theories of society have postulated six major types of links between units: *emotional attraction, mutual orientations* of actors to each other, *shared cognitive and evaluative perspectives,* mutual influence through *coercion* or because of economic or *functional interdependence,* and common participation in a *shared environment.* There is no reason to assume that any of these types of links constitutes the one true mechanism of social coherence. On the other hand, one or another of them may be dominant in particular process systems, and this possibility suggests important sociological problems. We are led to ask such questions as: "What is the consequence of the expansion of systems of economic interdependence beyond the boundaries of systems based upon shared emotional attachments?"

---

[35] Parsons, *Social System,* pp. 24–26.

Society and Societal Change

The concept of society as a set of overlapping process systems is more than a useful analytic device. It is peculiarly well suited to the analysis of some processes of social change which elude analysis under the assumptions of social-system theory. Two extremely important trends of historic and contemporary change, ecological expansion and modernization, seem particularly resistant to sociological analysis as long as we insist on the notion of society as a system with fixed and uniform boundaries.

Ecological expansion is the process by which organized human communities come to include larger and larger populations extending over wider and wider territorial areas.[36] Since the beginning of recorded history, ecological expansion has been a dominant trend. By population migration, conquest, annexation, economic penetration, political consolidation, and cultural diffusion, small independent communities have become incorporated into larger and more complex communities. This process does not occur evenly, but in fits and starts; some process systems expand more rapidly than others, and the consequent imbalances impart a dynamic thrust to social development.

In the last two hundred years, ecological expansion has been associated with modernization. "Modernization" refers to the development of deliberate and rational mobilization and organization of technical and human resources so as to produce a productive and efficient national society. As Western technology has impinged on the underdeveloped world, and as Western political and economic penetration has disturbed traditional societies, new nations have formed, and these new nations have all been required to come to grips with modernity.

Comparative studies indicate that the realistic analysis of modernization must maintain the problematic status of the boundaries of society. For example, C. E. Black's comparative analysis of modernization shows that patterns of modernization vary according to whether the process occurs in a society with continuity in its population and territorial boundaries, or in a society undergoing fundamental regroupings of lands and peoples.[37]

Further, the latter alternative is far more common: In Black's

---

[36] For a theoretical account of the ecology of expansion see Amos Hawley, *Human Ecology* (New York: The Ronald Press Co., 1950), chapters 18–20. For an account of world history from this point of view, see William H. McNeill, *The Rise of the West: A History of the Human Community* (Chicago: University of Chicago Press, 1963).

[37] C. E. Black, *The Dynamics of Modernization* (New York: Harper and Row, Publishers, 1966).

view, only ten of 170 societies studied could be described as having continuity in their population and territory during the entire period of transition to modernity. Therefore societal analysis, if it is to be relevant to the real world, should not assume static, fixed, and uniform boundaries for society.

A Definition of Society

The notion of a set of overlapping process systems is not a sufficient definition of a society. How does a society differ from other sorts of social groupings such as institutions, associations, and communities?

The concept of a "population" is the key concept for distinguishing societies from other sets of systems of social processes. Other social organizations have sets of members, but they do not have populations in the biotic sense.

A society is sustained by a population. To establish the boundaries of a societal population, we will adopt a definition of a population quite similar to the concept employed by bio-ecologists. A population consists in the self-perpetuating inhabitants of a territorial area.[38] In this context, the term "self-perpetuating" implies mating and the term "inhabitant" implies relatively permanent residence. Thus, the boundaries of a population that sustains a society are established by the limits of the largest territorial area within which mating is common and residence is relatively permanent. Such a population may be termed a *societal population*, and we may define a society as *all of the systems of action sustained by a given societal population*. This model provides a means for clearly excluding types of groups which are not societies. Many groups do not qualify because membership is not conferred by birth. Further, the populations of local communities are distinguished by the relatively frequent crossing of boundaries for the purpose of mating and establishing new residences.

This emphasis on the concept of a population should not obscure our previous emphasis on activity and process. Note that a society does not consist in the population, but in the systems of social action in which the members of the society participate. The boundaries of these systems may not correspond with

[38] T. A. Goudge, *The Ascent of Life* (Toronto: University of Toronto Press, 1961), pp. 26–34; John Paul Scott, *Animal Behavior* (Chicago: University of Chicago Press, 1958), pp. 219–232.

the boundaries of the population. Many process systems overlap two or more societal populations; hence our concern for the overlapping, nonuniform character of the boundaries of systems of social action. In a highly organized and stable society, the relations between members of its population and other populations may be very closely controlled. On the other hand, societal systems are often very permeable to influences from well-organized systems which cross-cut population boundaries. For this reason we must be flexible in our treatment of boundary problems.

Society and Intersocietal Relations

Historically, conceptions of society have had ideological implications and overtones. Perhaps the present conception is no exception, for it seeks to call attention to the emergence of larger and more inclusive networks of social organization. As man has expanded his ecological niche, there has been a continuous growth of national organization that transcends less inclusive traditional solidarities. At the same time, cosmopolitan and international organization have outrun national boundaries.

The process of modernization has fostered the growth of the national state; the aspirations of peoples for the rational and efficient mobilization of resources for human happiness have centered on the organization and development of national political units. The emergence of the well-organized national state, carefully protecting its territorial, social, and cultural boundaries, is consonant with the concept of society as a self-sufficient social system. But the same processes of modernization have destroyed traditional boundaries, encouraged the growth of intersocietal relations, and welded the world together in a complex and ramified system of relationships that cross-cut nations as units.[39] The modern world is regularly upset by shockwaves reverberating from local traditional cleavages, upward through national political systems, to the international arena. If sociological analysis is to adequately represent the constraints of the emergent global level of social reality, our analytical conceptions must not be inflexibly tied to the concept of the national boundary.

---

[39] Black, Modernization, pp. 26–34, 129–139.

2

Concepts for Societal Analysis

All of the concepts introduced in this chapter have been the topics of a voluminous and, in many cases, controversial literature. A closely reasoned defense of the many concepts and usages of this book would be a book in its own right, though a rather sterile one. This chapter does not seek to develop a complete sociological theory; only a few concepts will be introduced briefly to establish our basic assumptions and perspectives and to facilitate later exposition.

SOCIETAL ANALYSIS

Unit Concepts

The first premise of our approach to society is that the "stuff" of society is human activity. In this we respect the basic traditions of sociological thought as they were established at the turn of the century. Society is not a static entity made up of people or norms or institutions. It is a dynamic process. In the words of one early exponent of this position, Albion W. Small, "the subject matter of sociology is the process of human association. . . . The term 'society' has usually connoted virtually the same phenomena for which the term 'the social process' stands in our argument. . . . Society denotes, in general, that phase of the conditions of human life which consists of inevitable action and reaction between many individuals."[1]

The smallest unit of society as process is the *act*. An act is the smallest identifiable phase or segment of the purposive action of a human being. In adopting terms like "act" and "action," we clearly opt for a particular approach to human conduct. We reject the image of a passive human being who merely expresses or reflects biological needs, reflex learning, or the constraints of social structure. "Action" unambiguously denotes purposive, intentional conduct; action theory posits act that attempt to implement will or intention in the face of an environment, not mere responses to the stimuli presented by an environment. We would not expect a social reform group to christen itself "Behavior to End Poverty," but "Action to End Poverty" properly conveys the sense of goal-directed, purposive effort.

To adopt an action perspective is not to deny the existence of social structure or to assert that action is free of systematic constraint; action theory merely asserts that the raw materials of societal analysis are the purposive human actions of men who confront each other and an environment, and who attempt to cope with the conditions of life. Being purposive and human, activity tends to be innovative, creative, flexible, varied, pragmatic, and inspired by values.[2] Indeed, it is this pragmatic flexibility that produces such fluid, permeable, and expandable boundaries in the systems of society. Man, as a purposive actor, is not easily constrained by established social and territorial boundaries. Nor is he rigidly constrained by the fixed values and norms of social systems.

The flexibility of human conduct is founded on our capacity to respond to the meanings of objects as well as to their physical properties. This fact is often expressed in the statement: "Human conduct is symbolic." We are not dependent on a repertory of

---

[1] Albion W. Small, *General Sociology* (Chicago: University of Chicago Press, 1905), pp. 3, 45.
[2] For an outline of the components of the action frame of reference see Parsons, *Structure of Social Action*. For a forceful, consistent, and thorough (if extreme) analysis of the implications of one action perspective, see Herbert Blumer, "Sociological Implications of the Thought of George Herbert Mead," *American Journal of Sociology* 71 (March 1966), 535–544.

fixed responses; we "decode" complex symbolic messages about situations, and we adjust our activities in response to the information about contingencies expressed in such messages. There is nothing in the wave lengths of the color red to cause us to stop for red lights, nor did we learn to stop through trial and error. Rather we learned to decode the symbol of a red light so as to learn the contingencies and possibilities which it represents. Codes and meanings are learned through association with other persons and are the principle vehicle for carrying on ordered interaction with others. Acts are performed by *actors*, and, in this sense, the activities of a given person may be seen as a unit. Since persons interact with a wide variety of purposes, in variable contexts, and with various other people, sociologists have found it useful to separate the activities of persons into a variety of different *roles*. The acts performed within a given role are then termed "persons-in-role" and are treated as another sort of unit.[3] From this perspective, my activities as father, as sociologist, and as citizen are separate societal units.

Actors do not interact with random others, but with specific others, depending on the role that is being played. Any set of actors who interact with each other and mutually influence each other may be called a *group*, but, in studying larger social entities, such as society, our attention is drawn to groups of actors who interact relatively frequently in particular contexts and in an organized way. These are units of society, or, more exactly, their activities are units of society. Just as persons-in-role are the units corresponding to individuals, so organized group activities are the units corresponding to groups.

Organized groups are of two major types. *Communities* are organized around a territorial location of residence, and *associations* are organized around one or more specific interests or purposes. The household, the neighborhood, the village, and the city are examples of communities. Associations include such groups as clubs, business firms, political parties, and schools, which, though they have a territorial reference, are not usually themselves residential units. By these definitions, communities are groups that (whatever else they do) literally live together, whereas associations are groups that associate for various purposes.

A third type of social group may be called a *stratum*. Strata are not associations or communities because they have neither

---

[3] Parsons, *Social System*, pp. 24–26.

an explicit purpose nor a territorial reference. Strata are drawn from subpopulations of actors with more or less equal status on any of the dimensions along which persons may be arranged hierarchically—prestige, wealth, power, etc. Such aggregates differ in the extent to which they are internally organized, homogeneous, self-conscious, or clearly defined strata. Nevertheless, because actors compete for status and try to preserve status, and because status is associated with group memberships, patterns of association between people, and life styles, stratification has a pervasive influence on the interests of associations and communities and on the collective organization of social activity.[4]

System Concepts

The many acts which, taken together, comprise the activities of communities and associations do not form a random hodgepodge of behavioral bits. We start with an action frame of reference, insisting that human conduct is purposive, innovative, and flexible, but nothing in this perspective denies that the activities of men are interrelated and interdependent. Certainly, no one who lives in a modern society, who is completely dependent on a vast network of economic exchange spanning the entire globe, whose security is daily affected by political acts in distant countries, can possibly deny that he is implicated in systems of action transcending his individual goals and perceptions.

We can speak of *social systems* because the activities of men are interdependent. A great deal of technical analysis has extended the meaning of the concept of a social system in a number of intricate ways, but, in its most primitive sense, the term "social system" is quite simple. A system is any set of interdependent units; when the units in question are social acts, we have a social system. In its simplest sense, the term "social system" implies only the undeniable fact that human actors influence each other in systematic ways. Since this is true, we may,

---

[4] This usage of the terms "association," "community," and "stratum" does not agree precisely with common sociological parlance but has the advantage of simplicity and clarity. My usage is consistent with MacIver's distinction between community, as the common living of social beings, and association, as an organization of social life established for the pursuit of common interests. R. M. MacIver, *Community: A Sociological Study* (New York: The Macmillan Company, 1917), pp. 22–24.

as students of society, direct our attention not merely to the individual as he establishes a sequence of acts, but to the systematic influences men have upon each other. Differently stated, social systems are objects of study in their own right. Indeed, as was stated in the first chapter, society consists in a set of social systems.[5]

One of the most difficult tasks in societal analysis is to demarcate the various social systems within society. Human activities are so interconnected and interdependent as to give society something of the character of a seamless web. This is one of the main reasons that the idea of a social system has come to involve so much more than mere interdependence. In particular, it is one of the sources of the important idea of *social functions*. Given the somewhat seamless character of the web of interdependence, how do we break up the totality of interaction into smaller, more manageable complexes? The problem is exacerbated when one considers that one of the main methods of societal study must be comparative analysis of different societies. Although there may be relatively natural breaks and boundaries between the various action systems within a given society, when we look at various societies we find that the lines are drawn in different places. In one society we may find clear lines drawn between the economic system and the political system, and in others we may discover that similar natural boundaries cannot be found because political and economic activities are thoroughly fused. Such variation makes comparative analysis quite difficult, but the solution to the problem lies in the concept of a function, for if we can develop a list of functions common to all systems, then we can compare two or more societies on the basis of how these functions are performed. Thus, one component of every society is an economic system, that is, a system of action comprising all of those interdependencies between acts that have an economic character.[6] Similarly, for each function there is a *process system* consisting in the activity involved in performing that function; the separability of functions permits the use of analytic (rather than natural) boundaries to draw the lines "between" systems.

---

[5] Talcott Parsons, "Social Systems," in *International Encyclopedia of the Social Sciences*, Vol. 15, pp. 458–472; Charles Ackerman and Talcott Parsons, "The Concept of 'Social System' as a Theoretical Device," in *Concepts, Theory, and Explanation in the Behavioral Sciences*, ed. Gordon J. DiRenzo (New York: Random House, 1966), pp. 24–42.
[6] Talcott Parsons and Neil J. Smelser, *Economy and Society* (New York: The Free Press, 1956), pp. 13–29.

A Scheme for Classifying Functions

From time to time we will have occasion to refer to a particular scheme for classifying functions in social systems, the analytical categories proposed by Talcott Parsons.[7] Parsons objects to indefinitely long lists of social functions, such as the list developed by Aberle and his colleagues (outlined in the first chapter of the present book). Rather, he believes that it is necessary to develop a truly analytical scheme that permits derivation of a limited number of functions from the underlying dimensions of the basic problems facing all systems. According to Parsons, the basic system problems are four in number—adaptation, goal attainment, integration, and pattern maintenance. These four functions are derived from the cross-classification of two dimensions of system problems. Problems may be *internal* and concern the relations between units, or they may be *external* and concern the relations between a system and its environment. The other dimension is founded on the distinction between the *development* of resources and the application or *expenditure* of resources. The former problems are termed *instrumental* and the latter are called *consummatory*.

Adaptation

Adaptation is the external and instrumental function of social systems. It is external in the sense that it involves relating a system to an environment, and it is instrumental in the sense that it involves the development of generalized means for pursuing a variety of goals and for meeting a variety of environmental conditions as they fluctuate and evolve over time, rather than the actual pursuit of particular goals. The key word in this definition is "generalized." Systems increase their adaptive capacity by developing generalized facilities that are uncommitted to any particular use. Money is an example of such a facility. One who has money has "purchasing power" and is not committed to buying anything in particular.

---

[7] Talcott Parsons, "General Theory in Sociology," in *Sociology Today*, ed. Robert K. Merton, Leonard Broom, and Leonard S. Cottrell, Jr. (New York: Basic Books, Inc., Publishers, 1959), pp. 4–7. The present summary of the scheme is adapted from Leon Mayhew, "Ascription in Modern Societies," *Sociological Inquiry* 38 (Spring 1968), pp. 112–116.

Goal attainment

Goal attainment is the external consummatory function, external in that it refers to relating the system to its environment and consummatory in that it involves organization for the effective pursuit of particular systems goals, rather than the development of generalized instrumental resources. The key word in this definition is "effective." Systems are well equipped for goal attainment when they are organized to control activity in order to bring it to bear on collective goals. Energy is expended ineffectively when it is dissipated on diffuse goals or diverted to internal power struggles.

Integration

The third function, integration, is internal and consummatory, internal in the sense that it involves relating the constituent units to each other, and consummatory in the sense that it involves not the development of general facilities and resources of stability such as value commitment, good will, or emotional therapy, but the confrontation and solution of the specific coordinative problems that arise when the units of a system mutually interfere with each other. Mutual interference stems from conflict, the breakdown of mutual expectations, or a lack of complementarity in people's activities.

Pattern maintenance

The last function, pattern maintenance, is internal and instrumental. It refers to a problem in maintaining relations between units within systems, but, whereas "integration" refers to the problem of meeting specific coordinative problems and conflicts, pattern maintenance refers to the problem of developing generalized resources for dealing with internal disturbances of all kinds. In social systems, the function of pattern maintenance is met through mechanisms for teaching and reinforcing commitment to general patterns of normative order. Thus, stable values insure continuity in the normative order and stability in patterns of mutual expectations among actors. Values also provide a focus for the inculcation of generalized loyalty and commitment to the group. The concept of pattern maintenance is closely linked to

Parsons' theory of equilibrium in social systems, i.e., the idea that disturbances are solved by specifying and drawing on the established resources provided by a widely shared body of values. This theory assumes the existence of mechanisms of pattern maintenance, institutions devoted to inculcating commitment to common values.

Systems Boundaries

We have seen that drawing functional boundaries for social subsystems is an analytical problem. Drawing the boundaries of the extent of social systems across persons and space is also an analytical problem because natural boundaries are usually not clear and abrupt. The population and territory of an action system should be drawn in correspondence with the actual limits of interdependence, but, whether we are studying the boundaries of economic interdependence in territorial communities,[8] the boundaries of a space over which culture traits are distributed,[9] or the boundaries of interbreeding,[10] we find not a clear stopping point but a falling away, more or less gradual, which makes any given boundary more or less arbitrary. Strictly speaking, it is more accurate to speak of the slope of a *boundary gradient* than of a boundary as such.

Even though natural boundaries are not ordinarily abrupt, they are usually clear enough to permit judgments about the approximate and *relative* extent of different process systems. Some process systems are relatively narrow and closed, extending only over relatively small territorial areas; others unite vast populations spread over very broad areas. In chapter one, it was proposed that these differences are important in societal analysis. Because we will return to such differences repeatedly, it is useful to define a few analytical terms at this point. When the participants in an action system are all included in the population of a society, we designate that system *internal*. When a system includes participants who are members of more than one societal population, we call that system *intersocietal*. All societies include both internal and intersocietal systems.

[8] Hawley, *Human Ecology*, pp. 245–258.
[9] Clark Wissler, *An Introduction to Social Anthropology* (New York: Henry Holt, 1929), pp. 341–355.
[10] Goudge, *The Ascent of Life*, pp. 26–34.

Structural Concepts

The term "structure," like "system," is a highly abstract word with a very simple fundamental meaning. The *structure of a system* consists in those relations between its units that are relatively stable or constant over time.

There is nothing in the action frame of reference (with its emphasis on purposive, directed human conduct) to suggest that human actors do not develop stable modes of relating their activities to each other. In fact, several investigators have actually observed stable structures emerge from initially unorganized states as actors confronted individual problems, collective problems, and each other. One student watched leadership structures emerge in small experimental problem-solving groups as members differentially rewarded and punished each other's contributions. Another investigator observed the development of relatively stable patterns of attraction within a group of college students, initially strangers, as they came to have stable perceptions of each other and common or discrepant attitudes to social objects. A study of a law enforcement agency revealed that both stable alliances and a status hierarchy developed as agents sought each other to exchange advice and consultation. Yet another observer studied business executives as they attempted to cope with the demands of a novel role in their business organization. Through routine supervisory procedures, meetings, and programs, and through new definitions of their own selves, these executives developed stable and functional patterns of conduct in their new roles. A student of Jewish community life watched permanent organizations develop as the Jewish residents of a suburban community sought to cope with problems inherent in their cultural tradition and minority status.[11] These studies, which are illustrative of a much larger number of observations, all represent humans as active striving individuals, motivated by interests and self concepts. Yet, all show the emergence of stable

[11] See R. F. Bales, "The Equilibrium Problem in Small Groups," in *Small Groups: Studies in Social Interaction*, ed. A. Paul Hare, et al. (New York: Alfred A. Knopf, Inc., 1955), pp. 424–463; Theodore M. Newcomb, *The Acquaintance Process* (New York: Holt, Rinehart & Winston, Inc., 1961); Peter M. Blau, *The Dynamics of Bureaucracy* (Chicago: University of Chicago Press, 1955), pp. 99–130; Paul R. Lawrence, *The Changing of Organizational Patterns: A Case Study of Decentralization* (Boston: Harvard University, Graduate School of Business Administration, Division of Research, 1958); Herbert J. Gans, "Park Forest: Birth of a Jewish Community," *Commentary* 2 (April 1951), pp. 330–339. For a good account of various approaches to the emergence of organization, see Walter Buckley, *Sociology and Modern Systems Theory* (Englewood Cliffs, N.J.: Prentice-Hall, Inc., 1967); and Daniel Katz and Robert L. Kahn, *The Social Psychology of Organizations* (New York: John Wiley & Sons, Inc., 1966), pp. 71–109.

patterns of conduct as individuals adjust their activities to each other.

We are all familiar with this process in our daily lives. Consider the example of courtship and marriage. From the first moment boy meets girl, their interaction has some of the characteristics of a system, for their activities depend on each other; some activities may be sanctioned with a slap, others with signs of affection. At first acquaintance, activities are relatively fluid, experimental, and unexpected. Gradually, as acquaintance develops into courtship, our couple comes to develop habits, routines, agreements, common sentiments, stable conceptions of each other, and enduring expectations of each other's conduct.

With marriage, a new level of structural solidity is achieved, for at this point the couple forms an attachment constrained by more powerful socially binding obligations. Marriage implies obligations of support, sexual access, and child-rearing which may be enforced, directly or indirectly, by the state. It cannot be dissolved at will, and the content of the relationship cannot be defined entirely by the participants. For this reason we call marriage a *social institution*. Its definitions and consequences are not defined entirely by the parties but by the norms and sanctions of a larger social system.

The concept of an institution is one of the most important ideas used in societal analysis. The most brilliant demonstration of the significance of the concept (and the best introduction to the idea of an institution) is Emile Durkheim's famous analysis of contract in *The Division of Labor*.[12] Durkheim's argument was conceived as a polemic against Herbert Spencer's notion of a regime of contract. Spencer had claimed that modern society can be described as a regime of contract in which the main social ties are contractual obligations freely accepted by individual citizens because it is in their own interests to do so. The regime of voluntary contract expresses, or is a manifestation of, an underlying network of reciprocal interests created by forces of supply and demand within the free market. Durkheim rejected this picture of society, insisting that Spencer had described only the *interests people bring to contracts*, not the *institution of* contract. If we look closely at a contract, we see that the obligations of the parties are not exhausted by the terms they mutually and voluntarily accept. Many of the obligations of contracting parties derive from the law of contract, which defines the range of possible

---

[12] Durkheim, *Division of Labor*, pp. 200–229.

content for contracts, conditions of enforceability, minimum terms, and rules of interpretation, and which supplements the parties' agreement in order to take unforeseen circumstances into account. The institution of contract is prior to, external to, and constrains the acts of contracting parties. But, by the same token, the institution *permits* contracts by narrowing the range of negotiation. By providing a structure of generalized norms and procedures, the institution allows negotiators to form alliances without resorting to the creation of a complete social structure *de novo*. Similarly, various specific institutions — marriage, property, banking, policing, incorporation, the physicians role, representative government, etc. — provide a structure for activity in other realms by offering convenient, ready-made, stable, and socially binding arrangements for actors who wish to construct joint activity and organize their social life.

Institutions are so important as structural components of society that we will sometimes use the term "institutional sphere" as a synonym for process system. Nevertheless, there are other important structural concepts in societal analysis; not all of the stable relations between the units of social systems are institutionally defined by norms. Persons and groups establish differential control over economic and political resources; they exhibit patterns of location in space; and they display patterns of motives and interests. These are stable conditions of social action and, as such, contribute to the structure of process systems. Finally, regularities in the environment are reflected in the structure of process systems.

The Components of Action Systems

We are now prepared to view action systems as exhibiting several components or layers of structure. Every action system is sustained by a *population*, that is, a set of concrete persons who are engaged in the systemic activity. We refer to the structure of a population as its *morphology*, which includes its size, its composition by sex, age, and other attributes, and its pattern of distribution in space.

The second component is *technology*. The participants in an action system make use of a set of physical tools and instruments to implement their intentions. Technology is an obvious component in economic and political systems, but we must not overlook the fact that *homo religicus* has his medicine bundle or cathedral, the educator his blackboard or videotape machine, and the mother her cradleboard or automatic TV-set–baby-sitter. Technology affects the basic conditions of human association and communication and thereby shapes action systems of all types. The third component is *collective organization,* the organization of activity into relatively stable units sustained by communities and associations. To mention a few possibilities, an economic system may be organized into firms, a political system into legislatures, parties and government agencies, a religious system into churches, and a kinship system into families.

Organizations have several properties that enter into the structure of process systems. Organizations develop commitments to particular goals, and, in this sense, they may be said to have *interests.* They also develop stable relations with other organizations, and these relations are an element in the structure of process systems. Whenever an organization succeeds in implementing an interest by forming a stable relation with another organization, we say that interest has become *vested.* As we shall see, vested interests are crucial elements in process systems, especially when they are legitimized by institutional norms and values.

The fourth component is *institutional organization.* Action systems include a body of operative and enforceable norms and procedures to control activity and facilitate collective enterprise.

Neither groups nor institutions could be organized if it were not for *symbol systems,* which facilitate communication by providing convenient terms and signs to refer to complexes of ideas and sentiments. Language itself is a universal symbol system available to all process systems, but some systems have specialized systems of symbols appropriate to specialized types of endeavor. Mathematical notation, money, religious objects, and poetic imagery, though very different, are all specialized systems of symbols adapted to diverse communicative tasks. These symbol systems are the fifth component of action systems.

We do not need to delve into the historic controversies over the role of ideas as determinants of social structure and social change to recognize that idea systems are components of action systems. Human actors constantly utilize ideas in their conduct; they refer to them, teach them, argue about them, systematize them, use them to construct tools, and insist that others follow them. The influence of systems of scientific, religious, political, and moral ideas on human conduct is unmistakable. Since ideas are manifest in symbolic expressions, idea systems and symbol systems are closely intertwined. Myths, for example, are inextricably fused with symbols. Hence, for many purposes we can link idea systems and symbol systems in the term *cultural systems.*

To summarize, every action or process system has (1) an associated population, (2) a technology, (3) collective organization, (4) institutional organization, and (5) an associated cultural system.

In addition, several other determinants of social life can be seen as forming an *external environment* containing potential resources for the system. In the language of system theory, social systems are open or adaptive systems, as opposed to closed or mechanical systems. They exist only by drawing upon and processing the resources of an environment, and they must be responsive to variety and change in the environment.

In sum, human activity, though it is flexible, sensitive, contingent, and innovative, comes to cohere in organized, adaptive process systems. Interacting human beings exchange, sanction, evaluate, define, and make commitments, and these types of conduct lead to the emergence of organized systems, flexible and adaptive, yet exhibiting a discernible structure. Not only is the action frame of reference consistent with the idea of structure and organization, the degree of adaptive organization present in human social systems actually *presumes* units with a high degree of capacity to adjust their behavior to a flow of communicated information. No collective organization could be founded on shared acceptance of rules with a high degree of specificity. The rule, "Every third Thursday after a full moon, walk seventy paces west of the nearest oak tree and shoot a deer," could not possibly permit the organized pursuit of game animals. Such organization requires not detailed institutional control but complex machinery for communicating and responding to information.

Instrumental and Institutionalized Action Systems

The foregoing discussion implies that social systems can differ in their degree of institutional constraint on action. At one extreme, social institutions can specifically prescribe human action in great detail. A system of religious ritual may require the repeated intonation of formulae at precise times and prescribed places. Performing the ritual may be the task of a well-organized and established priesthood with vested interests in an established social structure, supported by economic and political power as well as their sacred aura and their high social status. Sanctions may be severe for failing to perform or for interfering with performance. Such a system can be described as *institutionalized*. On the other hand, a group of persons who wish to exploit a new invention by marketing a new product may form a more loosely organized action system. They cannot avoid the use of some established institutions—language, contract, etc.—but their cooperative activities and the content of their collective agreements usually have a more flexible and instrumental character, more adapted to the nature of the task than to the established social order. Such a system may be termed *instrumental*.

Instrumental action systems are characterized by:

1) willingness among the participants to attach themselves to others with whom they do not have any prior sentimental tie;

2) normative creativity, that is, willingness to treat the problems of social coordination and rule-making in novel terms according to the exigencies of situations;

3) willingness among the participants to accept leadership based upon the leader's success or his legitimate specialized office rather than upon traditional claims to leadership or social status;

4) sensitivity to new sanctions and relative immunity to the automatic sanctions built into the traditional social order. To cite an extreme example, the participant in an active revolutionary movement must be willing to find "spiritual" rewards in illegal activity and be willing to accept the risks of police sanctions. In alternative terms, his interests are not vested in an established structure of social groups.

In sum, the instrumental system is oriented to change, to the practical, to the novel. By contrast, the institutionalized action system is oriented to the established social order. Its normative order is preestablished and supported by regular and routine sanctions. It is supported by a pattern of social stratification so that those with authority are strengthened by the respect shown for their general social status. Normative precepts and social statuses are deeply embedded in close sentimental ties. Family ties, ethnic affiliations, and close associational ties link the participants to each other and to the demands of the system.

Several prominent thinkers, notably Max Weber, have been intrigued by the problem of institutionalizing the instrumental order. This problem might be termed the paradox of modernity: A modern social order clearly allows for a great deal of instrumental activity and for the incorporation of instrumental action systems. And yet, paradoxically, this occurs without destroying "society," the larger social order. Weber attributed this to the rise of new rational instrumental frameworks, such as rational law, which permits practical methods of norm-making for the whole society, and bureaucratic office, which specializes authority and limits it to specific instrumental ends. Further, such rational-legal instruments as contract permit actors to bring the power of the established state to bear upon their private affairs. Weber also thought that a revolution in motivation has made actors sensitive to novel instrumental sanctions without sacrificing the grounding of motivation in the societal moral order. The so-called protestant ethic founded rational, material pursuits on religiously anchored values.

Nevertheless, it would be a mistake to suppose that modern society has dispensed with institutionalized action systems. Many modern action systems are supported by strong links to a closely interlocked established order within which power still adheres to general social status and is supported by networks of personal links, traditional ties, and social barriers.

The usefulness of the distinction between instrumental and institutionalized social systems is illustrated in Franz Schurman's study of Communist China.[13] Schurman relies on a similar distinction between "organization" (what we call instrumental systems) and social systems (what we call institutionalized systems). The communist revolution represented a triumph of instrumental organization over a closely interwoven institutionalized social system welded together by the power and influence of the gentry. The social revolution was directed against the gentry and was directed toward the provision of new instrumental leadership to direct Chinese modernization. The geographically diffuse character of the Chinese revolution and its militant ferocity reflect the diffuse and pervasive influence of the old elite in the institutionalized system. The periodic reformation movements of the postrevolutionary era as illustrated by the Red Guard movement reflect a continuing attempt to assert the supremacy of instrumental organization against either residual pockets of traditionalism or the creeping rise of a new institu-

[13] Franz Schurman, *Ideology and Organization in Communist China* (Berkeley: University of California Press, 1966).

tionalized social system based on a new bureaucratic elite, with vested interests in established bureaucratic organization.

Structure and Change

If social structure consisted entirely in a set of behavior-determining norms and if these norms were handed down from generation to generation, then social change would be difficult to understand. For this reason, some students have supposed that the concept of structure is inconsistent with the concept of change. This is incorrect for several reasons. In the first place, the concept of structure does not imply that everything in a system is permanently constant, only that some relations are relatively constant over given time periods. Second, human conduct is not a mere expression of social structure. Institutional structure does not determine behavior; it merely influences conduct enough to organize the activities of disparate actors. Given the action frame of reference, which stresses the goal-directed, adaptive, deliberate character of human conduct, we are not surprised that actors innovate when they face changed conditions. Indeed, there is an innovative component in virtually every act, since established ways of doing things can never be spelled out in sufficient detail to even purport to *determine* courses of action.[14] Further, several of the components of action have an inherently dynamic aspect. For instance, the morphology of a population is constantly in process. The members of a population are continuously aging, and the members of any given age category are constantly being replaced. For this reason, recruitment is a continuous problem in social systems; since each replacement group is "socialized" at a different point in time, is exposed to different experiences, is likely to be a different size than the group it replaces, and comes from a different location, recruitment is a source of change.

Further, institutional norms are not necessarily static. Norms may *demand* flexibility and change. Finally, just as the rules of grammar permit the construction of novel sentences such as "Orange igloos never jump," so institutional norms and procedures permit the construction of innovative but comprehensible social arrangements. Indeed, modern societies incorpo-

---

[14] For a reasoned defense of the view that every man is an innovator see H. G. Barnett, *Innovation: The Basis of Cultural Change* (New York: McGraw-Hill Book Company, 1953), Chapter 1.

rate structures specifically designed to produce changes—planning agencies, development councils, research agencies, etc.

In this book, several types of change are particularly prominent: technological advancement, expansion, differentiation, centralization, and revolutionary change. *Technological advancement* refers to the growth of man's capacity to harness energy.[15] Over the millennia, man's power to increase production, speed communication, and impose his will on the environment has increased tremendously. Increases in the capacity to control energy permit the *expansion* of social systems. Expansion, which has been defined by Hawley as "a progressive absorption of more or less unrelated populations and land areas into a single organization,"[16] can occur in any social system, but social systems tend to expand at different rates and this is the cause of the overlapping character of societal boundaries stressed in the first chapter. Expansion has been a very conspicuous component in human history because it produces dislocation, conflict, disorganization, and other strains.

Expansion seems to be closely associated with the specialization of human conduct and the growth of diverse associations, institutions, and cultural systems, a process we call *differentiation*. Specialization and diversity imply problems of coordination and integration that are often met by the *centralization* of control in dominant groups and central locations. Indeed, expansion and centralization are so closely related that expansion is sometimes defined as the growth of a center of activity and the enlargement of its scope of influence.

Often the dislocations and conflicts that accompany expansion, differentiation, and centralization are neutralized by a continuous series of relatively minor adjustments, giving the process of change smooth contours. Sometimes strains become so intense that they become the occasion for collective outbursts which may culminate in *revolutionary change;* the collective and institutional organization of society then undergoes rapid and radical overhaul.[17]

Boldly stated, this synopsis seems to present an evolutionary scheme of technological determinism. Broadly speaking, this is a

[15] Leslie White, *The Evolution of Culture: The Development of Civilization to the Fall of Rome* (New York: McGraw-Hill Book Company, 1959).

[16] Hawley, *Human Ecology,* pp. 348–431.

[17] See Chalmers Johnson, *Revolutionary Change* (Boston: Little, Brown and Company, 1966).

fair estimate, but such generalized frameworks should not blind us to the problems of analysis in concrete societies. Because we can detect an increase in man's capacity to harness energy does not mean that such development is characteristic of every society in every period of time. The study of concrete societies presents problems resistant to broad generalization, problems requiring careful analysis of the organization of conduct in their constituent systems.

Emergence and Constraint in the Study of Social Change

The sensitive reader will have noted a certain tension in this chapter. On the one hand, there is an emphasis on process and change, on the free play of human activity. On the other hand, there is an insistence on such concepts as system and structure, on the stable self-perpetuating features of social life. Debate on this issue and on theoretical approaches which supposedly can or cannot deal with one or the other poles of this dilemma has been discussed in sociological writings for many years. We should not be surprised at this, for the issue reflects a tension inherent in social life itself. On the one hand, adaptation requires constant attention to variation and change. Actors and systems must adjust to developing situations by creating new routines, new arrangements, and new ideas. On the other hand, actors and systems have investments in established institutions and practices. Social order rests on some degree of stability in expectations, some degree of faith in prior promises, and some use of established values and loyalties. Therefore, social order is often best served when new problems and conflicts are resolved within the framework of established arrangements. But in many cases, the requirements of order and adjustment are incompatible. Given groups or ideologies are served by one or the other force, and we should not be surprised if many social theories emphasize one side of social life.

Unfortunately, in recent years this problem has been defined as an issue between "functionalism" and "conflict theory."[18] It is alleged that functionalism cannot deal with conflict and change or that conflict theory has no interest in social institutions. The

---

[18] For a collection of papers on this debate, see N. J. Demerath and Richard A. Peterson, eds., *System, Change, and Conflict: A Reader on Contemporary Sociological Theory and the Debate over Functionalism* (New York: The Free Press, 1967).

issue is a false one. The theory of the social system is, like other social theories, a strategy for understanding change.

It is much more useful to distinguish between two broad strategies for dealing with conflict and change. Both strategies deal with interests, collective organization, institutional arrangements, and cultural systems. Both would arrange these elements of social life in roughly the order given, that is, in a hierarchy from the most concrete to the most abstract. Both assume that conflict and strain is endemic in society. The two strategies differ in the assumptions they make about the hierarchy.

We will call one strategy the "model of structural constraints." According to this model, the hierarchy of abstraction is a hierarchy of control, with culture at the top and patterns of interests at the bottom. Culture "controls" or shapes institutional arrangements, which in turn control the broad groupings and coalitions in society. These in turn control the pattern of individual interests in society. Lower levels in the hierarchy constitute conditions which higher levels must meet in order to prevail; hence, lower levels have definite social consequences.[19] Nevertheless, higher levels can be said to control lower levels in the sense that disturbances at lower levels tend to be stabilized by a reaffirmation of the larger higher-level pattern. For example, a given change of interests for a given group is more likely to result in that group's changing sides in a coalition than to produce a fundamental change in the structure of coalitions. Similarly, a new institutional arrangement is more likely to draw upon and reaffirm a cultural tradition than to challenge fundamental cultural premises. The constraint model supposes that the function of pattern maintenance is vital in social systems.

The assumptions of the constraint model can be summarized in a few brief statements:

1) Changes in patterns of structure occur relatively rapidly at lower levels in the hierarchy of control and slowly at higher levels.

2) Disturbances at any given level are solved at the next highest level or, if they cannot be stabilized at that level, cause disturbances at higher levels until they reach a level where a solution can be found.

3) Whenever a solution occurs, it is shaped by the constrainst deriving from ·a preexisting stable structure which lies

---

[19] Talcott Parsons, "An Outline of the Social System," in *Theories of Society*, ed. Talcott Parsons et al. (New York: The Free Press, 1961), pp. 37–38, 70–79.

above it in the hierarchy, e.g., new political coalitions that form in response to changing patterns of interest will still compete within the framework of an established set of political institutions, and these institutions help to determine what groupings will be politically viable and effective. Consider the difficulty of establishing a third party in the United States.

4) Progressively higher levels of structure unite larger and larger groups of people.

5) History is the progressive institutionalization of values; as actors face problems they draw upon the high levels of structure that unite large numbers of people, and, in consequence, institutional arrangements come to be more accurate reflections of value traditions.[20] Thus, in the United States the fundamental legal norms of the society have come more and more to reflect the American value of equal opportunity.

The constraints model by no means denies conflict nor slights change; it posits that the processes of change and conflict resolution tend to create an integrated, uniformly bounded set of institutional systems within societies that are united by consensus on abstract value premises.

The other strategy we will call the "emergence model." According to this approach, we should not concentrate on how higher level stability shapes lower-level change. The interesting question is "How does any structure arise in the first place?" This question seems to apply a rather different set of assumptions:

1) The existence of order at higher and higher levels of abstraction is progressively problematic. Consensus on such values as equal opportunity is highly uncertain and must be demonstrated.

2) Disturbances are resolved by the creation of orderly arrangements at the minimum necessary level; for example, whatever order exists in the United States in the arena of racial relations is strictly a *de facto* truce between fundamentally hostile groups, not a consequence of any prior egalitarian norms.

3) Progressively smaller numbers of persons are united by systems at progressively higher levels. Systems boundaries are not uniform; very large numbers of persons are linked by interdependent interests, fewer participate in a given institutional framework, and these participants may be further subdivided by divergent allegiances to diverse cultural values.

4) Values and norms are not the source of deductive solu-

[20] Parsons, *Structure of Social Action*, pp. 751–752.

tions to social problems and conflicts; they are mere inductive summaries of *de facto* arrangements achieved at lower levels.

It would be absurd to attempt to decide which of these approaches is true; the assumptions of neither approach are universally valid. Taken to extremes, the model of structural constraints overstates the integration and stability of society. It is more applicable to societies with long-standing institutional traditions and less applicable to emergent societies characterized by a plurality of traditions and chaotic boundaries. We have already criticized the assumption of uniform boundaries among institutional spheres (which tends to be associated with the assumption that society is a social system whose participants agree on fundamental values). On the other hand, the emphasis on emergence, taken to an extreme, fails to appreciate the force of establishment. To take such a strategy literally would be to believe that actors always approach situations *de novo*, paying no attention to fixed investments, habits, or proven methods, and unaffected by any social forces beyond the perceptions of individuals. Exclusive preoccupation with the emergence of collective social action neglects the undeniable fact that there is a given in social life — a *social reality* that is not infinitely malleable to the wishes of any given group of participants, a social environment that sometimes changes according to an inner dynamic independent of the intentions or the wills of individuals.

The two sets of assumptions outlined here are merely general strategies of inquiry; they indicate which aspects of given situations should be taken by the investigator to be problematic. Neither set will suffice as general theory. The problem for the general theorist is to explain the process by which actors cope with the physical environment, social reality, and each other, and, in so doing, both draw upon and create viable social arrangements.

PLAN OF THE BOOK

The remainder of this book explores human society in more detail within the general framework established in these first two chapters. Having started with the assumption that society consists in human activity and that every society is sustained by a concrete population, chapter three continues to explore the concept of a societal population. How do the structural features of a population condition activities within the society it sustains?

Chapter three is devoted to the basic processes of population that constitute the morphological conditions of human society.

With chapters four through seven, we begin our analysis of the process systems of society. Each of these chapters deals with a distinctive type of process system. All four types of process systems are crucial components of every human society. Chapter four deals with systems of solidarity, the emotional base of society. Chapter five concerns economic systems, chapter six political systems, and chapter seven examines specialized systems for creating and disseminating culture. These chapters have a common plan. Each begins with an account of some of the classic approaches to analysis of the institution in question, with special emphasis on the theme of ideological usage of the concept of societal constraint, thus recalling a theme prominent in chapter one. The chapters then proceed to examine the nature of that type of process system and to construct a model of an integrated process system. The "integrated process system" does not describe reality; it describes a theoretical model in order to make problematic the difficulties involved in the organization of society. Indeed, in each of these chapters the next section is devoted to the constraints and limitations on institutional integration with particular emphasis on the consequences of the differential expansion of system boundaries brought about by several historical trends in the modern world. The chapters conclude with discussion of some of the principal techniques and trends of institutional organization found within process systems of the type in question.

Chapters eight and nine return to the total society, exploring how the various process systems of society fit together into a coherent whole. These chapters feature a critique of that version of social-system theory that would make the totality of society consist in exchanges between its constituent institutional spheres. The process systems of society are intertwined in a more inextricable web-like way by virtue of their common involvement, and are embedded in underlying structures of communication, stratification, networks of interests, and population. The work concludes with commentary on three selected problems of the comparative analysis of societies, beginning with the problem of cross-societal and cross-cultural method, moving to the use of typologies in societal analysis, and ending with a return to the theme of social change as it is presented in evolutionary schemes of societal development.

3

Social Morphology

INTRODUCTION

The most inescapable factor in human interaction is the sheer physical presence (or absence) of other actors with given characteristics. Because of the elementary significance of this aspect of interaction, *social morphology*,[1] the study of the size, composition, and territorial location of populations, is an appropriate starting point for societal analysis.

The fact that the size, composition, and location of populations can become a relatively fixed element of the situations confronting actors has often led students of society to make two errors in the treatment of population. In treating population as a given, it is tempting to see demographic variables as static conditions that actors face and to see them as external to social systems. Both of these assumptions are erroneous.

In the first place, the morphology of populations is in constant flux. Populations could neither adapt to their environments

---

[1] Cf. Emile Durkheim, "Note," *L'Année Sociologique* 2 (1897-1898), pp. 520–521.

nor become organized without regular and constant movement. Further, many changes in morphology occur through a process intrinsic to the nature of a population. A population is a set of persons with a given characteristic, but there is constant movement in and out of the population, so that its size and composition are constantly changing. Paul Glick's studies of the family life cycle in the United States provide excellent examples of the dynamic character of population.[2] Glick studied the changes in age of marriage, childbearing, and death that occurred between 1890 and 1960. In 1890, women married at a median age of 22 years and bore their last child at a median age of 32. A mother was, on the average, 55 years old when her last child married. If her husband died before her, he died, on the average, when she was 53 years old, or two years *before* her last child was married. By 1960, earlier marriage and childbearing, in combination with later death, had changed the situation markedly. Women married at a median age of 20, bore their last child at a median age of 26. Because of decline in death rates, women who survived their husbands attained a median age of 61 by the time their husbands died, nearly ten years *after* the marriage of the last child. Thus, a set of changes in age at marriage, childbirth, and death led to a change in the composition of the family. By 1960, couples lived more than one-quarter of their married lives after their children had left home. In effect, a set of demographic changes created an enormous increase in a given type of social relationship in the society, namely older husbands and wives living together without children. And this happened not because a set of social actors said, "Let there be more older couples," but as a consequence of the logic of the relationship between changes in ages of marriage, childbearing and death. Earlier marriage, early retirement from childbearing, and later death necessarily imply a large number of "childless" parents.

The second fallacious assumption, that population represents a condition outside of social systems, has been repeatedly attacked by students of the relation between sociology and demography.[3] It is true that social systems consist in action rather

[2] Paul C. Glick, "The Family Cycle," *American Sociological Review* 12 (April 1947), pp. 164–174; "The Life Cycle of the Family," *Marriage and Family Living* 17 (February 1955), pp. 3–9; *Population Index* 30 (1964), p. 314.

[3] Kingsley Davis and Judith Blake, "Social Structure and Fertility: An Analytic Framework," *Economic Development and Cultural Change* 4 (April 1956), pp. 211–235; Wilbert E. Moore,

than people, but it is also important to remember that the materials of demographic and ecological study—birth, marriage, residences, transportation, etc.—are *activities*. Like other human activities, these activities are collectively and institutionally organized. Such institutions as marriage and the family organize and regulate demographic processes. Accordingly, we may speak of systems of population process and subject their internal organization and their relations to other systems to the same type of analysis and investigation used in the study of economic, political, or religious systems.

Population systems are no more external to society than any of the other process systems of society. However, the outcomes of the processes within a system, such as the economy, constitute a set of environmental conditions for the other systems of society. The success of the economic system in producing wealth is a condition affecting the amount of surplus wealth available for expenditure in elaborate religious activity. Similarly, the various consequences of population process systems in the form of size, rates of growth, and patterns of location create pressures and constraints in other process systems. In this chapter, we focus not on the collective and institutional organization of population systems, but on the social conditions which they create for the other systems of society. These social conditions are of strategic importance for the study of society precisely because all the various process systems are implicated in the same societal population.

All the action systems of society must, to some extent, be located in the same space and share the same participants. Hence, the composition, location, and movement of a societal population constitute one of the major structural links between the process systems of society. Because of these links, patterns in some social realms are stamped upon others.[4] *De facto* school segregation is a familiar example of this phenomenon. Family activity, including residence, is segregated along racial lines. If educational institutions define school boundaries along neighborhood lines, then the segregation of familial activities will be reproduced in educational activities.

"Sociology and Demography," in *The Study of Population: An Inventory and Appraisal*, ed. Philip M. Hauser and Otis Dudley Duncan (Chicago: University of Chicago Press, 1959), pp. 832–851.

[4] Leon Mayhew, "Action Theory and Action Research," *Social Problems* 15 (Spring 1968), pp. 420–432.

ANALYSIS OF POPULATION

The Societal Population

In chapter one, the societal population was defined as the "self-perpetuating inhabitants of a territorial area." According to this definition, the boundaries of a population that sustains a society are established by the limits of the largest territory within which mating is relatively common and residence is relatively permanent. In order to further clarify the approach to society employed in this book, several features of this definition should be made explicit:

1) *The designation of the inhabitants of any given territorial area as a societal population (i.e., as sustaining a society) is always arbitrary to some degree.* In some cases it is fairly clear that movement across boundaries for mating and establishing new residences is entirely too frequent to justify labelling the inhabitants of some territorial areas as societal populations. New York City, for example, is clearly a local community, not a society. The northeastern United States is a region, not a society. On the other hand, it is difficult to locate a physical boundary at which residential mobility suddenly drops to zero. Human populations are characterized by movement rather than by immobility. The forces that move people have their sources in the networks of social systems that engage them. Wherever systems extend over vast areas, the interdependence within these systems will be expressed in patterns of movement. Thus, one economist has related patterns of trans-Atlantic migration to cycles and trends in the international economic system.[5] From this perspective, it is possible to speak of all the inhabitants of Europe and the Americas as comprising one vast societal population for "Atlantic Society." For other purposes it is more useful to think of "North American Society," and for yet other purposes to allow the political boundaries of the United States to establish the limits of a societal population. It is relatively easy to separate societies from local communities; but as territorial areas become larger, the student must choose units on strategic grounds. If he is engaged in comparative study, he should work with units small enough to permit the analysis of a sufficient number of

---

[5] Brinley Thomas, "International Migration," in *The Study of Population*, ed. Hauser and Duncan, pp. 510–543.

units. In a sense, the population of the world is a societal population, but because there is only one world, this unit is too large
for comparative study. Nevertheless, units must be large enough
to include the full territorial breadth of at least one of the process
systems that are of interest to the investigator.

2) *The "societal" character of a population is a variable.*
The implication of the foregoing remarks on the prevalence and
continuity of movement is that the degree to which a given territorial area bounds a societal population is subject to measurement. Awkward as the statement may seem, societies differ in
the degree to which their populations are "societal." This point
will be less confusing if we decompose this variable into two of
its constituent components. First, societies differ in the extent to
which long-distance internal mobility is frequent. The degree of
internal mobility of any societal population may be described by
a curve which plots rates of marital or residential mobility at a
series of distances. Second, societies differ in the degree of external immigration, emigration, and temporary movement across
borders. We will refer to the first of the two components as the
mobility of a societal population and to the second as the *closure*
of a societal population.

To illustrate: By the criterion of mobility, the mid-century
industrial United States has a "more societal" population than
did agricultural India. In the United States, long-distance movement is prevalent; in 1950, 26.5 percent of the population of the
United States were residing in states other than the state of their
birth. Even more impressive, more (56 percent) of the migrants
were born in noncontiguous than in contiguous states, an excellent demonstration of long-distance mobility.[6] In contrast, although Indian districts are only one-seventeenth as large as the
American states, only 9.8 percent of the Indian population resided
outside of their district of birth in 1927.[7]

Mobility and closure are important variables, for movement
implies contact between persons with different points of origin
and, thus, the establishment of relationships between persons
with different cultural backgrounds and organizational connections. Such contact should increase the integration of these so-

---

[6] United States Department of Commerce, *Historical Statistics of the United States: Colonial Times to 1957* (Washington D.C., 1960).

[7] Kingsley Davis, *The Population of India and Pakistan* (Princeton, N.J.: Princeton University Press, 1951), p. 107.

cial systems which extend across wide territorial areas. Thus, we are led to two propositions about societies: (a) The greater the internal mobility of a societal population, the greater the integration of the territorially extensive *internal* process systems of the society; (b) the greater the closure of a societal population, the less the integration of the territorially extensive *intersocietal* process systems of the society.[8] (For nonterritorially extensive, i.e., local process systems, the consequences of mobility and closure may be quite different, but we will deal with this problem in the next chapter.)

3) *The societal population is a physical rather than a cultural or organizational entity.* A societal population contains all of the inhabitants of a concrete contiguous territorial area. We do not attempt to isolate several physically intermeshed societal populations in the same territorial area. If, for example, several French-speaking communities are located in eastern Canada, we do not speak of a French and an English societal population. We speak of a societal population with ethnic diversity. A given population may contain a number of ethnic cleavages or cultural enclaves, but by our definition cultural differences or organizational cleavages do not create multiple societies. A societal population may even be divided among a number of independent sovereign states. The definition is physical; societal populations are not limited by cultural homogeneity, solidarity, or internal organization, only by mating and patterns of movement in a defined space.

There is often surprising cultural diversity within a contiguous highly mobile population. First Mesa in Arizona has harbored one Tewa Indian village and two Hopi Indian villages for more than two hundred and fifty years. The Hopi cannot speak the Tewa language, know little of Tewa culture, and are absolutely excluded from Tewa ceremonial. And yet, about one-half of all Tewa men and women marry Hopi partners, and a pattern of matrilocal residence moves spouses from one community to another.[9] Clearly, by our criteria, we cannot speak of Tewa and Hopi society as separate entities, for First Mesa has but one population. Indeed, in modern times all of these communities are a

[8] Cf. Donald J. Bogue, "Internal Migration," in *The Study of Population*, ed. Hauser and Duncan, pp. 486–488.

[9] Edward P. Dozier, *Hano: A Tewa Indian Community in Arizona* (New York: Holt, Rinehart and Winston, 1966), pp. 1–2, 20–31.

part of a society no smaller than the entire United States.

4) *The societal population and its morphological features are not the sole causes of social relations.* The boundaries and characteristics of populations are not completely set by man's geographic environment or his biological nature. As stressed earlier, the activities involved in residence, mating, and movement are constrained by social systems and institutional arrangements. Accordingly, with the rise of the nation-state, increasing control of movement across national boundaries, and the reduction of international migration to minimal rates, the state has become an entirely appropriate unit for societal analysis in many contexts. Even in contemporary times, however, there are massive movements of population that make it appropriate to treat units larger than nation-states as societies. Wars and revolutions displace large populations, and international organization and travel increase the temporary movements of population across boundaries.

Our choice of the societal population as the ultimate starting point for societal analysis reflects no bias in favor of demographic variables as primary. The choice is made on strategic grounds; if we wish to study the extent and character of the various social systems in which men participate, to examine the consequences of variation in the extent of social systems, or to study the emergence of congruent boundaries in various action systems, then we must not assume anything in particular about the boundaries of these systems. Thus, our approach is equally suitable for the comparative study of contemporary nation-states or for the study of the emergence of the nation-state as a novel form of social organization. To assume that contemporary nation-states merely serve to organize politically units that already existed as societies is to adopt gratuitously the notion of "manifest destiny" as a sociological postulate.

5) *In the modern world, societal populations are not small.* Given the technological capacity to communicate and travel and the territorial extensiveness of modern social systems, few, if any, societal populations are smaller than the lesser nation-states, and the populations of nation-states are increasingly "societal," that is, mobile. Perhaps it would not be necessary to make this rather obvious point if some recent commentators had not misinterpreted the concept of a "population isolate" and

---

[10] Bernard Berelson and Gary A. Steiner, *Human Behavior: An Inventory of Scientific Findings* (New York: Harcourt Brace Jovanovich, Inc., 1964), p. 319.

stated that "the total network of a group of intermarrying people is about the same size in modern Western society as is found in primitive society (from about 1,000 to 2,800 people)."[10] Such a statement implies that what the geneticist describes as a population isolate (which does not become very large) is a *concrete* group. The population isolate is a statistical concept which estimates the average effective size of the pool of potential spouses for each individual.[11] It is not a concrete network. Some nations are small and some are large, but societal populations, as we have defined them here, are larger and more inclusive than the regional groupings, ethnic and tribal enclaves, and dependent communities that are sometimes termed societies.

Population Structure

The structure of a population is described by three interrelated characteristics: size, rate of growth, and composition into categories. The size and growth of a population cannot be studied effectively without references to its composition. A population should not be seen as a mere aggregate, but as a series of groups of persons who entered the population at a series of time intervals. Our emphasis on process extends to the concept of population itself. Since man is not immortal, populations must be maintained by a constant "metabolism" of replacement of departing members. A population is not a static aggregate; it is a set of persons whose membership is constantly changing as old members leave and new members enter. Hence, a population can be seen as consisting in a set of *cohorts*, where each cohort consists in the persons who entered the population during a given time period. Demographers have demonstrated that the mathematics of population growth can best be formulated as a process of fertility and mortality within cohorts.[12]

The same approach to the composition of a population is useful to the sociologist in studying a variety of social processes. We are all familiar with the notion of the "baby boom hitting the

[11] Jean Sutter and Leon Tabah, "Les notions d'isolat et de populations minimum," *Population* 6 (July-September 1951), pp. 481–498; Jean Sutter and Jean Michel Goux, "L'aspect demographique des problemes de l'isolat," *Population* 16 (July-September 1961), pp. 447–462.

[12] Norman B. Ryder, "The Cohort as a Concept in the Study of Social Change," *American Sociological Review* 30 (December 1965), pp. 843–861.

colleges." What we mean by this is that in the years after World War II, women in the twenty to thirty-five year cohorts increased the production of children and produced a larger cohort of babies than had their predecessors. This cohort of children then began to grow older, and, as it aged, brought population pressure to the facilities of one institutional sphere after another; the turn of the colleges came in the sixties.

The sheer size of a cohort is not the only attribute which can have "cohort effects." Each cohort has a somewhat different set of experiences than its predecessors. Since man is not infinitely malleable to changing circumstances, some of the early experiences of a cohort can stamp it with relatively inflexible characteristics. As a cohort ages, it presents problems for institutions and for members of other cohorts because of its fixed cohort attributes. Such problems take many forms. Technological change may be so rapid that the training given to a cohort during its years in educational associations becomes obsolete while the cohort is yet relatively young. Some of the conflict between parents and youth derives not from the fact that they are at different stages in the life cycle, but that they were socialized at different points in time.[13] Here we see another illustration of the dynamic character of the populational component of society. A population is always renewing itself by replacement of its members. The continuing entry of new cohorts makes change probable.

A cohort is an instance of a category of composition that has a fixed or "ascribed" membership. A cohort moves through time, and its size changes as individuals leave, but one cannot move from one birth cohort to another birth cohort; his time of entry into a given population fixes his membership in a given cohort. There are a number of such fixed attributes which define subpopulations or compositional categories. Some analysts have said that specifically demographic analysis is the study of the composition of populations with respect to these fixed attributes—age, sex, race, etc. It is true that many of these attributes are particularly important in the study of population growth, and that many fixed attributes form the foundations of crucial social institutions in all societies. Every society, for example, must make distinctions by age and surround the stages of the life cycle with appropriate institutional arrangements for child rearing, education, mating, the care of the aged, and death. Nevertheless, the methods of demographic study can be applied to the composi-

[13] Kingsley Davis, "The Sociology of Parent-Youth Conflict," *American Sociological Review* 5 (August 1940), pp. 523–535.

tion of populations according to attributes that are not absolutely fixed. The composition of a population can be described as an array of occupations, income groups, levels of education, or linguistic or ethnic groups. A population (or subpopulation) is any "aggregate of individuals who conform to a given definition."[14] If the defining attribute is fixed, the members of a society are confronted by and must cope with a fixed social condition. But "fixity" is not an absolute. If a morphological attribute changes infrequently or for only a few members of a group, or if it is flexible within only a narrow age range, it defines a "quasi-population."[15]

Populations can be divided into relatively fixed morphological groups based on education, occupation, and ethnic origin. These morphological variables are a product of the operation of process systems. Occupational composition, in a modern society, is largely a consequence of the organization of the economy, but, insofar as the economic system produces a population of actors with a stable pattern of occupational locations, constraints are introduced into the actors' social world. The morphological description of a population must therefore include a depiction of its composition by socially defined as well as biological statuses.

The importance of this aspect of morphology is illustrated by its impact on social stratification. We speak of stratification precisely because strata are relatively fixed groups. If persons could change their hierarchical position, there would still be ranking in society, but there would be no system of social classes as we know them. Social stratification is maintained because an initial status is fixed at birth, and later statuses are strongly affected by education (which is variable only in early life) and by occupation (which becomes less flexible with advancing age). Hence, a system of stratification is affected by its own morphology: the process of allocating persons to occupational roles is not just a product of the occupational choices of the participants. New cohorts enter an occupational structure of opportunities that is limited by the current occupational distribution of older cohorts. The number and types of opportunities available depend not only on the number and distribution of tasks to be performed but also on the relative sizes of old and new cohorts.

[14] Kenneth E. Boulding, *A Reconstruction of Economics* (New York: John Wiley & Sons, Inc., 1950), pp. 182–202.

[15] N. B. Ryder, "Notes on the Concept of a Population," *American Journal of Sociology* 69 (March 1964), pp. 451–455.

The Morphology of Societal Populations: Growth

In the modern world, the most important demographic fact about societal populations is their rapid growth. In some Asian and Latin American nations, population is increasing by more than 3 percent per year, enough to double a population in as few as twenty years.[16] Rates of increase are slower (or even negative) in the nations of Europe and North America, but even in these regions such nations as Canada, the United States, France, West Germany, the Netherlands, Poland, and Yugoslavia are growing at rates in excess of 1 percent per year.[17]

Both now and in the past, the cause of rapid growth of world population has been the decline in mortality brought about by improvements in standards of living, public health, and medical care. The crude rate of natural increase of a population is determined by subtracting the number of deaths per year from the number of births per year and dividing the difference by the total population. It follows that when death rates decline, populations will grow, unless there are corresponding declines in birth rates.

In pre-modern times, population grew slowly. Annual birth rates were high, perhaps around forty per thousand of population, but death rates were equally high. Hence, populations grew slowly if at all. With the emergence of modern science and technology, mortality began to decline toward its present rate of fewer than ten per thousand. Declines in fertility lagged. Accordingly, tremendous natural increases of population occurred in Europe between 1750 and 1900. In that time period, Europe's population increased from about 150 million to well over 400 million, despite a substantial stream of transatlantic migration.[18] Gradually, beginning about the middle of the nineteenth century, fertility began to decline and rates of population growth declined. Social and economic development have now started to bring mortality down rapidly in Asia, Latin America, and Africa; but, aside from a few exceptions, notably Japan, birth rates remain high. In consequence, the nations of these regions are growing very rapidly. Annual death rates of ten to twenty per thousand, combined with birth rates of thirty to forty-five or even fifty per

---

[16] Ralph Thomlinson, *Demographic Problems: Controversy Over Population Control* (Belmont, California: Dickenson Publishing Company, Inc., 1967), p. 23.

[17] Ibid.

[18] John D. Durand, "The Modern Expansion of World Population," in *Population and Society*, ed. Charles B. Nam (Boston: Houghton Mifflin Company, 1968), p. 110.

thousand, produce net increases of from 2 to more than 3 percent per year. Such societies are said to be in the second phase of "the demographic transition"; they have moved from high birth rates and high death rates to high birth rates and low death rates. The third phase, low birth rates and low death rates, produces a more stable population again.[19] Nevertheless, constant population size remains the exception rather than the rule. In very few modern nations has the birth rate declined as much as the death rate, and continued growth is the most common trend.

Modernized, industrialized nations are usually able to absorb population increases of 1 or 2 percent per year. Indeed, such growth may stimulate continued investment in the renovation of institutional facilities because each cohort is somewhat larger than its predecessors.

The more rapid growth, which is common in underdeveloped nations that are attempting to industrialize their economies and produce a larger per capita output, presents more serious problems. It is precisely because population growth stimulates the need for investment that such growth is a problem for the developing nation. New members of the population must be equipped with the capacities, tools, and facilities of production, and this requires a constant flow of investment. It has been estimated that it requires about 4 percent of a nation's income to equip every 1 percent of increase in population.[20] If a societal population is growing by 2.5 percent per year, then about 10 percent of national income must be used to equip the new population at the same level as the old. For a very poor population, this represents a considerable need for savings and investment even to maintain a fixed level of income per capita. Under such conditions, increase in the levels of investment and per capita output is very difficult.

The problem is exacerbated by the compositional effect of rapid population growth, an effect neatly summed in the phrase "the burden of dependency." Rapid population growth is caused by the continuation of high birth rates despite declines in mortality. Paradoxically, as average life expectancy increases, a pop-

[19] George J. Stolnitz, "The Demographic Transition: From High to Low Birth Rates and Death Rates," in *Population: The Vital Revolution,* ed. Ronald Freedman (Garden City, N.Y.: Doubleday and Company, Inc., Anchor Books, 1964), pp. 30–46.

[20] Joseph J. Spengler, "Population and Economic Growth," in *The Study of Population,* ed. Hauser and Duncan, p. 67.

ulation becomes younger!²¹ This is so because the substantial increase in average life expectancy that occurs during the first phases of the cycle of population growth is achieved primarily by reductions in the mortality of babies and young children. Thus, rapid population growth increases the percentage of children in the population and decreases the percentage of persons of working age who must bear the brunt of sustaining the society. In most of the impoverished but rapidly growing nations of the world, more than 40 percent of the population are under fifteen years of age. Modernized European nations with stable populations sometimes have as little as 20 percent in that age group.²²

Consider the problems that the United States, the wealthiest nation in the world, has had in providing educational facilities for a moderately growing population with about 35 percent under fifteen, and then imagine how much more difficult it would be to establish educational facilities from scratch in a largely illiterate developing nation with both a higher proportion of children and a higher annual rate of growth.

The present rate of world population growth is without precedent. Nevertheless, population growth has always been an important dynamic factor in societies. Whenever technological advance (and the growth of institutional capacities for organizing technology) have permitted population growth, societal populations have expanded. Historically, such growth has been associated with the extension of societal boundaries and the spread of civilization. For example, the tremendous growth of the population of Greece in the middle third of the first millennium B.C. was associated with extensive Greek colonization of the Mediterranean and the Middle East, the migration of Greek merchants and teachers, and the extensive use of Greek mercenary troops by non-Greek states. Hence, Alexander's military exploits did not lead to the Hellenization of a world previously isolated from Greek influence. Rather, military conquest helped to consolidate the expansion of societal frontiers made possible by centuries of population growth.²³ Similarly, the modern growth of European population was associated with great waves of transatlantic migration and the establishment of European forms of civilization in the Americas.

²¹ Ansley J. Coale, "How a Population Ages or Grows Younger," in *Population*, ed. Freedman, pp. 47–58.

²² Ibid., pp. 52–54.

²³ McNeill, *Rise of the West*, pp. 280–282.

In the contemporary world the impact of population growth has been profoundly modified by the tightening of the boundaries of the nation-state, the depletion of frontier area for expansion, and the perilous approach to the finite limitations of usable resources. These factors have forced the attention of national leaders to internal development. At the same time, this trend is occurring in the context of the legacy of imperialism, the penetration of the economic systems of advanced societies into the territorial areas of the new nations. An understanding of these phenomena as context for international relations is prerequisite to the analysis of contemporary societies and will necessarily occupy our attention in later chapters.

The Morphology of Societal Populations: Composition

The dynamic potential of the morphology of population is not limited to growth and its concomitant compositional effects. Many other compositional factors have important effects, some obvious, others more subtle. For example, there are a number of cases when the ratio of men to women in the population (sex ratio) has become unbalanced because of wars and other sources of attrition. The combination of massive losses in World War II and revolutionary political transformations seriously depleted the males in several cohorts in the Soviet Union. In 1959, the productive cohorts of ages sixteen to fifty-nine had only seventy-five males per one hundred females.[24] To what should we attribute the fact that in 1959, 58.4 percent of females aged ten and over in the Soviet Union were in the labor force, as compared to 26.5 percent in the United States?[25] What is the cause of the surprisingly high rates of female participation in such "masculine" activities as construction in the U.S.S.R.? At first guess we might suppose that Communist ideology was responsible, but the merest glance at the sex ratios in productive cohorts is enough to convince us that the sheer physical absence of men was an important factor.

Several "quasi-population" categories are also of considerable interest in describing the morphology of a population. Since

---

[24] Computed from Warren Eason, "Labor Force," in *Economic Trends in the Soviet Union*, ed. Abram Bergson and Simon Kuznets (Cambridge, Mass.: Harvard University Press, 1963), pp. 38–95, table on p. 54.

[25] Ibid., p. 57.

every societal population must be related to a set of natural resources and be organized to exploit, process, and distribute
resources, the composition of a population by type of work is
very important. The most significant single index of occupational
composition is the percentage of the employed population engaged in agricultural pursuits. This percentage is frequently used
as an index of industrialization and economic and social development. The percentage of a societal population engaged in
agriculture affects the capacity of the population to engage in
some complex forms of political and social activity. The burden of
agriculture is such an important limiting factor that it should be
an established canon of comparative research on societies that
every generalization about societal organization must state
whether it holds for all societies or only for societies at a given
level of freedom from agricultural pursuits.[26]

The nations of the contemporary world display a full range of
variation on this variable. In the United States and the United
Kingdom, more than 90 percent of the working population are in
nonagricultural occupations. In virtually all of the nations of
Western Europe, more than 75 percent are in nonagricultural occupations. Some of the more developed nations of Asia and Latin
America (e.g., Japan, Pakistan, Argentina, Chile, Venezuela) now
have more than 50 percent in nonagricultural pursuits. On the
other hand, many underdeveloped nations have more than 75
percent of the working population in agriculture.[27]

Space will not permit even a catalogue of the various compositional features of a population that are useful in societal
analysis. Two brief final comments must suffice. First, when societies are compared, their populations display both intersocietal
and intrasocietal distributions quite similar to (and correlated
with) the distribution of the labor force into agricultural and
nonagricultural occupations. This is true, for example, of such
variables of composition as education, real income, and degree
of occupational specialization. Second, the heterogeneity of a
societal population provides information useful in locating potential sources of cleavage in societal systems. When persons are
physically confronted with others of different race, religion, or
ethnic origin, they sometimes make something of it.

[26] Cf. Marsh, who makes a similar point with respect to the degree of societal differentiation
using percent of the labor force outside of agriculture as one element in establishing differentiation. Robert M. Marsh, *Comparative Sociology: A Codification of Cross-Societal Analysis*
(New York: Harcourt Brace Jovanovich, Inc., 1967), pp. 33–37.

[27] Ibid., pp. 338–347.

SPACE AND RESOURCES

Location and Movement

Thus far we have considered the morphology of populations without reference to their location and movement in space. Like other morphological characteristics, location and movement are both cause and effect. They refer to human activities and reflect the patterns and adjustments of human process systems. At the same time, once an activity has been located in space with some degree of permanence, it represents a given for actors and a resource or a constraint for social systems.

Human Ecology: Resources and the Friction of Space

The study of the relations between organized populations and their environments is sometimes termed human ecology. The ecological approach views human societies as dependent on the exploitation of the resources of the natural environment. Hence, human organization can be seen as an adaptive response to the problems of extracting and transforming natural resources. Extraction implies access; therefore, the location of human activity must be related to the location of natural resources. Of course, resources, finished products, and human beings can be moved; but, since transportation is costly, the "friction of space" affects the allocation of activities in space. Accordingly, spatial patterns of location and movement often provide convenient indices of the underlying patterns of man's adaptive organization. Again, it should be emphasized that ecological theory does not state that location is the determinant of society. We are still talking about activities; we are merely stating that man must be "where the action is," or at least close to it. We do not find farmers living in New York City and commuting daily to Wisconsin to work the land. Nor do we find New York agriculturalists attempting to farm vacant lots on Wall Street. That area has become too devoted to the high-level coordination of the complex activity of financial and legal institutions, which requires a high level of density of persons per square foot. It is no longer economical to use the space for primary extraction of foodstuffs from the land. On the other hand, these people must eat lunch, so there is a niche for the sort of activity carried on in lunchrooms. In short, as activity is coordinated with resources and other activity, the resulting interdependencies are expressed in patterns of location.[28]

In the ecological perspective, we do not lose sight of action and process. Even resources are not static givens. In the words of Erich Zimmerman, "resources are not, they become."[29] What is or is not a resource depends on man's technological development, his organizational capacity, and his goals. Zimmerman cites as an example of this "functional theory of resources" the conversion of Brazilian "neutral stuff" into coal. This transformation required the organization of international cooperation between Brazil and the United States, the investment of capital, a domestic market for Brazilian steel, a Brazilian government willing to subsidize steel production, a foreign market for iron ore created by World War II, able and willing labor, modern sanitation to make the ore-producing area livable, and the technology of steel production. To be sure, the physical substance of coal was present prior to this social development. The development could not have occurred without it. But only a whole complex of culture, organization, and technology determine the way coal *functions* as a resource; it is far from a static environmental condition.[30]

One major contribution of the ecological concept of social organization is the idea that *key functions* exercise *dominance*. From the ecological perspective, resource systems are *dominant* relative to other process systems; that is, other process systems must adapt themselves to the systems which create resources in the environment.[31] Translated to spatial terms, this means that dominant activities have first call on space, and other activities locate themselves around and according to their relations to dominant activities. Thus, the activities in the center of a cluster of interdependent activities may be seen as exercising dominance radially from the center to the peripheries of activity. In a small community, for instance, we might see a cement plant located near a deposit of lime and an available transportation ar-

[28] For an excellent short statement of the ecological approach see Amos Hawley, "Human Ecology," *International Encyclopedia of the Social Sciences*, Volume 4, pp. 328–337.

[29] Erich W. Zimmermann, *Introduction to World Resources*, ed. by Henry L. Hunter (New York: Harper and Row, Publishers, 1964), p. 21.

[30] Ibid., p. 20.

[31] Hawley, *Human Ecology*, 1950, pp. 45, 221.

tery; labor locates itself in relation to available employment at the plant; and retail businesses in relation to the availability of workers as customers. The spatial relations involved are indicative of the patterns of differentiation and dominance in the activities.

The theme of dominance is related to the most significant trend in the location of societal populations in modern times. As the creation of usable resources has become more and more centered in complex and interdependent systems of mechanized production, these systems, and the overarching governmental, legal, and financial systems that coordinate productive activity, become the key functional systems of the society. Many of these activities require the massing of large numbers of people in central locations, giving rise to the phenomenon of *urbanization*. The activities of cities come to dominate activities in the hinterland. As techniques of transportation and communication improve, the areas over which central locations can exercise coordination and dominance increases, and, in a cycle of reciprocal causation, additional dominant activity comes to be located in the urban area. In consequence, a larger and larger percentage of the societal population come to live in large cities. The actual number of points of concentration may not increase, but the most important central locations become focal points for larger and larger complexes of activities.

Urbanization is a part of the process of expansion described in chapter two. It is not new on the world scene; there have been (and, to some extent there still are) preindustrial cities.[32] Urbanization occurred in Mesopotamia in the fourth millennium, as centrally organized systems of water control created new agricultural resources and the dominance exercised by these systems of control came to be located in the urbanized city states of Sumer.[33] This process has been a part of human history more or less continuously since that time, but only in the modern world have some societal populations become virtually entirely urbanized. About 70 percent of the population of the United States live in urban areas,[34] and many of those who are still classified as rural

---

[32] Gideon Sjoberg, "The Rural-Urban Dimension in Preindustrial, Transitional, and Industrial Societies," in *Handbook*, ed. Faris, pp. 127–159.

[33] V. Gordon Child, *What Happened in History* (Baltimore, Md.: Penguin Books, 1954), pp. 89–112.

[34] U.S. Bureau of the Census, *Statistical Abstract of the United States: 1967*, 88th edition (Washington, D.C., 1967), p. 16.

dwellers work in cities, shop in cities, and are continuously subject to a variety of urban influences.

Urbanization has been a dominant trend in all the nations of the industrialized world. Thirty percent of the population of Europe and more than 40 percent of the populations of North America and Oceania now live in cities of 100,000 or more persons. Many nations with an intermediate level of economic development have between 10 and 20 percent of their populations in cities of 100,000 or more. In most of the underdeveloped countries of Asia and Africa, less than 10 percent of the population reside in cities that large.[35] Nevertheless, world urbanization is proceeding at a rapid rate, and many fundamentally agricultural nations have developed immense cities, for example, Shanghai and Bombay; in some agricultural societies very large cities develop even in the absence of the urbanization of the population at large.

It has been estimated that in 1800 less than 2 percent of the world lived in cities of over 100,000; by 1900 the percentage had increased to 5.5 percent, and by 1960 to 20 percent. Spectacular as this growth appears, these figures probably *underestimate* the growing dominance of large centers of population over vast hinterlands.[36]

Urbanization has a number of important consequences on the basic conditions of interaction among societal populations. First, it increases the range and frequency of social contacts by increasing population densities. If the population of the United States were spread evenly around the nation's land area, we would have a population density of approximately 50 per square mile. By contrast, U.S. cities of 500,000 to 1,000,000 persons have an average density of nearly 6,000 per square mile; the density of the city of New York is about 25,000 per square mile. Urban densities in Paris, London, and Tokyo are even higher.[37] To feed and to house such large and dense populations requires considerable overhead costs and investments in facilities. Such investment is especially difficult for poor nations, and we have

---

[35] H. Wentworth Eldredge, "People, Urbanization, and City Growth," in *Taming Megalopolis*, ed. H. W. Eldredge (Garden City, N.Y.: Doubleday and Company, Inc., Anchor Books, 1967), p. 96.

[36] Ibid., p. 95.

[37] Raymond E. Murphy, *The American City* (New York: McGraw-Hill Book Company, 1966), pp. 158–159.

in consequence an array of very poor living conditions in the impoverished urban centers of agricultural nations.

A second consequence of urbanization is the increased mobility of the societal population. As transportation and communication facilities are improved and the city intensifies its influence over an expanding area, movement to and from cities becomes more frequent. Indeed, the growth of cities through migration implies an increase in the societal character of a population. As Belgians have moved in increasing numbers to Brussels from the French and Flemish areas of Belgium, it has become increasingly difficult to think of the nation as enclosing two societal populations, one French and the other Flemish. Brussels, set in the heart of the Dutch-speaking province of Brabant, is a society-creating center, causing residential movement across an ethnically mixed population. This example points to a third implication of urbanization. Urbanization, and its concomitant increase in mobility within societal populations, increases contact between linguistically and ethnically diverse societal groups.

CONCLUSION

The members of every societal population participate in a number of process systems. These process systems produce regular patterns of births, deaths, composition, location, and movement in the population; thus, we may speak of the underlying population as exhibiting structure. It is important to remember, as we study societal process systems, that the participants in these systems are members of structured populations. The structure of societal populations provides a set of underlying variables that exert powerful influences on the organization of systems of social action.

The influences of the structure of a population are many and varied, but one summary word describes the main dynamic factors in societal populations today—growth. Societal populations are growing; the number of persons emancipated from agricultural labor is growing; and urban populations are growing. Growth has been a more or less continuous trend in human history. In earlier times, growth was associated with the expansion of the territorial extent of societal populations. In the modern world, growth has reached unprecedented rates and is occurring in the context of the stabilization of national boundaries. In consequence, current rates of growth are causing the rapid "societalization" of populations; we are observing the development of well-bounded, highly mobile populations, dominated by large urban centers of coordination and influence.

Growth, because of its dynamic implications, is a crucial backdrop for the study of society. Growth is not merely dynamic in the tautologous sense that if a population is becoming larger it is *ipso facto* changing its size. Kenneth Boulding, drawing on the works of the biologist d'Arcy Thompson, has called our attention to the principle of "nonproportional change."[38] As something increases in size, the internal proportions of its components or dimensions cannot remain the same because the relations between the variables in a system are not all linear. To cite a simple physical example, the area of a circle increases as the square of the radius. Hence, as a circle becomes larger, the ratio of the radius of the circle to its area becomes smaller; the internal ratios change as the whole becomes larger. By analogy, as the territory of a population expands, the distance from the center of control to the periphery becomes a declining proportion of the total area to be controlled, a fact with important implications for the extension of influence. Since many communication functions (such as transportation) can only move in a linear manner, the expansion of area puts a tremendous strain on the communicative capacities of a social system. Such examples could be multiplied by reference to all the other social system variables that are related in a nonlinear way. Accordingly, growth is problematic for systems of social action; it is a constant source of strain and change. Our study of the process systems of society will attempt to keep the potent facts of societal and urban growth in the forefront of the analysis.

[38] Kenneth E. Boulding, "Toward a General Theory of Growth," *Canadian Journal of Economics and Political Science* 19 (August 1953), pp. 326–340.

4

Systems of Solidarity

THE NATURE OF SOLIDARITY

This section is founded on the assumptions that social actors have emotions about other people and that social emotions affect both stability and change in social life. Some people are loved and others are hated; some groups are "we" and others are "they"; we are attracted to some and repelled by others. Because of human emotional ties, patterns of solidarity emerge in society —attraction, loyalty, and identification. Solidary ties are expressed in human activity as men love or fight, care for or ignore one another, cooperate or work at cross-purposes. Like other activity, conduct based on emotional ties is collectively and institutionally organized. The grouping of a population into a set of families whose activities are organized by the role-defining institutions of kinship and marriage illustrates the social organization of emotional ties and provides an example of a *system of solidarity*.

A *system of solidarity* is any social process organized around the function of encouraging, stabilizing, and regulating patterns of attraction, repulsion, loyalty, and identity within a population. The members of every societal population participate in one or more such systems, and at least one system of solidarity. Kinship, is found in all societies. But solidarity is not limited to kin units; it exists in communities, in ethnic groups, in work groups, and in religious associations. In many cases, men's identities, that is, their intense feelings of membership in groups, extend to nations or even to cross-societal groups. Because of the multiplicity and complexity of solidary relationships, it is useful to see populations as involved in a number of separate but interwoven systems of solidarity. In this section, we will explore the organization of societal populations into these systems.

We will not be concerned primarily with the social psychology of personal bonds. There is a voluminous and very interesting literature in social psychology on "interpersonal attraction." Why are people drawn to some people and not to others? Is it that we like people who share our beliefs and attitudes? Or are people attracted to each other when they have complementary needs? We will not attempt to answer this type of question. In societal analysis, the focus is on the patterns, functions, and institutional organization of networks of emotional ties and solidary groups.

In examining the process systems of society, we begin with systems of solidarity because of the widespread belief that such systems have an evolutionary primacy. The pervasive influence of solidary groups in primitive societies is frequently asserted. Social anthropologists and students of social evolution have often noted that the institutional organization of all kinds of activities—economic, political, religious, and educational—is deeply embedded in the kinship organization of pre-literate societies. From this perspective, the process of evolution consists in the specialization of social organization and the emancipation of social functions from kin groups and the local community.[1] The same process viewed from another perspective can be described as a loss of function for solidary groups. Hence one of the main concerns of theories of social change: Does social development imply the decline of solidary ties—"the loss of community"?

[1] Talcott Parsons, "Evolutionary Universals in Society," *American Sociological Review* 29 (June 1964) pp. 339–357.

Solidarity: Battleground of Social Theory

Most of the classic and influential theories of solidarity were conceived as attempted solutions to the problem of the reality of the collective. Wherein lies the unity or the integrity that makes the group more than its individual members?

Freud, for example, approached the problem of group solidarity in the context of an attempt to account for the unity and suggestibility of crowds as they had been described by Le Bon.[2] Freud found his solution in the concept of identification; the members of a cohesive group identify with a leader for his heroic or otherwise admirable qualities, and identify with each other because of their common tie to the leader. Out of this network of emotional bonds arises a group with collective properties.[3]

Marx, in discussing the solidarity of the workers, speaks of the transformation of a "class-in-itself" to a "class-for-itself." The former is a group whose members are objectively similar in their place in a system of production; all work for wages but the group is a mere aggregate of wage earners. When this group becomes aware of its common interests and its historic mission, it has become a class-for-itself, a proletariat, a solidary group. For Marx, this transformation is brought about by class struggle and conflict, which manifest and teach the underlying polarities of interest in the economic system.[4]

Simmel, who also stressed the role of conflict in defining the tensions and solidarities in human relations, was fond of ironic demonstrations of the collective character of the seemingly anti-social. Conflict, isolation, the stranger, and secrecy are, despite superficial appearances, *social* forms, examples of the mutual influence we call society. Conflict, because of the mutual solidarities that it defines and maintains, is one of the constituents of the specifically collective character of group life.[5]

---

[2] Sigmund Freud, *Group Psychology and the Analysis of the Ego*, trans. by James Strachey (New York: Liveright Publishing Corporation, 1951) pp. 5–32.

[3] Ibid., p. 80.

[4] For an explanation and discussion of this point, see C. Wright Mills, *The Marxists* (New York: Dell Publishing Co., Inc., 1962) pp. 87–88, 113–115.

[5] Georg Simmel, *Conflict and the Web of Group Affiliations*, trans. by Kurt H. Wolff and Reinhard Bendix (New York: The Free Press, 1955); Lewis Coser, *The Functions of Social Conflict* (Glencoe, Ill.: The Free Press, 1956).

Among contemporary thinkers, Parsons provides an example of the linking of solidarity and the collective level of social action. For Parsons, solidarity is "institutionalized loyalty"; it occurs when actors come to value the integrity of their association for its own sake. When this occurs, mere loyalty is transformed into solidarity, and the maintenance of the integrity of the group becomes a basis for placing binding obligations upon its members. Only at this point may we say that a group has achieved collectivity. It is interesting to note that Parsons recognizes the continuity of his conception of solidarity with the historic tradition of sociological thought. In particular, Sumner's concept of the "mores" involves the idea that some group habits become associated with ideas of the welfare of the group and therefore become a strongly binding force.[6]

Because of the close affinity between the concept of solidarity and the search for social reality outside of the individual, solidarity has become a battleground of social theory. As we have seen in chapter one, the search for encompassing social reality is also a search for a standard for political action or a justification for political control.

These ideological affinities are particularly manifest in the French tradition to which Durkheim was heir. Among the French political theorists of the second half of the nineteenth century, the term *solidarité* had become virtually synonomous with fraternity, the third term in the republican formula, *liberté, égalité, fraternité*. For these thinkers, *solidarité* became a shorthand expression for the real and discoverable social order from which men's obligations to each other may be derived.[7]

Durkheim's special genius transformed this rather sterile tradition into a stimulating and influential series of contributions to the study of human solidarity. He used the term to refer to the overall integration and cohesion of a society, but the general form of his argument is applicable to the problem of solidarity in the narrower, less inclusive sense in which it is used here. Durkheim proposed a basic distinction between types of solidarity which has influenced sociologists of many stripes and persuasions over the last seventy-five years: The members of a population may be bound together by their like-mindedness; to use the Durkheimian language, they may participate in a common-consciousness and construct the social and moral order in the

[6] Parsons, *Social System*, pp. 97–98.

[7] Leon Bourgeois, *Solidarité* (Paris: Librarie Armand Colin, 1926).

same terms. Or they may be bound by the division of labor, by the complementary interests that derive from the differentiation of interdependent social roles. The division of labor forces interdependent people to establish mutually beneficial relationships of exchange.[8] At the same time, Durkheim stressed that the two forms are not mutually antagonistic, for the latter form, integration by complementarity, presupposes an institutional framework. In any exchange, there must be a common set of premises in order to permit the participants to construct a stable relation.[9] According to Durkheim, primitive societies are based more exclusively on common consciousness or *mechanical solidarity*. The course of social evolution has intensified the division of labor and produced more *organic solidarity*. Nevertheless, a stable complementarity implies the continued development of common constructions of social reality among the population. It was Durkheim's hope that the formation of solidary groups among newly developed professional and occupational specializations would contribute to the continued creation of moral order in the modern world.[10]

Tied as he was to the polemics of the French tradition, Durkheim originally set his argument up as an answer to the claim that solidarity was declining in the modern world. Toennies, in his distinction between *Gemeinschaft* and *Geselschaft*, had argued that *Gemeinschaft*, or community, is losing hold in modern society. The natural bonds of affection and communal feeling are giving way to ties based upon mere calculation and self-interest.[11] In *The Division of Labor*, Durkheim argued that ties based on mutual interests always imply some sort of institutional framework which in turn implies solidary order outside the relationship. Durkheim, though he stressed this solidary level in his theoretical argument, also recognized that the breakdown and dislocation of the social ties of mechanical solidarity can create serious problems. In his concepts of "egoism" and "anomie," he called attention to endemic problems of malintegration and normlessness in industrial societies. In doing so he entered in a raging and still current controversy about solidarity in mod-

[8] Durkheim, *Division of Labor*, pp. 70–132.

[9] Ibid., pp. 200–229.

[10] Ibid., pp. 1–31.

[11] Toennies, *Fundamental Concepts of Sociology*.

ern societies.[12] What happens to primary direct communal ties
when social systems are no longer loosely connected sets of
segmentary local kin groups? What happens when communities
become large, highly differentiated, territorially extensive systems, founded on rapid, frequent, and extensive movement, rational calculation, and the intrusion of outside interests into local
solidary groups? These questions have become a major battleground for social theory, and alternative answers animate much
of the discussion of solidary relations. Does growth of the scale
and complexity of society destroy solidary ties, dislocating people and leaving them isolated, without meaningful identities and
relationships? Or do new sorts of meaningful groups develop
within the context of large-scale organization? Do primary solidary ties maintain themselves but become more specialized and
differentiated? Do new forms of more extensive solidary ties
develop in complex modern societies? Is it possible that modern
societies will develop solidarity through the elaboration of secondary associations such as professional and occupational
groupings?

Various theorists have answered all of these questions in the
affirmative. Many have, in the tones of Cassandra, bemoaned the
isolation of modern man. Others have recognized that tightly
knit groups develop within large organizations—work groups in
factories, "buddy" groups in armies, friendship networks in
unions; the important question is whether these groups support
the goals of the larger organization or are alienated. Parsons has
claimed that some solidary institutions, the family, for example,
maintain themselves in modern society; they simply become
more specialized in their functions. Families lose economic and
other functions to specialized institutions, but the modern family
becomes more devoted to emotional, therapeutic functions.[13]
Further, solidary ties are not limited to small face-to-face groups;
new forms of solidarity, different in character from the solidary
primary ties between members of small groups, emerge in the
large-scale differentiated society.

According to this view, one of the historic moral concerns of
American sociology has been somewhat misdirected. Cooley,
who coined the term "primary groups" for groups "characterized

---

[12] Emile Durkheim, *Suicide*, trans. John A. Spaulding and George Simpson (Glencoe, Ill.: The
Free Press, 1951).

[13] For a good discussion of this issue see Dennis H. Wrong, "The Break-up of the American
Family," *Commentary* 9 (April 1950), pp. 374–380.

by intimate face-to-face association and cooperation,"[14] joined a number of American social theorists in asking how community can be extended beyond the limits of the small group. How, in the face of the extension of social organization to a variety of ramified and segmental associations, can the ties and ideals of primary groups be maintained in social life? Will we be frustrated in our search for society as larger reality and moral context?[15] When the problem is formulated in this way, the direct face-to-face emotional bond becomes the prototype of solidarity. In the genetic sense this is probably true, but to define the problem of the extension of solidarity in these terms is to risk overlooking the rise of new manifestations of solidarity.

Nevertheless, in one sense this American tradition is fundamentally correct; the *extension* of solidarity *is* always problematic. We cannot assume that as the size and territory of populations increase, as these populations become more dominated by urban centers, and as the scope of economic and political systems expand, systems of solidarity will extend to the boundaries of other widely inclusive systems. Economic and political systems tend to outrun the boundaries of solidarity, to force the confrontation of opposing populations, and to create cleavages in solidary organization. To assume, as social-system theory frequently does, that solidary systems are coextensive with political and economic systems is to fail to appreciate the origins of such important societal phenomenon as racial and ethnic divisions and the rise of nationalism. Worse, such an assumption ignores the structural impetus to the development of new forms of solidarity.

The extension of solidarity is problematic because solidary systems tend to be institutionalized rather than instrumental. They are based upon sentimental ties built up over a long period of time and reinforced by clear and established rituals and norms; they are deeply embedded in an established social order, the very order whose network of relationships created a set of commitments of actors to each other. In contrast, economic systems can more readily be instrumental in character. The participants can interact on a more superficial basis and can create novel, practical, and expedient institutional settings for their transactions. In the realm of solidarity, the creation of new and

[14] Charles Horton Cooley, *Social Organization* (New York: Charles Scribner's Sons, 1920), p. 23.

[15] Ibid., pp. 32–37.

more inclusive forms is not impossible, but it confronts more deeply rooted obstacles.

INTEGRATION OF SOLIDARY SYSTEMS

Forms of Solidarity

Our strategy at this point will be to outline a model of an integrated system of solidarity in a modern society. We will then note the points at which the assumptions of this model are unable to describe the dynamics of solidarity in the face of the expansion of populations and process systems.

An integrated solidary system requires the existence of four forms of solidarity. First, there are primary ties of affection based on direct emotional attractions between people. We will call this type of solidarity *attraction*. Every person is attracted to an aggregate of others, and this produces a network of circles of attraction in every population. When a member of an operative social group is attracted to that group and comes to view it as a unit whose integrity and aims must be protected, we may speak of *loyalty*, the second form of solidarity.

Attraction and loyalty are both based on direct positive emotional attachments for persons and groups. The difference between them rests on whether the objects of attachment are aggregates, defined by the choices of given persons, or established, institutionally defined, operative groups, such as families, work groups, or army units. The other two forms of solidarity are founded not on direct emotional attachments but on a sense of membership or inclusion in a group. We speak of *identification* when a person sees himself as a member of a group, when part of his identity, his conception of himself, derives from his sense of membership in a group. Identifications often refer to broader groups than do attractions or loyalties. An American Negro need not like all other Negroes to recognize a common fate with other Negroes and experience identity as a Negro. Established institutionally defined groups that have this sense of membership will be termed *identity groups*. Identity groups range in scope from a few members to whole nations, and every actor has a wide range of manifest identities as well as a number of latent identities that are mobilized in the social process.

The term for the fourth form of solidarity, *association*, is used in this context more narrowly than in common parlance. When actors reach out and establish common cause with others who do not share an established group membership, we may call this process association; it is a process of the creation of solidarities that cross-cut established groups and identities. Following Parsons, we may interpret the process of exercising influence as establishing solidarities of this kind. In the Parsonian paradigm, influence consists in affecting another's behavior by pointing out that what is wanted of him is in his own interests. The subject and the object of influence create a new solidarity, for he who influences creates a "we" by saying, "Let us do this for it is in our interests."[16] Extensive social differentiation creates a multiplicity of roles and interests and, thus, a variety of opportunities for associations that transcend and cross-cut established identity groups. The ties of cooperation and trust created by association are as important a component of solidarity systems as the more immediate ties of attraction and loyalty, though the former may be more brittle and difficult to institutionalize.

The Integration of Systems of Solidarity

A societal population participates in an integrated complex of systems of solidarity when six conditions are met:

1) *All members of the societal population must have intense attractions, loyalties, identities, and associations.* An integrated system of solidarity requires the extensive development of all four forms of solidarity.

2) *There must be a vertical alignment of attraction and loyalty.* Students of the primary group have repeatedly called our attention to the fact that organizations cannot maintain cohesion and effectiveness without strong solidarity within their small operative groups. Further, these groups must not be alienated, that is, they must not develop subgroup norms or goals in opposition to the aims of the larger organization.[17] For example, studies in industrial sociology include many examples of the restriction of industrial output by small solidary work groups that command the loyalties of the individual factory worker. Follow-

[16] Talcott Parsons, *Sociological Theory and Modern Society* (New York: The Free Press, 1967), pp. 366–378.

[17] Edward A. Shils, "The Study of Primary Groups," in *The Policy Sciences*, ed. Daniel Lerner and Harold D. Lasswell (Stanford, Calif.: Stanford University Press, 1951), pp. 44–69.

ing the analogous terminology of Durkheim, we will call the direct attachment of individuals to the other members of operative groups and the vertical alignment of the goals of groups and subgroups *mechanical solidarity.* Following the terminology of chapter two, we may also refer to mechanical solidarity as "the collective organization of solidarity," for it refers to the social organization of attraction through its location in the operative goal-seeking groups of society.

The importance of the collective organization of solidarity is illustrated by studies of the cohesion and disintegration of armies. During World War II, students of the American soldier learned that the effectiveness of combat units does not depend merely on an effective chain of command; it depends on intense loyalties to immediate comrades and a consequent willingness to fight for the security of the primary group.[18] Similarly, a study of the German *Wehrmacht* revealed that the German soldier fought doggedly during the last months of the war, even though the German army was hopelessly overpowered from a strategic standpoint; he fought not for secondary political or cultural symbols but because of the solidarity of his immediate primary groups.[19]

3) *In a modern urban society, mechanical solidarity requires the extension of ties of attraction beyond the boundaries of established identity groups and bureaucratically defined categories.* In a highly mobile society containing many large scale organizations, persons from diverse racial, cultural, and ethnic backgrounds are thrown together in operative groups. Further, in large-scale organization, bureaucratic hierarchies develop; by definition, their development means that some operative groups will contain members of varying statuses. Hence, in modern society mechanical solidarity is problematic for it requires persons to become attracted to others who are socially distant. There is, of course, a similar problem in stratified premodern societies, but the rise of democratic ideologies exacerbates the situation.

4) *There must be an alignment of association and identification.* Association is a tentative process which requires institutional ratification. There are two basic types of association. In one

[18] Edward A. Shils, "Primary Groups in the American Army," in *Continuities in Social Research,* ed. Robert K. Merton and Paul Lazarsfeld (Glencoe, Ill.: The Free Press, 1950), pp. 16–39.

[19] Edward A. Shils and Morris Janowitz, "Cohesion and Disintegration in the *Wehrmacht* in World War II," *Public Opinion Quarterly* 12 (Summer 1948), pp. 280–315.

type, persons in differentiated positions reach out to form an *alliance* based on common or complementary interests. In the second type, a person assumes the position of spokesman for an alleged common interest. For such a person we will resurrect the term *prolocutor*. A prolocutor is not the appointed spokesman of an established, unified, tightly organized group, but a person who *alleges* a solidarity by presuming to speak for a "we." In this sense, the leader of an emergent social movement, the journalist or publicist, and the leader of any somewhat heterogenous group are prolocutors. In these cases, the "we" formed in the process of association is tenuous and tentative. An alliance or a prolocutorship must be ratified by the formation of new identities to cement the newly emergent ties. Because of Durkheim's analogous use of the phrase "organic solidarity" to denote the institutional integration of diversity, we may use that phrase to describe the alignment of association and identification. Also, following Durkheim, it is important to recognize that organic solidarity is possible because of the existence of institutional forms which can be used or modified to express, regulate, and stabilize new associations. To illustrate, Joseph Smith and his associates acted as prolocutors in founding the Latter-Day Saint (Mormon) Church. They asserted a community of interest that could bind all men. But Mormonism emerged as one of the constituent solidary identity groups of American society when the members of the Church adapted the available institutional forms of religion—priesthood, the sunday school, baptism, sacraments, etc. —to their collective activity. Nevertheless, Mormonism continues to be a form of association, for it continues to claim a universally valid path to salvation and proseletyzes for the association of new members, who may or may not adopt and maintain the Mormon identity.

5) *In a modern, highly differentiated society, organic solidarity requires the extension of identities.* The free play of a variety of interests and the loosening of the bonds of traditional groups create favorable conditions for the rise of association; alliances, mass movements, and the expansion of mass media of communication are frequent concomitants of modernization. Nevertheless, the stabilization of association is always problematic, for association cannot become institutionally ratified unless old identities are transcended in order to form new, more inclusive ones. To return to our example, the Mormon church made many converts of immigrants of diverse Northern European national backgrounds and from a broad range of social strata.

Hence, it was necessary to make Mormonism a transcendent identity.

6) *The ties of attraction, loyalty, identification, and association must cross-cut each other.* Students of society have long appreciated the significance of cross-cutting ties in integrating a system of multiple and conflicting solidarities. E. A. Ross, writing in 1920, said:

> Several . . . oppositions may be in full swing at the same time but the more numerous they are the less menacing is any one. Every species of conflict interferes with every other species in society at the same time, save only when their lines of cleavage coincide, in which case they reinforce each other. . . . For each new cleavage contributes to narrow the cross clefts, so that one might say that society is sewn together by its inner conflicts.[20]

Thus, out of a large number of solidary attachments of relatively limited extent may be born a vast system of cross-cutting ties so that large numbers of persons are bound in a common network. What from one perspective is conflict is from another perspective a process whereby the subgroups of society increase their cohesiveness. Through conflict, persons discover new common interests and are drawn into wider circles of association. Conflict may bring latent identities to the surface, and the net result is to strengthen the unit loyalties from which the system of solidarity is built. The crucial question is not whether conflict exists between solidary subgroups but whether the lines of opposition reinforce or cross-cut each other.

In modern societies, actors are brought together to participate in a wide variety of large, extensive systems. These actors often have strong roots in disparate cultural and ethnic groupings. Populations once relatively separate are welded into a single societal population, and the emergence of strong cross-cutting ties is problematic. In this situation, one common form of emergent cross-cutting ties is the overarching inclusive tie to the total society as a community. In modern parlance, this community is usually called the *nation*, and the development of nationalism is one of the most important subjects in the study of modern systems of societal solidarity.

[20] Edward A. Ross, *Principles of Sociology* (New York: The Century Company, 1923), pp. 164–165.

Cleavage and Fragmentation

Many social theorists have expressed the hope that mechanical and organic solidarity are possible in large-scale societies, that man's tasks can be well-motivated by placement in attractive primary groups, that a varied and complex associational life can express a wide variety of interests and meaningful identifications. Reality obviously falls somewhat short of these aspirations, for the conditions of an integrated solidary system as outlined in the previous section are not fully met in any large society. The scale of solidarity does not increase as rapidly as the expansion of societal populations. The constraints on the expansion of solidarity do not come about because of an inability to expand ties beyond immediate associates. To attribute the problem to the notion that man can only find meaning in intimate and personal relations is to indulge in an argument parallel to the mercantilist argument in economic thought: Only gold is wealth. Analysis of solidarity in modern society requires sensitivity to the more subtle forms of association. When a spokesman assumes a prolocutorship, that is, when he presumes to speak for a "we," he creates a solidarity. The ratification of this solidarity does not require a positive, active endorsement of all of the relevant people any more than the solvency of an economy depends on holding sufficient precious metal to back up every dollar in the system. All that is required is sufficient endorsement to produce trust in the spokesman's claim.[21]

The limits of solidarity are not an expression of man's need for intimacy; they reflect structural problems associated with the expansion of social systems through *conglomeration*. The territorial and numerical expansion of societal populations and of political and economic process systems involves conglomerating culturally, racially, and nationally diverse peoples, who have disparate institutions of solidarity, into larger populations and systems. In consequence, it becomes difficult to create solidary ties across the constituent groups in the conglomerate, especially when such groups form social strata of differing rank or class. The oppositions within society come not to cross-cut but to reinforce each other. Such reinforced cleavages occur whenever diverse racial, ethnic, cultural, religious, regional, or political groups or strata fail to participate in common solidary groups. The members of the opposing groups participate in segregated

[21] Parsons, *Theory and Modern Society*, p. 368.

subgroups and develop separate institutional facilities even, in the extreme case, confining some groups to specific occupational roles.[22]

Conglomeration and reinforced cleavage have several related sources. Conquest, or the expansion of a frontier, may incorporate separate groups into one population as when, with the Spanish and Portuguese conquest and the subsequent expansion of Iberian influence, the Indian became a part of the societal population of Latin America. A newly arrived conquering group may transform an old economy, creating new occupational niches to be filled by subsequent immigration, voluntary or involuntary. In the case of the United States, the plantation economy of the South led to the forced movement of Negro slaves from Africa. Plantation development in Hawaii proceeded by a series of voluntary migrations from Asia.[23]

The growth of inter-regional interdependence is an extremely important source of conglomeration. When large territorial areas come to specialize in limited types of economic activity, *export economies*, which are dependent on a system of interregional trade, develop. These territorial areas become economic units, and political apparatus is established to develop regional resources and to protect trading opportunities. With the growth of larger territorial systems, diverse local groups find themselves brought together in a single population. Such was the base for the political development of societies as diverse as Greece in the fifth century B.C. (founded on olives and wine) and Germany in the eighteenth and nineteenth centuries (based on iron and rye).

In the contemporary world, conglomerate societal populations have been formed as a heritage of Western imperialism, for Western powers often established administrative units in Asia and Africa that extended beyond the boundaries of traditional solidarities. As these units gain independence, they enter into a world political system which takes nations as its units, even if they are somewhat arbitrary conglomerations.

One rough index of the degree of fragmentation of a societal population is the percentage of the population that speaks a single dominant language. The index ranges from virtually 100 percent in the countries of Western Europe, except Belgium and Switzerland, to less than 33 percent in a dozen former African

[22] Pierre van den Berghe, *Race and Racism* (New York: John Wiley & Sons, Inc., 1967).

[23] Stanley Lieberson, "A Societal Theory of Race and Ethnic Relations," *American Sociological Review* 26 (December 1961), pp. 902–910.

states.[24] The power of colonial administration to produce conglomerate nations is manifest in the fact that of the bottom thirty-
three nations in a sample of sixty-six nations ranked according to
the percentage of speakers of a dominant language, twenty-six
are former European colonies.

Finally, urbanization and mobility, by drawing together persons from diverse regions and backgrounds, create populations
that are, in effect, more conglomerate, even in nations with a relatively long political history. All of the sources of conglomeration
—conquest, frontier movement, migration, urbanization, regional
interdependence, and international imperialism—have something in common. All are concomitants of the expansion of social
systems. Here we have another example of the importance of
recognizing the multiplicity of systems in society and the overlap of their boundaries. Intersocietal political and economic
systems often expand rapidly, and the interdependencies within
the new expanded systems are expressed in large scale movements of population and in the formation of large conglomerate
societal populations whose members participate in diverse solidarity systems of relatively limited extent.

In this context the rise of the nation-state in modern times
must be seen as a response to the emergent incongruence of system boundaries. Nationalism may be a mere instrument of those
whose interests demand the formation of a more inclusive and
intensive sense of identity within the large units of modern intersocietal systems, but nationalists, whatever the immediate
interests served by their actions, assume the role of prolocutor by
presuming to speak for an inclusive solidary group. Whether he
be spokesman for a rising bourgeoisie seeking a place in the political order (as in the case of England and France in the nineteenth century) or politician attempting to create an indigenous
political order (as in the case of many new nations), the nationalist creates a larger solidarity *by placing his goals in the framework of debate about the "common" good.* In so doing, new
commonalities are defined.

By a similar logic, the classic sociological theorists were
prolocutors. The theory of society asserted the existence of a solidary foundation for regulatory standards. By asserting the existence of "society," the sociological theorist refused to accept the
expanding political and economic systems of the nineteenth cen-

tury as uncontrollable givens, beyond the influence of any moral imperative implicit in the existence of a wider social community.

Solidarity and the Constraint Model

The problem of creating solidarity in conglomerate populations raises questions about the adequacy of a "constraint model" in the study of social change in emergent nations. As outlined in chapter two, the constraint model proposes that social conflicts and disturbances are resolved by "specifying" or drawing upon high levels of value-consensus in the population. Therefore, as new institutions of order are created, the overall value system of the society is reaffirmed. But the conflicts endemic in the solidary fragmentation of a conglomerate society cannot be referred back to higher levels of value-consensus, for, if the societal population is truly conglomerate, such consensus does not exist. There is no common cultural tradition to draw upon. In consequence, new cultural bases of identity must emerge. The "emergence model" seems more appropriate. Insofar as institution builders draw upon preestablished cultural forms, they are forms that are not implicit in the cultural heritage of the nation. Rather they are ideas, values, and symbols imported from other traditions, drawn from *international* political movements, such as communism or the world nationalist movement itself. In other words, paradoxically, the search for *nationhood* in a world of conglomerate populations tends to foster *international* social and cultural systems.

Plural Society and Mass Society

Conglomerate societies made up of disparate and separate cultural groupings have been termed "plural societies." This usage is confusing for a number of reasons. In the first place, the term has been used in a number of ways, by a number of authors, to describe a variety of degrees of conglomeration and institutional segregation.[25] M. G. Smith has convincingly argued that

[25] See J. S. Furnivall, *Colonial Policy and Practice* (London: Cambridge University Press, 1948); Lloyd Braithwaite, "Social Stratification in Trinidad," *Social and Economic Studies*, 2 (1952), pp. 3–175; Raymond T. Smith, *The Negro Family in British Guiana* (London: Routledge and Kegan Paul, 1956); M. G. Smith, *The Plural Society in the British West Indies* (Berkeley, Calif.: University of California Press, 1965). There is a review of the issue of

the term not be used to describe mere cultural heterogeneity or the existence of ethnic minorities in the population. It should be reserved for the case of maximal reinforced cleavage, when a population is divided into sections, each with a full range of totally segregated institutions, but with only one minority group maintaining political dominance. A society with a continuous, integrated class system with an ethnic minority group at the bottom would not, from this perspective, be a plural society, though it would have some reinforced cleavage.[26] Smith uses as his primary example the British West Indies, with its dominant white minority and institutionally segregated black, colored, East Indian, and Amerindian sections.[27]

The application of the term "pluralism" is further confused by its long recognized usage to describe a system that includes a wide variety of categories of people who are well organized and whose interests are effectively represented in the political arena. According to the theory of democratic pluralism, modern democratic societies permit the representation and articulation of a wide range of specialized interests; farmers, laborers, ethnic groups, and business interests all find their place in the competitive political process. Because the theory of pluralism asserts the existence of effective groups cross-cutting the major cleavages in society (broadly based publics and parties for example), it is in opposition to the theory of conglomerate societies.

The theory of democratic pluralism is called into question not only by the existence of conglomerate societies with weakly integrated systems of solidarity, but by the problem of the general breakdown of all solidary ties. Some commentators have alleged that industrialization and urbanization cut people off from all kinds of solidary groups. In consequence, the public is unable to become effective. The citizen, since he is not well integrated into independent groups, is subject to manipulation by the organs of power and of mass persuasion; his poorly-organized identity groups are unable to combat or resist the power elite.[28]

Although we will reconsider this issue in the chapter on polit-

---

plural societies in Lee A. Despres, "The Implications of Nationalist Politics in British Guiana for the Development of Cultural Theory," *American Anthropologist* 66 (October 1964) pp. 1051–1077.

[26] M. G. Smith, *Plural Society*, pp. 75–91.

[27] Ibid., pp. 18–74.

[28] C. Wright Mills, *The Power Elite* (New York: Oxford University Press, 1956), pp. 298–324.

ical process, the topic properly belongs under both headings. It is proper to introduce the issue in the context of a discussion of solidarity, for the two aspects of pluralism are closely linked. Moreover, though it is not commonly recognized, one of the major weaknesses in the democratic theory of pluralism is its failure to explicitly recognize the implications of the stratification of solidarity.

The Stratification of Solidarity

In every complex society, the degree of solidary integration varies among social strata. High-status persons are more likely to participate in extensive, even intersocietal, solidary systems. The attractions, loyalties, identities, and associations of low-status persons are more local and limited, involve fewer cross-cutting groups, and provide few ties with centralized dominant organizations.

The roles of the aristocracy and the church in medieval society illustrate the stratification of solidarity. In both church and aristocracy, particularly in their upper reaches, solidary ties extended across territorial divisions. The church was a Pan-European institution, and its professional participants were an educated and powerful elite. The upper aristocracy had kin and marital ties throughout and beyond the dynastic states of Europe. The ordinary peasant was more tied to a purely local scene; his horizons seldom extended even to the nascent units bounded by national borders.

Similarly, nationalism is, in the first instance, an elite movement. When the solidarity of the European church was destroyed by the Reformation, and the power of the aristocracy eclipsed by the rise of powerful central monarchs, a greater sense of national consciousness developed. Nevertheless, elites were the carriers and prolocutors of that developing movement; the rising middle class spoke for the nation in order to secure a place in national political life. Again, in the new nations of the twentieth century, the educated elites are more integrated into national life and the various associations that extend across the entire nation than are the lower classes. Those who speak of a power elite in the modernized industrial state are also speaking in part of the stratification of solidarity. The elite holders-of-power base a part of that power on organization; they have a territorially extensive set of solidary ties deriving from a wide network of memberships and associations, the "old school tie," for example. The ordinary citizen, and especially the members of segregated minorities, have fewer memberships, and their associations are more limited to immediate neighbors, associates, and kin.

It is not difficult to appreciate the sources of the stratification of solidarity. The members of high strata have both more resources to invest in creating and maintaining associations across long distances and across established groups and a more immediate interest in making such investments. Elite status is high status *within a social system*. The highest status goes to those whose status is high in the most extensive systems. Hence, as social systems expand, a person must be mobile and must maintain widespread connections in order to hold a position of influence. Neither the national leader nor the builder of nationhood can operate from a fixed local position and a set of purely local ties to kin and community. Prestige and influence require resources and a willingness to invest in affiliations throughout the whole territory of a system.

Hence, the expansion of social systems tends to produce not only conglomerate populations but also stratified systems of solidarity wherein the six criteria of integrated solidarity discussed above are more applicable to elites than to what are appropriately called the masses. In both cases, the expansion of social systems works against the assumptions of integrated solidarity.

THE INSTITUTIONS OF SOLIDARITY

Kinship

Solidarity, like other social functions, is regulated, facilitated, and encouraged by institutional frameworks. One such framework, kinship, universally defines a basic set of solidary relationships, and one specific institution, the *nuclear family*, is itself virtually universal.[29] In every population (with a few marginal exceptions), there is an institutionally recognized unit consisting of a married man and woman with their offspring. Operative familial units are often larger, including for example, more than one wife or more than two generations, but the larger aggregates include as components the basic nuclear unit. George Peter

[29] George Peter Murdock, *Social Structure* (New York: The Macmillan Company, 1944), pp. 1–21.

Murdock has concluded that this basic unit universally performs four social functions: It is a unit for expressing and regulating sexual urges, a unit of economic coöperation, a unit for producing children, and it is a unit that takes some responsibility for socializing and educating these children.[30] Of course, all of these activities also occur outside of nuclear families, but every human population participates in a kinship system, and every kinship system establishes a nuclear unit with sexual, economic, reproductive, and educational functions.

A second feature of kinship structure is also almost universal. Again with debatable exceptions, sexual intercourse (and hence marriage) is prohibited within the nuclear family by an *incest taboo*. This taboo has a profound impact on the structure of solidary institutions, for it forces the members of societies to create a ramified set of kin relations extending beyond the basic family unit. If mates must be chosen from outside of the nuclear family, then persons must establish solidary ties with the members of other nuclear families. The offspring of these ties are related to two separate groups of kin, one through the mother and one through the father. Thus, every member of a human population becomes a member of a bilateral kinship tree with a variety of types of biological relatedness. Such relations as maternal aunt, paternal uncle, paternal uncle's daughter, and many others are biologically universal. Various kinship systems recognize a variety of combinations of these relationships and treat them in varied ways, but the relationships are always there to provide a readymade network of ties which can be used as an institutional framework to create and define solidary units, ties, and social obligations. And, universally, the positions in a kinship network are used both to define stable structures and to provide a "language" for more fluid interaction.

The cross-cultural similarity and the ordered character of networks of biological kinship permit precise (indeed mathematical) formulation and rigorous cross-cultural testing of the uniformities in relations among the various features of kinship systems. The literature that has developed along these lines is too vast to review here.[31] For our purposes, the major cumulative contribution of kinship studies has been to demonstrate on a

[30] Ibid., pp. 4–10.

[31] For a review of this literature, see Morris Zelditch, Jr., "Family Marriage and Kinship" in *Handbook of Modern Sociology* ed. Robert E. L. Faris (New York: Rand McNally and Company, 1964) pp. 680–733.

massive scale the universal use of kin networks to provide solidary units and solidary ties. These units and ties provide a framework for the institutional definition of a wide variety of social functions. All manner of social responsibilities, obligations, and privileges can be defined in terms of obligations to one's kin. Thus, it is possible to embed all of the social functions in kinship. Because this is not uncommon in preliterate societies characterized by relatively small size and relatively unproductive technology, some of them have been referred to as "kin-organized" societies. The embedding of all types of social relations in networks of kinship is so prevalent in nonindustrial societies that Murdock, who drew a sample of such societies and examined their kinship organization, boldly entitled the resulting monograph *social structure*.[32] In the kin-organized society, the family is the main unit of production and exchange, and the individual's clan or kindred his main source of political protection.

Even in the kin-organized society, there are other institutions of solidarity which cross-cut kin ties and permit the institutionalization of other bases of association. For example, among the Sebei of East Africa, a man may trade a heifer for a bullock with the understanding that when the heifer is grown to a cow and has itself produced a heifer it will be returned. Sebei men may enter into dozens of long-term contracts, and each one implies mutual obligations of hospitality and good faith. Thus, a network of personal associations cross-cuts the lineage solidarity of the Sebei tribes.[33]

More inclusive solidary units are also common in kin-organized society. For example, age-sets may unite a group of males who undergo initiation together, uniting a male cohort across an entire community. The same initiation ceremony may also reinforce the solidarity of the entire male community, creating overarching ties across all lineages and families.[34] The principle of multiple cross-cutting solidarity is especially important in kin-organized societies because, in groups without central government, the peace of the community must depend upon the absence of reinforced cleavages. Diverse ties to patrilineal kin, matrilineal kin, and relatives by marriage, to partners in gift ex-

---

[32] Murdock, *Social Structure*.

[33] Walter Goldschmidt, *Sebei Law* (Berkeley, Calif.: University of California Press, 1967) pp. 189 250–251.

[34] Frank W. Young, *Initiation Ceremonies: A Cross Cultural Study of Status Dramatization* (Indianapolis: The Bobbs-Merrill Company, Inc., 1965).

changes, to age-sets, to local communities, and to ceremonial lodges prevent any one set of ties from polarizing the enmities and feuds within the group. This process has been nicely described for some of the stateless tribal societies of Africa. Among the Nuer, for example, the individual is bound to fight for his paternal clansmen, but a state of feud puts him into conflict with maternal relatives, toward whom he has especially tender feelings. These constraints, plus the need to live at peace with immediate neighbors who are not of the same lineage, are powerful forces for unity in the group. Nevertheless, in such a society, the solidary bonds across the entire population are rather weak and decline rapidly with distance. Such societies have relatively little sense of being an entire people.[35]

Religious Solidarity

In primitive society, the sense of solidarity in family, clan, and community is often reinforced with ritual, an important institution of solidarity. According to Durkheim, ritual serves to reunite the individual and the community. Religious symbols are collective representations of society itself; the totem animal, for example, represents not the forces of nature but the clan. Ritual activity around such religious symbols inculcates unity with and respect for the group.[36] The idea that God *is* society may seem rather farfetched, but the similar idea that religious beliefs reflect the actual *constitution* of the social order has helped to illuminate the problem of intersocietal variation in religious belief. Guy E. Swanson has discussed a variety of such relationships, including a connection between belief in a high God and the existence of a social order whose participants are able to perceive a higher order of sovereignty regulating the relations between lower-order sovereign groups.[37]

The intimate connection between religious ideology and ritual and the unity of the constituent groups of society suggests that religion is a second institutional focus of solidarity equal in importance to kinship. Historically, most social orders have been

[35] E. F. Evans-Pritchard, *The Nuer* (Oxford: Clarendon Press, 1940).

[36] Emile Durkheim, *The Elementary Forms of the Religious Life*, trans. Joseph Ward Swain (London: George Allen and Unwin Ltd., 1915).

[37] Guy E. Swanson, *The Birth of the Gods* (Ann Arbor: The University of Michigan Press, 1960).

sacred in character; the members of society have a shared identity of being believers in the reality of the symbols of their own collective life.

Modern Institutions and Constitutive Symbolism

If religion is such a force for solidarity, how can we also explain its divisive force in so many historical epochs? We do not fully understand the transformation of religion from a symbol of collective unity to a weapon of intrasocietal conflict. Nevertheless, we know enough to document the suspicion that to solve this problem would be to reveal the distinctive character of the problem of solidarity in the modern world.

Apparently, only societal populations with limited heterogeneity and limited complexity of organization are capable of maintaining sacred constitutive symbols. With increasing societal expansion, the symbols of collective solidarity fail to adequately represent new degrees of ordered heterogeneity. The old religious symbols no longer represent new levels of political and social complexity, new movements of power, new centers of sovereignty. G. E. Swanson has used a similar line of argument to provide an intriguing account of the breakdown of Catholic Europe and the origins of Protestantism. Between the late fourteenth and early fifteenth centuries, many of the centralist regimes of Europe, regimes capable of expressing by their own sovereignty the immanent sovereignty of the social group, broke down. The political conditions of early modern Europe made it possible for regimes to survive only if they adopted constitutional techniques appropriate for larger and more complex societies than had previously been known. In many instances, the new types of regimes were, in some sense, more socially remote and were symbolized by a more transcendent, that is, protestant God.[38]

In Europe and America, sacred symbols have increasingly come to symbolize and reinforce order only within subpopulations, and we see the development of more encompassing secular constitutive symbols, such as the nation. In the face of serious integrative problems, such secular symbols may be very tenuous. Where cultural heterogeneity and the social isolation of subgroups are an underlying social reality, constitutive symbols of

[38] Guy E. Swanson, *Religion and Regime* (Ann Arbor: The University of Michigan Press, 1967). See especially pp. 245–247.

unity have a somewhat prolocutory and fragile character. Where national symbolism holds out hope to all groups for complete participation in the affairs, ideals, and rewards of national life, but society fails to deliver on the promises implied by the symbolism, severe and value-laden conflict is the result. Thus, the black population of America has come to question its place and future in American life. The symbol of free democratic society, equal participation in American institutions on a color-blind basis, does not jibe with the facts of institutional exclusion, which is solidly structured around segregated housing and segregated primary groups. "Afro-Americanism" and "black power" represent an attempt to construct an alternative basis for inclusion, that is, inclusion as an organized, autonomous, and culturally distinct group. The social and cultural problems involved are but one illustration of the endemic problems in modern society, or in any society sufficiently complex to complicate the terms of participation of constituent solidary populations.

Subgroups and the Nation

A recent study of the comparative success of nineteenth-century American utopian communities by Rosabeth Moss Kanter suggests that it may not be possible to study solidarity on the simple assumption that group cohesion rests on making membership attractive. Kanter's study shows that commitment to continued participation, to emotional attachment to the group and its demands, did not depend on how easy the community made life for its members. On the contrary, commitment rested on devices to secure *investments* from members, devices of sacrifice, renunciation, ego-submersion, mortification, and surrender. Only by renunciation is the member made to transfer his commitments from the outside world to the communitarian group.[39] By a similar logic, commitment to the nation may require similar mechanisms to transfer loyalty away from traditional groups and roles. This may explain the prevalence of the ideology of dedication, sacrifice, and selflessness prominent among nationalizing elites.

Although such messages of moral rigor are often addressed to the nation at large, they achieve more effective expression in elite organizations, e.g., dominant national parties that them-

[39] Rosabeth Moss Kanter, "Commitment and Social Organization: A Study of Commitment Mechanisms in Utopian Communities," *American Sociological Review* 33 (August 1968), pp. 499–517.

selves stand as symbols of nationhood. This suggests that the problem of national solidarity must be approached at two levels. First, there is the level of constitutive symbolism. How are definitions of the terms and modes of membership created to permit a broad and inclusive societal community? Parsons has suggested that one of the main causes of historic failures of society has been their inability to develop sufficiently *universalistic* definitions of membership. Roman and Islamic civilization failed to overcome the disabilities inherent in maintaining two classes of membership that were in principle unequal and, accordingly, suffered in their capacity to expand "societal community" to the limits of their political and military influence.[40]

On the other hand, the development of nationhood has an organizational level. How can commitment be developed within specific groups? Considered from this point of view, a simple universalistic definition of membership may *not* be the most effective and convenient formula at some stages of national development. Specialized elite groups who symbolize total commitment to nationhood and renunciation of all subsidiary loyalties may be useful. Or, another strategy is to establish national unity not by destroying traditional groups, but by expanding their horizons, aligning their goals with national purposes, and incorporating them into the national political process as semiautonomous participants.[41] There appears to be more than one model for institutions of inclusion. Against the assimilationist, "melting-pot" model asserted by traditional American values we must juxtapose the long and viable histories of the more plurally organized nationhood of Canada and Switzerland.

Functional subgroups and other special interest associations may play a similar part in the solidarity of the total society. It was Durkheim's hope that solidarity within occupational groups could be the foundation of solidarity in differentiated modern societies.[42] While there is nothing to indicate that Durkheim's hopes are being literally realized, it is nonetheless true that a variety of specialized associations can link their own internal solidarity to membership in a larger community. One of the foundations of an integrated system of solidarity within a societal population is the *institutional* definition of the constituent

[40] Parsons, *Societies*, pp. 10–18, 33–35, 85–86, 91–92.

[41] Mayhew, "Ascription in Modern Societies," pp. 118–120.

[42] Durkheim, *Division of Labor*, pp. 1–31 (the so-called Second Preface).

associations within the population as units of a larger whole. Whether one is a Democrat or a Republican, a member of the National Association of Manufacturers or of Americans for Democratic Action, another more inclusive membership in a larger society is implied, and concern for the meaning and purpose of that society creates the sort of debate about the common good that in itself defines a "we."

5

Economic Systems

THE NATURE OF ECONOMIC SYSTEMS

All human beings participate in a number of economic systems. As we work at producing goods or providing services, as we receive a share in the distribution of produced wealth, use our shares to obtain the items we desire and, finally, consume these items, we engage in the four economic functions—production, distribution, exchange, and consumption. These functions are termed "economic" because they all bear on the problem of *economizing*. The materials to sustain life and satisfy human wants are never available in limitless abundance. The materials of life are not only scarce, they are constantly being consumed. In their raw natural state, they usually are not ready for immediate consumption and must be transformed for use by the application of human labor. Since materials are scarce and work is onerous, the objects of human desire are in short supply relative to the magnitude of the desire; in consequence, there is a constant process of human activity in which goods are produced, distributed, exchanged, and consumed in a constant economic battle against scarcity.

Economic activity is collectively and institutionally organized and coheres in economic systems. The grouping of a population into a set of producing and consuming units whose economic activities are organized by institutions of distribution and exchange constitutes an *economic system*.

There is at least one economic system in every society, but the members of every societal population participate in a number of different economic systems. Earlier we made a similar point about systems of solidarity. The members of any given societal population may participate in a number of overlapping systems of solidarity. But there is a fundamental difference between solidary and economic systems in this respect, for the extensiveness of solidary systems is determined by the limits of emotional attraction. Emotional attraction tends to exist only within circumscribed limits and tends to drop off very rapidly with the extension of territorial areas. As we saw in the last section, this feature of solidarity impedes the extension of solidarity to the boundaries of expanding populations.

By contrast, economic systems are vehicles of the expansion of social systems. The boundaries of economic systems are defined by the limits of trade, which, in comparison with systems of solidarity, has great powers to transcend other forms of human boundaries. Therefore, the members of societal populations usually participate in a number of economic systems that extend beyond the boundaries of the population, systems that are in our terminology *intersocietal*. This characteristic of economic life is as crucial to an understanding of economic systems in society as is the relatively inelastic character of solidary systems. Sociologists often insist that the stabilization of complex and productive economic systems requires a high degree of institutionalization. In this sense, economic activity, far from being merely ad hoc, instrumental, and utilitarian in character, is deeply embedded in a complicated institutional apparatus involving entrepreneurship, business law, the inculcation of motivation to work, and so on. True as this point is, it should not make us overlook the fact that a minimal economic transaction can be very instrumental indeed. Hence, economic systems can expand quite rapidly.

The tendency of man to engage in far-flung trading relations appears to be an ancient feature of human history. Indeed, archeologists have some evidence that it is virtually as old as man in his role of technological animal.[1] Man, a habitually peripatetic

---

[1] J. G. D. Clark, *Prehistoric Europe: The Economic Base* (Stanford, Calif.: Stanford University Press, 1966), p. 241.

animal, has regularly migrated from place to place. In the course of these migrations, men became dependent on some of the raw materials available at their former homes and eventually developed trade relations with those who succeeded them as residents of these places.[2] There is also evidence that tool "factories" existed in mesolithic times, and that the economic forces encouraging specialization and trade existed even with a very simple technology. The best raw materials for stone axes are concentrated at relatively few choice locations and, since the production of stone axes is very wasteful of raw materials, it is not economical to transport the stone across long distances. In consequence, families and tribal groups who gained control of the resource areas became professional axe makers.[3] Local specialization and intergroup trade is a very old phenomenon indeed.

It is easy to dismiss the importance of this interregional trade in primitive societies since it is ordinarily a rather small proportion of the total economic life of any given group. Nevertheless, it may be a very strategic component of the group's apparatus for adaptation to its environment. For example, some central Alaskan Eskimo groups participated in a far-flung barter system extending to the Alaskan coast, Siberia, and Eastern Russia. These groups used only a few trade items; yet, when the growth of the whaling industry made the old trade patterns obsolete for most participant groups, the central Alaskan groups were forced to move to the coast, destroying their former patterns of life.

In the course of economic development, intersocietal systems of trade become increasingly significant. It would be very difficult to study realistically the contemporary economic scene without reference to the expandability of economic systems and their tendency to cross-societal interpenetration. Bert Hoselitz, in the course of developing a typology of economic growth, has suggested three important dimensions of variation in the pattern of economic development. First, he distinguishes *expansive* from *intrinsic* systems. The former grow through expanding unified control over larger territorial areas, and the latter by developing more intensive exploitation within a fixed resource base. Second, he distinguishes *dominant* from *satellite* economies. The former are independent, and the latter are, by virtue of intensive specialization, dependent on trade with other econo-

---

[2] Ibid., p. 244.

[3] Norman A. Chance, *The Eskimo of North Alaska* (New York: Holt, Rinehart & Winston, Inc., 1966), pp. 12–13.

mies. Finally, he distinguishes economies based upon *autono-mous* growth from economies based upon the deliberate *in-ducement* by centralized agencies of control. Hoselitz argues persuasively that these variations are an important key to under-standing both historic and contemporary strategies of economic development.[4] If he is right, it follows that any theory that is limited to the use of domestic resources within a system with established boundaries can account for development in only two of the eight types of economy depicted by the intersection of Hoselitz' three dimensions. Because of the flexible and interpene-trating character of economic boundaries, economic process systems are among the most resistant to analysis by theories founded on postulates of societal independence and isolation.

The subject of economic growth is a particularly apt illustra-tion of the methodological significance of intersocietal systems. Simon Kuznets has shown that generalizations about the corre-lates of economic growth made on the basis of comparisons at a given moment of time between stages of development often fail to hold true in longitudinal studies of the development of econo-mies over time. For example, the proportion of national product entering into capital formation is now higher for more-developed countries than for underdeveloped countries. However, this ratio has not necessarily been increasing during the historic develop-ment of the advanced countries.[5] One reason for the lack of cor-respondence between cross-sectional and longitudinal data is that economic growth is occurring in the context of a world economy. Growth is a process that began in Europe and is *diffus-ing* throughout the world.[6] Advanced economic systems have an impact on backward systems; backward systems are deeply pene-trated by the economies of the richer societies. Economic growth is, in short, an intersocietal system, and various populations entered into the system at different phases of its development. Failure to recognize this fact is at the base of the fallacy of inter-preting cross-sectional regularities as indicators of necessary developmental sequences. Such inferences would be more justi-fiable if each society could be treated as an independent instance of a repeating sequence of societal evolution.

[4] Bert F. Hoselitz, *Sociological Aspects of Economic Growth* (New York: The Free Press, 1960), pp. 85–114.

[5] Simon Kuznets, *Six Lectures on Economic Growth* (New York: The Free Press, 1959), pp. 69 ff.

[6] Ibid., pp. 114–116.

The Autonomy of the Economy

If the most debated issue in social thought regarding solidary systems concerns the possibility of expanding solidarity to
boundaries as broad as those of the more elastic process systems,
the comparable issue regarding economic systems is the converse: Can any other social systems control economic systems?
The ready expandability of the economic process implies a
measure of autonomy for economic systems. Economic transactions—trade or the creation of economically specialized collectivities—tend to outrun the boundaries of other well-organized
social systems. The establishment of an economic relationship
does not require the prior existence of other well-established systems. For this reason, one of the most cherished theorems of institutional theory must be subjected to careful examination and
redefinition. Sociologists often state that stable systems of exchange imply a common framework of institutional order and
that, in this sense, integrative systems have an independent and
controlling significance in social life; economic systems are not
self-integrating. However important this theorem might be in
studying the development of well-integrated economies, it does
not follow that the formation of an economic process requires
prior establishment of another type of social system. Given the
capacity of human beings to construct joint action as described
in chapter two, given the human ability to engage in adaptive,
flexible activity, to come to pragmatic working terms of cooperation, it is possible to construct economic transactions in the
context of only minimal prior understandings. Such minimal institutional apparatus as a trading language, specialized trade
agreements, or even such facilitative institutions as merchant
courts or money exchanges, do not imply the full panoply of regulative systems we associate with a full-blown social system. In
fact, as at least one shrewd observer has pointed out, the motivation to exchange between groups is strong in proportion to how
different the groups are. The homogeneity implied by incorporation into a single system with uniform values, institutions, and
life experiences reduces the probabilities of the existence of the
comparative advantages that motivate exchange.[7] The differences
in environment, history, and social organization that make Brazil
a coffee-producing country and the United States a producer of

---

[7] Mancur Olson, Jr., "Economics, Sociology, and the Best of All Possible Worlds," *The Public Interest* 12 (Summer 1968), pp. 96–118.

manufactured goods imply some segmentation or lack of unity in whatever larger system contains both the United States and Brazil. In sum, economic interests have a tendency to outreach established social arrangements and to lead actors to create new human ties and new collective interests.

This dynamic character of the economic process has led social theorists to wonder whether economic systems can be socially controlled. Much of the ideological discussion involved in the study of what has been called "political economy" revolves around the possibility and means of bringing systems of economic interests under the influence of political and normative regulation.

Ironically both the most "conservative" and the most "radical" economic doctrines stress the autonomy of economic organization. Classical liberal economics and Marxian political theory assert that economic interests either are or should be uncontrolled in a capitalist society. According to the former doctrine, economic interests need not be controlled because the free play of economic interest insures the most rational allocation of resources. Further, such a system is automatically integrated, for the division of labor makes each producer dependent on exchanges with other producers. According to Marxian thought, a capitalist economy unleashes the free play of economic interests so that no external system of moral regulation is capable of subjecting pure economic motives to ethical control. Ethical systems merely legitimize the interests of the economically powerful. However, since the uncontrolled economic relations of capitalism are exploitative, the system is only temporarily integrated. In the long run, the system will be destroyed by the exploited segments of the population. In this respect, capitalism is like all other economic systems of the past; the interests embodied in the system of economic production are an autonomous force not subject to the control of any independent regulatory system.

By contrast, the program of the modern liberal has been to subject economic interests to ethical and legal control for the benefit of the common welfare. The sociological ideas of modern liberalism have, accordingly, stressed the independent integrative force of social systems external to the economy. In chapter one, it was suggested that this was an important source of the idea of society as external and constraining reality.

The program of modern liberalism is in opposition to the faith of classic laissez-faire liberalism in an automatic and beneficial identity of interests in a market system of pure economic competition. Classic liberalism became embodied in academic economics, in consequence, the debate between classic and modern liberalism has included a corollary academic debate between economics and other social-science disciplines over the adequacy of economics as a conceptual framework for the study of human conduct. Sociologists insisted that noneconomic factors influenced economic behavior and that economic systems could not be understood without prior understanding of their social contexts. Even today, much of the sociological writing on economic life exhibits residual overtones of this historic debate. Current works in the area are often organized around a series of alleged social influences on the "economic," as if the purely economic were somehow not social. For our purposes, an economy is one type of system of social process, and social variables are "economic" if they refer to the production, exchange, distribution, or consumption of goods. Activity is no less social if the actor is motivated by utilitarian considerations.

ECONOMIC SYSTEMS AND THEIR INTEGRATION

Elements of an Economy: Production

Every economy includes a system of production; the creation of consumable goods is by definition the prime function of the economy. Economists divide the sources of productivity into four "factors of production": land, capital, labor, and organization.

In *Economy and Society*, one of the most sophisticated attempts to develop the symmetry of economic and sociological theory, Talcott Parsons and Neil Smelser suggest that the factors of production can be interpreted as a special case of the four functionally requisite subsystems of any organized social system: pattern maintenance, integration, goal attainment, and adaptation.[8] "Land" refers to those resources of production that are relatively fixed in the sense that the supply is not responsive to sanctions in the short run. This would include not only land in the literal sense but also such human resources as the basic commitment to work that is socialized into the personality at a relatively early age and cannot be easily increased by merely in-

---

[8] Parsons and Smelser, *Economy and Society*. A more detailed exposition of the fourfold system of functional requisites is included in chapter two of the present volume.

creasing wage rates. For productive systems, land is the fixed economic structure constraining and stabilizing short-run processes; it is the resource for *pattern maintenance*. Capital, the relatively mobile investment in the tools of production, increases the *adaptive* potential of the economy by providing generalized capacity to produce wealth. Labor provides for the attainment of the goals of the economy because it involves immediate participation in the activity of transforming raw materials into desired objects. Finally, economic or entrepreneurial organization integrates the economy; organizational activity combines the other three factors in accordance with a changing set of opportunities, integrating available resources in a productive and economic way.[9]

Parsons and Smelser believe that this is a valuable way to view an economy, for it permits the integration of economic and sociological theory. By asserting that a society consists in a set of functional subsystems that carry on a set of interchanges with each other, the authors are in a position to analyze the exchanges between economic subsystems and the other subsystems of society, using exchange theory as it has been developed in economics.[10] In this context, the distinctions between perfect competition and various types of imperfect competition, such as monopoly, are particularly important. The fact that various subsystems are structured in response to different types of functional needs prevents the interchanges between subsystems from being organized as perfect markets.[11] For example, consider the interchange between the family household and the labor subsystem of the economy. In modern industrial society, the source of labor is the worker who exchanges his labor for wages to fulfill his obligations of family support. He has been cut off from any traditional claims on productive organization such as might have existed in a system of agriculture based on the extended family. The isolation of the worker reduces his bargaining power and produces an imperfect labor market. Hence arise such associational devices as the labor union to increase bargaining power and further complicate the market structure of this particular subsystem interchange.[12]

[9] Ibid., pp. 39–46.

[10] Ibid., pp. 46–100.

[11] Ibid., pp. 143–175.

[12] Ibid., pp. 147–149.

Sociological Aspects of the Factors of Production

Several other sociological interests have focused on problems relating to the factors of production. With respect to "land" in the Parsonian sense, attention has focused on the problem of labor commitment. How does a mobile work force develop? What forces produce a body of wage workers who are willing to accept the disciplines and conventions of roles in an industrial market economy and are responsive to economic incentives? The problematic character of labor commitment rests on a distinction between, on the one hand, responsiveness to the short-run sanctions of a labor market and of industrial discipline and, on the other hand, the *development* of such responsiveness as a generalized resource in an economic system. The latter cannot be created by merely applying short-run economic incentives. It requires more radical structural transformations in patterns of social relations and human motivation. The classical theory of wages, which asserts that workers flow to roles with maximum money income, has been criticized by sociologists on the grounds that potential workers who are well-embedded in a network of traditional social organization are reluctant to accept the insecurity involved in breaking loose from their web of solidary affiliation. Nor will such a worker necessarily appreciate the notion that more money will give him more status. He may prefer the status and respect that are accorded to his position, possessions, and skills by his traditional group. Further, he may prefer traditional work to industrial work. Thus, an East African peasant may not be attracted by money incentives if acceptance requires him to leave his place in his tribal group, his clan brothers, and his age mates, and to leave the cattle and the herding that he loves so well. He is more likely to accept only temporary employment on an emergency basis than to develop a generalized commitment to industrial labor as a way of life.[13]

This line of argument originally developed as a part of the sociological critique of economic theory, but in recent years there has been a growing recognition that the extreme poverty of the countryside can in fact push persons into industrial employment. As the horizons of the peasant expand, he becomes more susceptible to economic temptation, and, provided that the in-

[13] See Wilbert E. Moore, *Industrialization and Labor* (New York: Russell and Russell Publishers, 1965), and Wilbert E. Moore and Arnold S. Feldman, eds., *Labor Commitment and Social Change in Developing Areas* (New York: Social Sciences Research Council, 1960).

centives offered promise a *realistic* hope of improvement of his lot, he will develop commitment to industry. For example, one observer has recently criticized previous accounts of the difficulty of pulling Indian peasants loose from the ties of village and caste. According to David Morris, previous accounts of the traditional commitments of Indian labor have failed to distinguish between large and small industry and between seasonal and temporary employment. There has been, to be sure, a historic pattern of temporary migration of Indian males to urban places for short-run stints of work, but this does not mean that Indian industry has found it difficult to form an adequate labor force.[14] The realization that workers from traditional groups can develop a commitment to industry has shifted attention to *opportunity,* that is, to the capacity of the economic system to create meaningful structural roles for employment.

With respect to the second factor of production, capital, the most important problem has concerned the sources of capital for economic development. Economies that have experienced rapid and sustained development have also maintained high rates of capital formation, rates of 20 percent of national income per year and more. In underdeveloped economies, characterized by very low rates of income per capita, consumers find it very difficult to provide the savings to invest in capital. But beyond the vicious cycle of low income, low savings, low investment, and slow growth, there are a number of sociological problems relating to capital formation. First, there is the problem of population pressure. If an economy is developing more slowly than the population is increasing, the benefits of growth cannot be reinvested in further growth without decreasing already precarious standards of living. As Barbara Ward has noted, the underdeveloped world is caught up in problems of unsynchronized timing in the transmission of the revolutions of the Western world to the underdeveloped world; the revolution in population growth and the revolution of rising material expectations preceeded the revolution in productive capacity, catching the poor lands in a vicious cycle of population pressure and slow economic growth.[15]

Second, there is the problem of institutionalizing the channels that lead from savings to investment. Social structure may

---

[14] David Morris, "The Labor Market in India," in *Labor Commitment and Social Change in Developing Areas,* ed. Moore and Feldman, pp. 173–200.

[15] Barbara Ward, *The Rich Nations and the Poor Nations* (New York: W. W. Norton and Company, Inc., 1962).

impose impediments to the free flow of savings into productive investments for economic growth. Thus, it is said that in Malaysia, Moslem women, fearful of sudden dissolution of their marital status under Islamic law, store wealth in the form of personal possessions, such as jewelry,[16] that are legally theirs. The modernization of an economy implies not only the overcoming of specific obstacles of this kind but also the positive development of the institutions of finance and credit.

A third heavily debated issue is more directly germane to the principal themes of this volume. To what extent is the international economy a source of domestic capital? In some cases the profits from international trade have provided surplus for capital formation. Some historians attribute much of the capital of the industrial revolution not just to savings of the profits deriving from technological improvement of domestic production, but also to profits from the expansion of the European economy made possible by improvements in transportation. For example, England profited from the three-way trade in slaves, sugar, rum, and manufactured products between Africa, England, and the New World.[17] It is easier to save for investment out of increased earning than to cut back expenditures. Accordingly, any rapid increase in income is likely to permit capital formation. Reduction of transport costs by over 60 percent after 1800 made possible an even larger international division of labor, and the consequent productivity increases were an important source of capital for European development.[18] Contemporary economists and political leaders now debate whether underdeveloped economies can effectively use increases in international export as a source of acquisition for capital goods.[19] We will reexamine this issue later.

In the case of the third factor of production, the process of labor, sociological theory has been most concerned with the degree of specialization in the economy; economic specialization

[16] Peter Gosling, personal communication.

[17] Eric Williams, *Capitalism and Slavery* (Chapel Hill, N.C.: University of North Carolina Press, 1944).

[18] Paul N. Rosenstein-Rodan, "The Modernization of Industry," in *Modernization: The Dynamics of Growth*, ed. Myron Weiner (Washington D.C.: Voice of America Forum Lectures, 1966), pp. 297–298; Fred Cottrell, *Energy and Society: The Relation between Energy, Social Change, and Economic Development* (New York: McGraw-Hill Book Company, 1955), pp. 52–78.

[19] Gerald M. Meier, *Leading Issues in Economic Development* (New York: Oxford University Press, 1964), chapter 7.

takes the form of a system of differentiated occupational roles. Advanced technology and modern techniques of distribution have produced an intensive division of labor. Although there is always an arbitrary element in how finely occupations are classified, it is interesting to note that the United States Labor Department lists well over 20,000 separate occupations.[20] By contrast, the economy of a hunting and gathering group often contains only as many differentiated economic roles as there are basic divisions by age and sex in the population. Even in the early days of the industrial revolution, occupational specialization had not begun to reach present levels. Although the figures are not exactly comparable, there is a rough lesson in contrasting the English census of 1840, which provided a detailed occupational classification depicting only 431 occupations, and the current United States governmental system for designating occupational specialties, which provides fifty times as many occupational classifications.[21]

This intense division of labor has stimulated a voluble debate on the fragmentation of work and its social consequences. Broadly speaking, there are two competing traditions of thought on this issue. One suggests that the division of labor fragments specific jobs to the degree that the workers feel alienated from them. The other stresses the organizational response to economic specialization, that is, the formation of worker organizations —unions, professional groups, and the informal associations by which the workers transform the purely technical organization of the task and cope with the pressures of the labor market and the job.

Sociological interest in the final factor of production, *organization* in the sense of entrepreneurship, has focused on the legitimation of the entrepreneurial role. What motivates the peculiar willingness to assume the risks of entrepreneurial activity, to become committed to ceaseless change and adjustment as one rationally calculates the best modes of organizing social resources into productive activity? How does the entrepreneur come to have respectable social status? Study of these problems has been heavily influenced by Max Weber, who believed that

[20] U.S. Department of Labor, *Dictionary of Occupational Titles*, 1965 (Washington D.C.: U.S. Government Printing Office), pp. xiii–xvi. This edition lists 21,741 separate occupations under an even larger number of occupational titles. Of course, many of these occupations are closely related.

[21] Theodore Caplow, *The Sociology of Work* (Minneapolis: The University of Minnesota Press, 1954), pp. 21–22.

Protestantism, with its insistence on the virtue of participation in a variety of types of worldly roles and its unanticipated encouragement of rational and systematic worldly activity, was instrumental in providing legitimacy and motivation for entrepreneurial activity.[22]

In a more recent study in the Weberian tradition, attention shifted to how entrepreneurs as a class have justified their social position and, particularly, their authority over the worker. This is an especially strategic way of defining the problem, for it ties the problem of gaining control over workers (as mobile factors of production) to the more general problem of social stratification and class conflict. Reinhard Bendix has compared the emergence of entrepreneurial groups in England and Russia, contrasting the independence and autonomy of the English entrepreneur with his politically dominated Russian counterpart.[23] The English entrepreneur sought status and authority within a set of loosely conjoined social groups and, in the process, came to argue for the loosest possible status arrangements. He wanted individual autonomy and independence from traditional social settings and tried to justify tearing the English peasant-worker from traditional moorings. Increasingly, the British entrepreneur became oriented to the intersocietal division of labor, which necessarily implied radical transformations of the domestic occupational structure as it became more specialized and industrial. His rival for social status, the aristocrat, had an interest in the traditional agricultural order and came to form what was, in effect, an ideological alliance with the worker. In consequence, worker ideology tended to retain a conservative, antimodern outlook. By contrast, the traditional intimate association of economy and state in prerevolutionary Russia was conducive to a more radical and politically revolutionary formulation of the workers' demands.

Distribution and Exchange

The division of labor implies some mechanism for distributing the products of labor. Of course, the distribution of wealth is

[22] Max Weber, The Protestant Ethic and the Spirit of Capitalism, trans. Talcott Parsons (New York: Charles Scribner's Sons, 1930).

[23] Reinhard Bendix, Work and Authority in Modern Industry (New York: John Wiley & Sons, Inc., 1956), pp. 1–21.

always problematic, even, to some degree, in subsistence economies. Further, as surplus develops, the social organization of distribution becomes especially important because of the crucial role of capital formation. This is the sense in which urbanization and economic growth are necessarily organizational phenomena. Surplus alone is not enough to insure development; it is necessary that there be some form of social organization for concentrating surplus and committing it to the tools of production and the equipment of civilization. Hence the intimate connection between systems of economic distribution and social stratification. The distribution and concentration of surplus defines the social strata that can control wealth and power and make the crucial allocative decisions.

Herein lies one of the major points of intersection of political and economic systems, for in all known societies there has been a measure of political control over the allocation of surplus. When urban civilization initially emerged, political control reached new levels and it became possible to wrest a surplus from the population to invest in the activities and the monuments of urban life. Underdeveloped nations in the modern world, with their problems of acquiring capital, investing efficiently for national growth, and maintaining political independence, power, and pride, lean heavily on governmental action to increase capital and control its allocation. In this respect, they admire and seek to emulate Soviet success in controlled rapid development. Although the growth of European and North American capitalism is sometimes seen as "free market" growth, it was associated with a variety of forms of governmental support and political direction from the beginning. European development was inextricably linked to political expansion and foreign trade, which required committing resources to military protection and support. American capitalism grew in the context of strong governmental support for industry and subsidization of the basic facilities of development—roads, canals, railroads, and productive agriculture.

Despite variation in the extent of political control of economic distribution, the intense division of labor characteristic of a highly productive economy is always associated with a modernization of market structure. The division of labor implies exchange and, if the division of labor is elaborated to a high degree, the system of exchange must accommodate a proportionately large number of exchanges. Further, these exchanges must occur rapidly, must reflect the exigencies of the efficient use of resources, and must be articulated with the pattern of wants or demands in the population. These needs are very difficult to coordinate by detailed and direct political control and must be serviced by a market-like system of allocation. A market exists for a given commodity when the price of the commodity depends on the impersonal decisions of a large number of buyers and sellers.[24] Price then becomes a signal to actors who are weighing the benefits and costs of various alternative courses of action, and the market becomes a means of allocating goods between alternative uses. Markets may exist not only for consumer goods but also for the factors of production, wherein they play a similar allocative role. One of the varying features of economic systems is the extent to which decisions about the factors of production, especially surplus in the form of capital, are removed from the political arena and located in free markets.

Cyril Belshaw, who has analyzed a broad cross section of exchange systems as they are depicted in anthropological, historical, and economic literature, has provided several criteria for judging the modernity of market structure: impersonality, the systematization of exchange values through a price system, the specialization of buying and selling roles, an extensive range of goods bought and sold, an extensive range of buying and selling across the productive process from raw materials to consumer goods, competition, and the separation of exchange into buying and selling through the use of money.[25]

Modern systems of exchange may be distinguished from systems stressing ritual and reciprocity. Belshaw points to systems of cattle exchange in East Africa as an example of the merger of political, economic, and solidary functions in a single system. Cattle exchanges have an economic aspect; a given exchange may be motivated by the desire to obtain an immediately consumable animal. On the other hand, exchanges may be used to reaffirm or create solidary relationships and to build up "social capital" in the sense of a network of obligations of reciprocity.[26]

A more specialized form of exchange is found in monetary peasant economies. Here exchange is more strictly economic, involves specialized roles, and in many ways resembles the

[24] L. M. Fraser, *Economic Thought and Language* (London: Adam and Charles Black, Ltd., 1937), p. 131.

[25] Cyril Belshaw, *Traditional Exchange and Modern Markets* (Englewood Cliffs, N.J.: Prentice-Hall, Inc., 1965), pp. 8–9.

[26] Ibid., pp. 29–34.

economists notion of a perfect market, for there are a large number of small buyers and sellers. However, these markets tend to lack bureaucratization. Traders operate on a very small scale and often establish a network of preferred customers. Both of these features reflect the face-to-face character of exchange in the monetized peasant economy, which in turn reflects the lack of modernized communication and literacy.

Eric Wolf has suggested that the intercommunity markets of peasant economies can be further classified as either closed sectional markets or as open network markets.[27] In *sectional markets*, given communities within a closed region specialize in certain types of production. The members of a community engage in some trade among themselves, so that each community forms a small scale internal market. The link to other communities is limited to a given specialized product, and the patterns of trade within a given group of communities are fixed by tradition. Thus, there is formed a closed exchange system founded on traditional monopolies within a fixed division of labor. It is similar to the traditional division of labor between castes and complementary exchange found in some Indian villages except that it extends to a specialization between communities. In a *network market*, on the other hand, the circle of trade is not closed. There is a seamless web of exchange which links each community to an overlapping set of other communities. In consequence, the local community is caught up in the economic forces of the international economy, and remote events in the larger world alter the fate of peasants in the village. No longer is the intercommunity division of labor fixed by traditional monopoly. Production becomes geared to market forces; the boundaries of the community have been penetrated by an international community; and domestic events become difficult to control in traditional ways.

Thus we may add another criterion to Belshaw's dimensions of modernity in markets—international scope. However, like Belshaw's other criteria, this is a dimension rather than a fixed type. The seamless web of a network is not truly seamless. Although even extremely remote places always have some link to larger markets, some boundaries do exist; the patterns of exchange are neither random nor equally spread through space, and the economic activity within any given population is linked to activity in other populations in varying degrees. Nevertheless, we cannot suppose that boundaries formed by the extent of

[27] Eric R. Wolf, *Peasants* (Englewood Cliffs, N.J.: Prentice-Hall, Inc., 1966), pp. 40–48.

market interdependence will correspond to political boundaries, because some states have poorly integrated economies. As the following sections will point out, some sectors of a given economy are closely linked to international trade and some are cut off; in consequence, the internal integration of the economy suffers.

The Integration of Economic Systems

Once again we will adapt the strategy of describing an integrated societal economic system and from there move to the realistic constraints on economic integration. By an *integrated* economic system we do not mean a system which is without conflict or one which is successfully regulated by some other type of social system. An integrated economy is one in which all members of a societal population participate without reference to their membership in other social and cultural groupings and all economic units participate in a single, unified system of transactions.

In some respects, the model of an integrated economy is similar to the economists' model of a perfect market. For example, in a perfect market all of the participants have full access to information and are equally mobile. However, economic integration, as conceived here, should not be confused with either economic development or the degree of mobility of economic efforts. An economic system is highly developed when it has great productive capacity, which might be measured with some indicator of energy mobilization, such as kilowatt hours of energy produced. A highly developed economy is associated with complex technology, an intensive division of labor, developed markets, and a high degree of freedom of movement of the factors of production. In turn, high mobility implies a lack of ascription to traditional occupations, willingness to seek and accept economic opportunities, and the saving of surplus wealth in a mobile and investable form. In a traditional economy based upon subsistence, and little trade or investment and largely organized around familial and kin organization, the mobility of economic resources may be very constrained. At the same time, such an economy may be well integrated, for integration does not imply mobility per se; it only implies that all the members of the societal population participate in and are linked to whatever network of transactions and cooperative activities are present in the economic system. Thus, if economic transactions and organizations do not cross-cut a certain regional boundary within a societal population, or if the societal economy excludes a certain ethnic group who participate mainly in their own enclosed subeconomy, we would say that the larger economy was poorly integrated.[28] On the other hand, all of the participants in a rather traditional and primitive economy may participate in the various available economic networks, however minimal, and we would speak of an integrated economy.

An integrated economy meets four structural conditions:

1) *The distribution of relevant economic capacities.* To participate in an economic role requires health, knowledge of the relevant technical skills, ability to communicate with fellow workers, and other skills. Hence, if human resources in the population are not developed so as to correspond to the technical requirements of the available roles in the system, malintegration occurs. This may happen when ethnic or regional groups do not learn usable economic skills or when employment opportunities of a given type expand but few members of the population have the requisite qualifications. The condition of broad participation cannot be met if some groups lack the capacity to participate.

2) *Willingness to participate.* People who are able to perform economic roles may decline to because they prefer other kinds of activities, even though the other activities are less remunerative or profitable. This is the problem of labor commitment, which was discussed earlier.

3) *A supply of opportunities.* People who are able and willing to participate in the national economy may not because of a shortage of available opportunities. This often produces a structured malintegration, in that those who are excluded from participation are barred on "ascriptive" grounds. In other words, indigenous natives, castes, ethnic groups, or social classes may be systematically excluded from participation or limited only to a fixed sector of the economy.

4) *Information.* Assuming an able and willing population and an absence of discrimination in the provision of opportunities, it is still necessary to communicate information about abilities, intentions, and opportunities so that the buyers and sellers of productive assets, goods, and services can get together. To this end, specialized organs and channels of communication may be created — the labor exchange, the employment agency, the stock broker, the yellow pages.

[28] Gunnar Myrdal, *Economic Theory and Underdeveloped Regions* (London: Gerald Duckworth and Co., Ltd., 1957).

The economist's concept of a perfect market and this concept of an integrated economy have one very important common implication. The market system, which permits everyone to maximize his utilities by trading things which are less useful to him for things that are more useful to him until he has achieved an optimum combination, presumes an integrated economy. Further, if an economy is not integrated, the presumed collective benefits of such an exchange of utilities cannot occur. As we shall soon see, this is an important point for it bears upon such questions of great concern to developing nations as whether a national economy will benefit from international trade.[29] The answer may depend on the degree of integration of the national economy. The benefits of trade and the division of labor are transmitted through the links within an economic system; they can only be communicated to those who participate in the system.

Note that an integrated economy is a type of social structure; it is not (as some sociological opponents of economic theory would have us believe) an absence of social structure. The economy, as an ongoing network of economic activity, may have a variable structure in relation to the elements just outlined—the distribution of economic capacities, commitments to participate, available opportunities, and information. When these elements are distributed to the full extent of a population, we may speak of an integrated economy.

Only a severely restricted definition of the social would exclude these structural patterns. Nor is it useful to see these elements as "contributions" to the economy, or to see economies as integrated only insofar as "social" influences do not operate. To label an economy as "integrated" or "not integrated" is to refer to its structure as a social system; it is to depict a pattern of interaction and participation within a social system.

Limitations on Integration

To insist upon the social character of the economy itself is not to deny that political, cultural, solidary, or other systems impinge upon its integration. The domination of a privileged class may lead to the systematic exclusion of less favored seg-

---

[29] Gerald M. Meier, *The International Economics of Development* (New York: Harper and Row, Publishers 1968).

ments of the population from economic opportunities. Religious values may support equal opportunity. Membership in a solidary subgroup may restrict economic participation. Modern market institutions facilitate integration in complex economies. On the other hand, some of the most important sources of malintegration in economies stem from the character of economic expansion. The tendency of economic transactions to extend beyond and blur societal boundaries may create malintegrated economies in populations that are on the receiving end of the expansion of economic systems. Malintegration is then reinforced by the political power of the expanding economy. In the modern world, this phenomenon is intimately associated with the expansion of the West through the medium of colonialism.

Western colonialism originally developed as an attempt by nation-states to impose political controls on the expansion of the international division of labor. In the original "mercantilist" stage of colonialism, the goal was to increase the wealth of the state by tapping the wealth of the East and of the New World. Originally the doctrine that precious metals would provide the means to pay for war was most prominent, but very soon a more sophisticated mercantilist philosophy developed. By the middle of the seventeenth century, the doctrine of gold was only a minor part of the mercantilist policy; the major thrust of the doctrine was that states could decrease their dependence on other rival states by obtaining secure sources of raw materials in new locations outside the orbit of European politics. At the same time, the loci of raw materials could be made into assured markets for the manufactured goods of the West.[30] Thus, by expanding the international division of labor, one could increase the wealth and power of the nation. Acting on this philosophy, Spain, Portugal, Holland, England, and France had become major colonial powers, drawing upon Latin America for sugar, cotton, tobacco, hides, and dye-woods, North America for cotton and furs, and Asia for spices, silk, and a variety of other goods.

Though the motives for expansion were in the first instance economic and were the motives of individual entrepreneurs, the strong political element involved in the idea of the control of trade for profit made colonialism a partially political phenomenon from the very beginning. Once independent entrepreneurs had begun their activities, the independence of the mother coun-

[30] Glyndwr Williams, *The Expansion of Europe in the Eighteenth Century* (New York: Walker and Co., 1967); D. K. Fieldhouse, "Colonialism: Economic Aspects," in *International Encyclopedia of the Social Sciences,* Vol. 3, pp. 6–12.

try vis-à-vis rival European states was held to require political control of the source of raw materials in order to ensure a trade monopoly. Further, indigenous governments could not be relied upon to create a framework for encouraging and facilitating production and trade. Accordingly, Western nations assumed political control of their economic satellites.

By the early nineteenth century, Britain had assumed a position of preeminence in international trade and was so entrenched that free competition could only increase her dominance as a trading nation; the antimercantilist doctrine of free trade began to hold sway. Monopoly profits seemed less significant. Nevertheless, so widespread was the belief that European states must acquire guaranteed markets, sources of raw material, and outlets for capital, and so intense the belief that national strength and pride depend on the wealth of empire, that the latter half of the century saw a new thrust of colonial expansion into the remaining parts of Asia, the South Seas, and Africa. The Belgians and Germans accelerated their quest for colonies and joined the great colonial powers. Coffee, rice, copra, and other products of tropical agriculture were added to the list of colonially produced products.

The actual benefits of colonialism to the colonial powers is much in dispute. The Marxist critics of colonialism have always taken the colonial apologists at their own word. The Western states expanded their economies because they had no choice. Because the system is inherently unstable, the dynamic of capitalism demands constant search for new markets and new sources of investment. More skeptical analysts have argued that it cannot be shown that the arguments of the exponents of colonial expansion were well-founded. Rates of return on investment in colonial enterprise can be shown to be only slightly higher than domestic rates of return.[31] Further, the fact of foreign investment does not demonstrate that domestic opportunities were drying up.

We cannot settle that argument here. Suffice it to say, the expansion occurred and the motives were varied. More interesting from the present perspective is the argument that Western economic expansion, because it meant an intensification of the division of labor, should have brought benefits to both sides. Because of the principle of comparative advantage, that is, because the division of labor permits each economy to specialize

[31] Jan Tinbergen, *Shaping the World Economy* (New York: Twentieth Century Fund, 1962), pp. 20 ff.

in that which it does best, total productivity should increase in the system. The increased income from trade permits the colonial dependency (or the struggling new nation) to invest in more diversified development. The development of an export industry stimulates opportunity for the peasants to follow the lead of the colonial entrepreneur, to improve their techniques, and to enter the international market.

The facts have never quite jibed with this theory, and there is a voluminous literature in economics devoted to asking what went wrong. One of the first important contributions to this literature was a study of the economy of the former Dutch East Indies by the Dutch scholar, J. H. Boeke.[32] Boeke asked precisely our question: Why did the lot of the Indonesian peasant not improve according to the predictions of the theory of trade? Boeke's conclusion was that the failure of the peasant's lot to improve was related to the fact that the Indonesians had not one economy but two: an export sector, modern and technologically advanced and largely organized by Europeans, and a subsistence peasant economy, primitive, backward, and isolated from the export sector. In our terms, the Indonesian economy lacked integration. The Dutch economy had expanded and incorporated a segment of the East Indian population, but that segment was closed off from the native segment, forming, in Boeke's terms, a "dual economy."

Boeke attributed the failure of integration to the difference between Western values and peasant values. The peasants had not learned the value of economic rationality and were not sufficiently sensitive to inducements. In our terms, there was a "failure of willingness." This aspect of Boeke's doctrine has been severely criticized. There is now much more emphasis on opportunity; the export system simply failed to produce available roles and realistic inducements. Thus, according to one version of dual economy theory, the problem lies in a radical difference in the factors of production in the two sectors of the economy. The modern sector uses *capital intensively* and at a fixed ratio to labor. The subsistence sector is *labor intensive* and can absorb labor at variable ratios to capital. Given a growing labor force, the *realistic* choices for the peasant are either a marginal opportunity in the traditional agricultural sector or unemployment in the modern sector.

In recent years, the explanation of the disappointing per-

---

[32] For his most recent account of his theory, see Julius H. Boeke, *Economics and Economic Policy of Dual Societies as Exemplified by Indonesia* (New York: Institute of Pacific Relations, 1953).

formance of international trade as a factor in development has taken a number of turns. Some theorists point to prematurely high consumption standards that prevent saving the profits of trade; others emphasize long-term secular declines in the terms of trade caused by lagging demand for the products of export agriculture. But the most persuasive and realistic accounts continue to stress the mode of articulation of the international and domestic sectors. Does the international sector create effective stimuli for complementary domestic products? Is the domestic economy characterized by factor immobility, poor communication, ignorance, price rigidity, and lack of entrepreneurship?[33] Has the modern sector failed to legitimize claims to the right to productive employment that are as strong as the peasant's claim on family organized agricultural enterprise?[34] In short, how well-integrated is the national economy? This question is crucial for the developing nations. The heritage of colonialism and the continuing international organization of trade make almost all underdeveloped economies heavily dependent on the export of a few basic products, either minerals or the products of tropical agriculture. The problem is to unify the profits from this trade with an emergent, diversified, and unified national economy.

It would be a mistake to suppose that the problems of economic integration are limited to the underdeveloped world. Considered more generally, malintegration is a consequence of expansion, and colonial expansion is but one of the problematic forms. Developed nations have had recurrent problems in integrating the rural and industrial sectors of the economy. The expansion of urban life creates a number of dislocations and disequilibrating market forces. The reorganization of farm production implied by rapid movement from rural to urban areas disrupts routine existence not only for the migrant but for the farmer as well. His reordered participation in the changing national economy is problematic. In the most extreme cases, national leadership has supposed that the proper articulation of rural and urban sectors requires a complete transformation of agricultural production, even at the costs of great social turmoil. The forced collectivization of Soviet agriculture and the displacement of the agricultural population in England in consequence of the specialization of England in wool production are, from this perspective, closely related phenomena.

[33] Meier, *International Economics*, pp. 214–254.

[34] Gayl Ness, personal communication.

More generally, the problems of lag in the expansion of solidarity systems can also be seen as barriers to economic integration because integration is primarily a matter of universal participation. Any barriers to participation are *ipso facto* barriers to economic integration. The integration of expanding economies requires the elimination of ascriptive solidary barriers and, more positively, the creation of a new institutional framework for facilitating collective activity, one not based on the assumption of ties of traditional solidarity.

DIFFERENTIATION AND THE INSTITUTIONS OF INTEGRATION

Differentiation and Industry

If the world history of human solidary systems is a history of the emancipation of human activity from the constraints of elaborate institutions of solidarity, then the history of economic systems must be seen as the converse development. Economic activity has become progressively more specialized and disembedded from solidary contexts.

The differentiation of economic activity is very ancient; accordingly, the origins of specialized institutions for economic coordination can be traced to very remote eras. It is clear for example, that the ancient Sumerians were familiar with a variety of complex legal instruments to facilitate contracts, sales, and credit, instruments as abstract and "modern" as negotiable paper, whereby a paper representing a debt of X to Y is assigned to Z in payment of obligations of Y to Z.[35] Specialized economic activity and its concomitant special institutional instruments seem to be as old as commerce itself, and this fact represents the tendency of economic forces to outrun, cross-cut, and break through the preestablished channels of solidarity.

Nevertheless, no previous system of economic activity had the specializing and differentiating force of industrialism. The application of scientific techniques of production within a set of large-scale factories has pushed the intensity of the division of labor and the width of the separation of economic and solidary

---

[35] Samuel Noah Kramer, *The Sumerians* (Chicago: The University of Chicago Press, 1963).

bonds to an unprecedented level. The radical specialization implied by industrialization has widespread ramifications for the whole range of social roles and institutional organization. This has led a number of analysts to posit a "convergence" of development among the societies of the world. According to this view, the "logic of industrialization" will lead all societies to become more and more alike.[36] As traditional societies industrialize, their social and institutional organization will become more and more similar to the patterns developed by the societies of western Europe and North America.

The idea of convergence is based upon four assumptions:

1) Industrialism, because it represents the rational application of science and scientific technology to production, creates the most productive form of economic organization.

2) Because of its high productivity, industrialism will ultimately destroy traditional forms of economic organization.

3) The application of scientific technology to production requires specific forms of economic organization at the social level, which will lead to greater similarity between economic systems.

4) Industrial economic organization requires a particular set of human resources and creates a set of problems of coordination and control which will lead to greater similarity not only within economic systems but in their surrounding social contexts.

This, of course, is only the skeleton of the argument. The flesh can be filled in with a variety of substantive arguments. For example, one team of observers argues that the application of science to production implies a highly skilled work force and that from this requirement flows the ever increasing level of education and commitment of resources to education in industrial society. They further argue that science is always growing and changing. In consequence, productive techniques are constantly changing. This process implies an open society in which men are not permanently and ascriptively committed to given roles, but are free to respond to new opportunities.[37] In our terms, the integration of a rapidly changing economy implies a low level of restrictions on economic movement. By a similar line of reasoning, the authors state that large-scale organization, urban dominance, a large role for government, a highly special-

[36] Clark Kerr, et al., *Industrialism and Industrial Man* (Cambridge, Mass.: Harvard University Press, 1960). See also, Hoselitz, *Sociological Aspects.*

[37] Kerr, et al., *Industrialism*, pp. 33-46.

ized labor force involved in a complex structure of job relationships, a complex web of instrumental rules, the valuation of modernity, change, and work, and the reduction of population constraints are all implied by the logic of industrialization.

Focal Industrial Institutions

From a sociological perspective the core of the phenomenon of industrial organization is to be found in three concepts: the economic enterprise, the specialized labor force, and the instrumental institution. In an industrial order, neither the nuclear nor the extended family, nor any other solidary group such as the guild or caste, is the unit of production. Production is carried on within the specialized economic enterprise—the factory or department store, the corporate farm, the brokerage house, etc. Family enterprise may remain in a few agricultural or service sectors, but, by and large, the scale of production and distribution outruns the family, and the economic enterprise is dependent on purchasing labor as a saleable resource or commodity.

The large-scale economic enterprise must buy, combine, and organize a complex array of economic activities from a work force willing and able to engage in a tremendous variety of specialized, often highly skilled tasks. Thus, the integration of an industrial economy implies both a high level of skill and mobility in workers, who sell their economic activity, and an absence of restrictions on opportunity.

The absence of restrictions on opportunity does not imply an absence of political and institutional regulation. On the contrary, the coordinative problems involved in organizing highly varied task-roles, productive groups of vast scale, and the relations between specialized large-scale organizations reach immense proportions. One need only consult the catalogue of a large law school to appreciate the vast web of institutional regulation required in an industrial economy. Apart from the basic institutions of contract and property, various specialized institutions govern and facilitate particular types of relations and transactions—labor law governs the contract of employment as well as unions and collective bargaining; credit law governs bills, notes, mortgages, negotiable instruments, money, and banking; welfare law regulates the problems of security inherent in any free labor force; the law of enterprise governs the formation of corporations and other business combinations. Other laws involve insurance, taxes, and administrative regulation. Within each of these general fields are an astonishing variety of special instruments and devices for regulating economic activities, and, in addition to the relevant law of the state on these matters, there exists a body of institutional rules at the level of business understandings, industry side-customs, professional rules, and, of course, the web of agreements between organizations.

All of this array of normative regulations has one common feature, its *instrumental* character. In view of our previous distinction between instrumental and institutionalized systems, the concept of an "instrumental" institution may seem to be a contradiction in terms. But we must also remember Weber's point; it is possible to organize institutions in a relatively rational, utilitarian way. They need not be founded on traditional statuses, traditional norms, or fixed interests.

In an industrial economy, there is an immense amount of normative regulation, but the normative rules tend not to have an immediately moral significance. The rules of industrial regulation are relatively far removed from ultimate value premises; rather, they are derived from the practical problems of coordination encountered in a differentiated economy. For example, the medieval law of contract was based quite directly on the premise of the sanctity of promises. By contrast, the modern law of contract is founded on the desire to protect reasonable commercial expectations so as to create a stable environment for decision-making in economic enterprises. The movement away from the sanctity of promises in the economic arena is effectively symbolized in Holmes' famous dicta, which says, in effect, that one has a *right* to break a contract upon payment of damages.[38]

The utilitarian character of the institutional framework of modern economic activity makes it possible for economic organization to outrun solidary organization and to cross-cut societal populations. Many utilitarian economic institutions are not intimately founded on shared cultural values and solidarities. Conversely, the instrumental character of the normative institutions of an industrial economy are made possible by the separation of solidary and economic systems. The institutional framework of economic transactions need no longer symbolize the solidarity of the transactors, their relative status, or their structural position in the community. Accordingly, the content of regulative norms can flow from the character of the coordinative problem rather than the solidarity of the group.

[38] Paraphrased from Oliver Wendell Holmes, "The Path of the Law," *Harvard Law Review* 10 (1897), p. 462.

Convergence in Instrumental Institutions

According to the theory of convergence, the foregoing should ultimately lead to more similarity in normative order across societies. Instrumental norms do not reflect historically and culturally variable value-premises; they reflect the universal coordinative problems of industrial activity. However, this view may exaggerate the similarity of industrial systems. Each system began industrialization from a different starting point and came to industrial society by a different route, leaving historic legacies that continue to support cross-societal variation in economic systems. This variation is reflected in the institutional order. For example, the existence of contract law in the Soviet Union provides support, to an extent, for the theory of convergence, since orthodox communist theory would consider the law of contract to be a specifically bourgeois institution. But it would be a mistake to overlook the fundamentally different character of contract in a communist system. Although its existence may be testimony to the universality of problems in the stabilization of interorganizational relations in any industrial economy, its special use and flavor reflects the authoritarian legacy of governmentally sponsored and controlled economic development. In the Soviet Union, the ultimate premise of the system of contract is not the protection of expectations (and thus of interests) but the protection of the accountability of the manager to the system. Contract is viewed as a device for implementation of the central development plan, not a device for freeing the organization to respond to market forces. Obligations flowing from contracts are viewed as subordinate to the basic obligation to implement the collective economic plan.[39]

Political Domination of the Economy and International Systems

The difference between contractual institutions in the United States and the Soviet Union reflects a difference along the most fundamental dimension of variation in industrial systems, the extent of political domination of the economy. Even the authors of the notion of a logic of industrialization recognized that all industrialized economies are not alike. They argued that one

---

[39] Harold J. Berman, *Justice in the USSR*, rev. ed., (Cambridge, Mass.: Harvard University Press, 1963), pp. 124–144.

of the most important sources of variation is the character and strategy of the industrializing elite. When middle classes are the bearers of the forces of industrialization, the industrialized economy tends to be organized around free market forces and to be relatively free of direct political controls. When industrialization is borne by traditional elites, revolutionary intellectuals, or nationalists, political controls are more dominant. Either the modernizing elite is merely fighting a rearguard action against the forces of change, or it wishes to bring the mobilizing powers of the state to bear upon economic development.[40] Under these circumstances, economic activity is separated from solidary contexts only to be engulfed by the political realm.

In the underdeveloped countries of the world, the modernizing elite is seldom middle class. Therefore, the fusion of the economic and the political realm is prevalent among underdeveloped nations. This fusion constitutes another example of the difference between an orthodox functional perspective, looking primarily to the internal functions within social systems, and the perspective of this book, looking to the overlapping, intersocietal character of systems. According to the functional arguments of social-system theory, there should be pressures toward differentiation between economic and political institutions. Since economic and political functions are based upon somewhat different premises, the functional capacity of a society should be increased by the separation of the two spheres so that economic and political ends can be pursued independently, according to their own needs. We would expect to find pressures toward the separation of a relatively free and decentralized market economy, with its advantages of flexibility and responsiveness, and a more centralized and hierarchical political structure, with its advantage of efficient control of the population. Why then do we see the opposite tendency, the fusion of political and economic activity?

The problem takes on quite a different appearance when viewed from an intersocietal perspective. Drawing on a line of argument established by Gustavo Lagos[41] and developed by J. P. Nettl,[42] we can look at the process of economic development as a process within an intersocietal system.

[40] Kerr et al., *Industrialism*, pp. 47–76.

[41] Gustavo Lagos, *International Stratification and Underdeveloped Countries* (Chapel Hill, N.C.: The University of North Carolina Press, 1963).

[42] J. P. Nettl and Roland Robertson, *International Systems and the Modernization of Societies* (New York: Basic Books, Inc., Publishers, 1968).

First, there is an international system of economic stratification. The most striking fact in the comparison of economic systems is that some nations are rich and some are poor. In 1961, the developed nations of Western Europe, Oceana, and North America, together with Japan and South Africa, included about 20 percent of the world's population but accounted for 60 percent of the world's wealth as measured by annual national product. The United States alone, with only 6 percent of the population, produced nearly 30 percent of the wealth. The communist bloc countries, with 35 percent of the population, produced 24 percent of the wealth. The poorest countries, the underdeveloped countries of Africa, Latin America, Asia, and the Middle East, had 46 percent of the world's population and only 17 percent of the wealth.[43] According to Lagos' calculations, 60 percent of the world's population lived in nations with a gross national product of under $300 per person.[44] Moreover, in relative terms, the poorer nations are becoming ever poorer, in contrast to the wealthier ones.

At the same time, the nations of the world, and especially their elites, have come to accept the egalitarian ideology of the West and to believe that the nations of the world should be equal. Further, the elites within nations know that the real power of their polity depends upon its economic and industrial capacity. Consequently, as national elites confront each other in the international arena, as they jockey for national power and prestige, they are motivated to modernize their national economies. In societies with plural sectors, especially in societies with traditional sectors cut off from participation in the national economy, national modernization means the use of political power to build national economic institutions, to penetrate traditional sectors of the society, to mobilize the population in the pursuit of economic growth, in short, to assume political direction of the economy. The fusion of political and economic institutions becomes quite comprehensible when viewed in the context of the historic penetration of the East by the West. It cannot be understood as an immanent movement within isolated and integrated economies. It must be examined against a background of malintegrated economies, international ideologies, internationally oriented elites, and international economic stratification.

---

[43] Lagos, *International Stratification*, p. 4.

[44] Ibid., p. 5.

6

Political Systems

THE NATURE OF THE POLITICAL

Power and influence are ubiquitous in human activity. Human beings are regularly political; they attempt to secure the things they want from other people by argument, persuasion, flattery, cajoling, threats, and brute force. As husband and wife, parent and child, teacher and student, as bus driver and commuter, as policeman and citizen, as foreman and worker—indeed, in all of our roles, we confront each other in the arena of power. Conflicts within this arena are the stuff of politics. Because power and the conflict of interests are so important in political life, some observers insist that we must avoid functional approaches to the study of politics. They believe that any theory that stresses the contribution of political activity to organization in social life loses sight of the grounding of politics in the pursuit of special private interests, in power conflicts, and in compulsion[1]

On the other hand, from the point of view of the functional

---

[1] Reinhard Bendix, ed., *State and Society: A Reader in Comparative Political Sociology* (Boston: Little, Brown and Company, 1968). See the introduction, pp. 1–13, and "A Comparative Approach to Political Sociology," by Randall Collins, pp. 42–67.

analyst, the very existence and threat of unregulated and unorganized force and conflicts of interest imply a set of specifically collective problems. How is the use of force socially regulated? How is force organized to be brought to bear on problems of territorial defense? How are private interests translated into collective policies? These are collective problems; political life is no mere set of unrelated battles between individuals at each moment of their lives. To be sure, virtually every human act has a political aspect, for most social acts are intended to influence other actors in some way. However, all conflicts are not equally relevant to the problem of *organizing* power.

The collective problems of organizing power are met by collective and institutional devices, therefore we can say that patterns of political activity cohere into *political systems*. The members of societal populations participate in a number of political systems, some relatively local, some far flung, some limited to other members of the population, and some cross-cutting societal boundaries.

In modern society, the main unit for the study of political systems is the nation-state. Some theorists would even make the state the exclusive subject matter of political sociology. This preoccupation with the state reflects the tendency within modern society for the state to acquire a monopoly of the legitimate use of force. In fact, this attribute, monopoly of legitimate force, is the usual defining criteria for a state. One common solution to the problems of political life is the concentration of authority in the hands of a particular institutionally regulated group, the state. However, one can object to the structural definition of the political in terms of the state on the grounds that it provides inadequate leverage on political processes and systems in primitive, "stateless" societies, in premodern states which fail to thoroughly penetrate the other orders of power in society, and in the international arena.

From this point of view, the realm of the political is more properly delimited by first defining a set of universal political functions and then examining the variable structures that perform political functions more or less successfully. Such an approach makes problematic how and why the political functions come to inhere in the state and in its associated institutional apparatus of citizenship and party. This formulation not only suggests the problem, it implies the outline of an answer. The modern state emerges because of its great capacity to meet the functional problems of politics.

Political Functions

The problem of identifying political functions is more complicated and controversial than the parallel problem of isolating economic functions. There is considerable consensus among economists that the economy involves the production and distribution of wealth and the function of economizing. Lists of political functions are frequently much longer.

One of the most sophisticated functional theories of politics, that of Gabriel Almond, proposes twelve political functions.[2] First, there are six "conversion functions" whereby political *input* in the form of public demands and supports is translated into political *output* in the form of public policies and decisions. Conversion functions include *interest articulation*, or the formulation of demands, and *interest aggregation*, or the combining and merging of interests. Three of the conversion functions, *rule making*, *rule application*, and *rule adjudication*, correspond to the three functions or branches of government in classic democratic theory, legislative, executive, and judicial. The final conversion function, *communication*, involves the transmission of information about all five of the other conversion processes within the public and the state.

Next, Almond describes four political capabilities or capacities for producing political outputs. The *extractive* capacity is the capacity to secure resources and efforts from the population. The *regulative* capacity is the capacity to control activities in the population. *Distributive* capacity refers to the ability of government to control the allocation of valued objects within the population. A political system's *responsive* capacity is its degree of sensitivity, attention, and compliance with the political demands of the public.

Almond proposes two additional functions, which he refers to as system maintenance and adaptive functions. The persistence of political systems requires (at the structural level) continuing participation through a process of *recruitment* and (at the cultural level) the continuation of understanding of and loyalty to the system through a process of *political socialization*.

Almond also speaks of another set of political capacities, which involve the ability of the political system to respond to the challenges of development. The first developmental challenge

[2] Gabriel A. Almond, "Introduction: A Functional Approach to Comparative Politics," in *The Politics of the Developing Areas,* ed. Gabriel A. Almond and James S. Coleman (Princeton: Princeton University Press, 1960), pp. 3–64.

questions whether the system can respond to the problem of the integration of state power and its penetration of society through *state-building*. The second asks if it can respond to the problem of developing uniform loyalty and commitment through *nation-building*. The third challenge is the need for the political system to respond to the pressures of including more and more members of the society by building *participation*. The fourth developmental challenge is the need to increase capacity to control *distribution*.

The developmental challenges are more than mere abstract types of functions. They are real historical problems which the competing nations of the world have faced over the last five centuries, and Almond has shown how this scheme for outlining political capacities can be used to produce a useful classification of types of polity and an intriguing interpretation of the historical development of various modern political systems.[3]

For example, Almond contrasts the "immobilist" democracies such as France with the more stable and effective democracies such as Great Britain. Britain solved the problems of building state and nation gradually and early, during the fifteenth to seventeenth centuries, before the rise of modern pressures on capacity for participation and distribution. France, on the other hand, developed neither a comparable institutional structure nor the national inclusion of her population. The French revolution and its aftermath left a permanent legacy in the form of a proclerical, conservative, and somewhat aristocratic right and an anticlerical, radical left, and neither were firmly committed to any given historic institutional structure. France then faced the pressures for mass participation and redistribution with a divided and institutionally impoverished polity.

Almond's functional scheme seems both conceptually exhaustive and also productive of insights into political history. However, in some ways it is analytically weak and cumbersome. It includes functions at different levels; communication, for example, refers to a subelement of all the other functions. Some of Almond's functions refer to contributions of the political system to the society and some to the requisites of the political system itself. The developmental capacities merely repeat in a different context what are elsewhere called output capacities.

For our purposes, a related scheme of four interdependent

[3] Gabriel Almond, "Political Systems and Political Change," *American Behavioral Scientist* 6 (June 1963), pp. 3–10.

functions will be adequate. All four functions involve the organization of *dominance* in the population. In every group, members control resources that enable them to dominate others. Control of force, or of wealth, reputation, knowledge, or other valued objects, permits actors to affect the fortunes of others through the exercise of *power*. Power may be defined as the capacity to control the behavior of others through force, threats, or the withholding of resources. Power is held by many people, and it can be distributed in a variety of patterns, but in every society the distribution of power is so organized as to ensure a measure of domestic peace and collective capacity.

The organization of power can produce four types of functional capacity in a population:

1) *Internal peace.* Power can be organized in such a way as to limit internal power-struggles and thus to prevent the expenditure of resources on internal conflict.

2) *External protection or expansion.* When power is socially controlled, it can be brought to bear on other societies, either defensively or in an expansive, aggressive way.

3) *Goal attainment.* To obtain collective goals, it is necessary to secure a variety of coordinated contributions from the population. This necessitates a measure of control over their behavior. Further, because competing courses of action will be supported by competing social groups, one political function is the formulation of those collective goals which bind members of society to particular courses of action.

4) *Interest alignment.* If power has been organized, it is possible to recognize and implement the interests of subgroups through the instrumentality of collective power. It is possible to allow for the expression, combination, and compromise of subgroup demands and their incorporation into public policy.

Clearly, these functions can support each other in an integrated way. For example, the successful alignment of interests may buy off subgroups who could use their power for internal disruption. Conversely, subgroup interests cannot be implemented unless the larger group has collective political capacity. If power is not dissipated in internal stalemates, it can be used in pursuing collective goals.

The mutual support of the power functions implies that power is not necessarily a "zero-sum" resource. It is not true that one person must always have power at someone else's expense. The organization of power can increase the capacity of the larger political system to achieve the interests of constituent groups.

Goals beyond the power of the various subgroups of society may be achievable if they can become the object of public power rather than remain tied to private force.

Components of Political Systems

It is possible to separate the components of political systems according to the Parsonian functional paradigm in a manner analogous to Parsons and Smelser's separation of the components of an economy into labor commitment (pattern maintenance), entrepreneurship (integration), labor (goal attainment), and capital (adaptation).

The pattern maintenance component of a polity consists in those basic commitments to political authority that are not responsive to short-run political sanctions. Here, as the remainder of this chapter should demonstrate, sociological attention has centered on the organization and transformation of authority. Authority may be defined as the acceptance of the legitimacy of those who hold power in a political system and of their legitimate right to make and enforce collective decisions. The goal-attainment component of the political system is the apparatus of compulsion itself; it is used to ensure conformity and collective effort in the population. Here, sociological attention has been primarily directed to the rise of the modern state with the capacity to penetrate other autonomous centers of power.

The adaptive component may be seen in the process of public political participation, or, alternatively stated, the process of the representation of interests in the political arena. The basic resource of any political system is the political motivation of its participants, their willingness to engage in organized politics in the pursuit of their goals. The measure of adaptive capacity is the success of the political system in aligning the interests of participants and the goals of the system and in adjusting to changing social needs as they are expressed in the demands of social groups. Sociological interest in this area has centered on the study of the associational life of societies, especially the political capacity of independent associations and political parties. Parties are usually studied in relation to the underlying political cleavages and power groups in society,[4] and associational life is

---

[4] See the excellent reader edited by Seymour Lipset and Stein Rokkan, *Party Systems and Voter Alignments* (New York: The Free Press, 1967), which includes an interesting introduction by the editors.

studied for its bearing on the structural foundations of a democratic polity in which a variety of interests are effectively represented.

Finally, the integrative component, which parallels entrepreneurship in the economy, is political leadership, the ability to combine the factors of "political production" in effective and responsive ways. The political leader draws upon his authority, utilizes the instruments of political compulsion, and mobilizes the political interests of the populace, all in the interests of the implementation of policy. Studies of political leadership have emphasized the analysis of elites. Such studies vary in their sensitivity to the problem of elites as the organizers of emergent political resources and interests. Nevertheless, successful studies of this type range from general studies of the rise of new levels of political consolidation when leadership classes mobilize new resources[5] to political biographies of individual statesmen who have founded their success on the consolidation of a number of emergent social forces.[6]

The remainder of this chapter, while not devoted to elaborating this scheme of components, does assume that the Parsonian categories define the main areas of sociological interest in political systems at the societal level.

The Modern State

In modern times, the major vehicle for organizing power for the creation of domestic peace, foreign policy, collective capacity, and interest alignment has been the monopolization of the legitimate use of force by the differentiated bureaucratic state. This is the definition of the state in classic sociological literature.

Max Weber defined the state with reference to four criteria: (1) *continuous organization*, that is, a full-time staff of officials devoted to full-time political administration; (2) *legal authority* defining the powers and duties of office; (3) *compulsory jurisdiction* by public officials over all the activity within the territory encompassed by the state; (4) *a monopoly of the legitimate use*

---

[5] S. N. Eisenstadt, *The Political Systems of Empires* (New York: The Free Press, 1963).

[6] For example, see the brilliant biography by David C. Douglas, *William the Conqueror* (Berkeley: University of California Press, 1964).

of force resting in the hands of the officials of the state.[7] By contrast, in earlier forms of political organization, the central authority operated with only the power and influence that could be mustered over other institutional functionaries, local magnates, or other social strata. Such was the case in traditional China, where the extended families of the gentry had autonomous power and monopolized bureaucratic positions within the empire. Similarly, the early medieval monarch in Western Europe was only first among equals. His chief vassals and local officials had independent power in their own domains, power that rested on precisely the same resource base as the king's own power. Only when the monarch had more land or more retainers, or when he could manipulate the traditional bonds of personal loyalty, was he able to exert royal influence within the territory of local officials. Further, ' the medieval monarch was forced to compete against the claims to independent authority put forward by the church, an institution that extended beyond the boundaries of any royal domain. Central authority and the integration of power through the institution of the state came only when the monarch was able to rest his power on a dependent army and on a staff of bureaucratic officials. Only then could he successfully negate claims to legitimate and independent jurisdiction put forth by other institutions.

State-Building and Political Leadership

The process of the consolidation of state power has been effectively illuminated by S. N. Eisenstadt's study of the political systems of empires.[8] From a comparative study of Egyptian, Mesopotamian, Incan, Aztec, Indian, Chinese, Persian, Hellenistic, Byzantine, Arab, and early European examples, Eisenstadt concludes that the imperial level of political consolidation has some common features wherever it occurs. "Historical bureaucratic" empires emerge whenever the interests within a society become sufficiently varied and complex to permit a local monarch with limited authority to develop machinery for turning varied interests into new resources of power. Differentiation in

---

[7] See the analysis of Weber and the state by Scott Greer and Peter Orleans, "Political Sociology," in *Handbook of Modern Sociology*, ed. Robert E. L. Faris (Chicago: Rand McNally and Company, 1964), pp. 808–810.

[8] Eisenstadt, *Political Systems of Empires*.

the larger society creates new interests that an ambitious monarch can mobilize against the traditional, aristocratic, patrician elites who have opposed the extension of monarchial power. New productive groups (for example, a bourgeois class), new achieved statuses, and new religious commitments provide such resources of power for an "entrepreneurial" empire builder.

Eisenstadt proceeds at such a high level of abstraction that it is often difficult to see just what it means, in behavioral terms, for a ruler to "make use of new resources" to increase his "generalized power." Nevertheless, the best political biographies of leaders who have successfully consolidated power show us in some detail the type of political entrepreneurship Eisenstadt has in mind. David Douglas vividly depicts William the Conqueror building the Anglo-Norman state through his capacity to draw upon social trends in eleventh-century Normandy to his own advantage. Novel use of new military technology, adept manipulation of growing religious piety, and masterful use of familial ties to weld together a group of newly powerful Norman magnates enabled William to overcome his political rivals, all of whom seemed more tied to traditional resources and techniques.[9] Reinhard Bendix has examined the methods of such contemporary charismatic leaders as Prince Sihanouk of Cambodia, Kim-Il-song of Korea, Nehru, and Mao-Tse-tung. In each case, he sees the use of symbolic techniques, either traditional or revolutionary, to capture a new resource—the mass public's hope for national progress.[10]

State and Society: Battleground of Political Theory

The process of state building is sometimes referred to as the "penetration" of society by the state because it involves acquiring control over force and denying its use to any other of the constituent elements of the social order. Castes, aristocratic strata, local leaders, powerful families, and religious associations are stripped of all power that rests on the direct use of independent force. Beyond the negative aspect of destroying or neutralizing intermediate centers of power, the penetration of society involves

[9] Douglas, *William the Conqueror.*

[10] Reinhard Bendix, "Reflections on Charismatic Leadership," in *State and Society*, ed. Bendix, pp. 616–629.

the establishment of direct links between the state and the individual participant in political affairs.

Much political theory has been devised with the implicit purpose of justifying the penetration of society by the state. In Plato's utopia, all other social segments, including the family, are to be eliminated, for they represent obstacles to the effective formation of the one institution which embodies man's highest abilities and aspirations, the state. Other advocates of unity through the state have been less radical. They have not demanded the absolute elimination of other types of human association, but whether they are royalists defending the divine right of kings, philosophers elucidating the concept of sovereignty, or nationalists arguing for the formation of the nation-state as the one effective link between the individual and humanity, the theorists of state power have argued that collective unity and purpose require an undivided and ultimate locus of power.[11] From Hobbes, who argued that the power of insubordinate citizens implies total anarchy, to Lenin, who argued that, within the encircled communist state, private interests are selfish and counterrevolutionary, the advocates of the penetration of society by the state have seen private centers of power as essentially antisocial. Only the state can guarantee social unity and collective purpose; therefore, state and society must be one.

On the other hand, political liberals have continued to argue that state and society are separate. Though few would argue that the right to apply force should be well-distributed in society, the thinkers in the pluralist tradition believe that the state, as custodian of legitimate force, should be controlled by and responsive to a society outside of the state. In pluralist thinking, this society consists in a number of centers of autonomous influence — the various constituent communities and associations of the societal population. The pluralist argues for a rich and politically relevant associational life, which he asserts is a condition of the continued separation and interdependence of state and society and, indeed, the only social base for a democratic state. To the pluralist, the only alternative is a totalitarian state which either forbids or dominates all human association.

Here we find another example of the familiar use of the concept of society as a designation of the external and controlling social reality from which flow standards for the social control of

---

[11] For an analysis of unity and plurality in social thought about the state, see Leslie Lipson, *The Great Issues of Politics* (Englewood Cliffs, N.J.: Prentice-Hall, Inc., 1965), pp. 134–195.

social subsystems. As indicated in chapter one, this was the first
secular basis for justifying the accountability of the state. In
medieval Europe, the distinction between state and society, that
is, the recognition of independent institutional spheres outside
of the state, was founded on the distinction between man's spiritual and material lives. The Christian church claimed independent
jurisdiction over the souls of men, and from this claim flowed a
series of encounters and contests between church and state. In
the first instance, the claim to absolute royal authority was made
over and against the claims of the church; eventually the sovereignty of the state was to prevail. The next challenge, which was
to the absolute dominion of secular authority, was itself secular.
The social-contract doctrine of eighteenth-century liberals asserted a natural order of interdependence between men, an order
on which the state is founded and, hence, an order the state must
respect.

In the nineteenth and twentieth centuries, the theory of the
social control of power shifted away from the idea of a natural
interdependence of individuals to the concept of organization
of group life. Alexis de Tocqueville believed that the break-up
of society into a set of isolated individuals makes the citizen easy
prey for the manipulation of arbitrary central authority. Indeed,
torn away from his historic social roots, the individual actually
looks to the central state as the only locus for collective experience. Only the possibility of a rich associational life, a degree
of local autonomy, and the maintenance of some isolated semiautonomous institutional spheres, such as the church and the
legal profession, can support democracy. De Tocqueville thought
he could discern the outlines of such a social order in the emergent American society of the early nineteenth century.[12] De
Tocqueville and the other advocates of social pluralism have
had a dominant influence on contemporary political sociology
Political sociology has taken the problem of the social structural
preconditions of democratic polity as the central question of
the field; pluralism, in the foregoing sense, has been considered
a basic requisite of democratic life.

The works of Seymour Lipset and William Kornhauser provide two examples of this type of analysis. Lipset argues for a
strong association between the degree of economic development
and the extent of democracy in nations, and he marshalls various

[12] Alexis de Tocqueville, *Democracy in America*, trans. Henry Reeve (New York: Schocken
Books, 1961), especially vol. two, book two, pp. 113–194, and vol. two, book two, pp.
345–400.

cross-national indices in support of that position. One of the main mechanisms of economic support for democracy is the formation of a large middle class. Middle-class support for democracy is based on a number of factors, and one of the most important is the extensive participation of middle-class persons in independent associations which are a source of political education, insulation from manipulation, and autonomous influence.[13]

Kornhauser gives an even more central role to social pluralism.[14] Drawing on both aristocratic and liberal critiques of mass society, Kornhauser points to an inherent vulnerability in democratic polity. Democratic government presumes elites that are accessible. Elites must not be in permanent possession of power; rather, the social structure must have the capacity to both absorb new elements and replace old elements as ideologies, groups, and interests wax and wane. But the very accessibility of an elite can also mean its vulnerability to take-over by antidemocratic elements. If non-elites form a *mass*, they are "available" for easy manipulation by elites, and democratic polity is imperiled, for antidemocratic elites can take over and form an inaccessible elite. Then this elite can take advantage of the availability of the masses to organize a totalitarian society in which all types of associations are penetrated by the state or are mere creatures of it. Only when the non-elites are organized by a complex array of plural institutions and associations is democracy placed upon firm social foundations. The existence of plural, organized social groups is the integrative foundation of the democratically ordered, societally controlled political system.

The Uncontrolled Polity

Because of the long history of the use of the word *pluralism* to describe the societally controlled political system, it is unfortunate that the term *plural society* has also come to mean, in another context, a type of society that is incapable of exerting meaningful social control over its political system. As the term is

---

[13] Seymour Lipset, *Political Man* (Garden City, N.Y.: Doubleday and Company, Inc., 1959). See also Lipset, et al., *Union Democracy* (Glencoe, Ill.: The Free Press, 1956). For an alternative view, see Harold Lasswell, "The Psychology of Hitlerism," *The Political Quarterly* 4 (1933), p. 374, and *Politics* (Cleveland: The World Publishing Company, 1958), pp. 113–130.

[14] William Kornhauser, *The Politics of Mass Society* (New York: The Free Press, 1959).

used by such writers as J. S. Furnivall and M. G. Smith,[15] a plural
society is not a society in which a variety of associations and institutional representatives negotiate and compete within a single,
institutionally organized political community. Instead, a plural
society exists when a population under a single government contains a number of distinct subgroups, each with its own institutions and cultural life, and without a sense of common identity.
Furnivall was referring to such societies as colonial Burma,[16] in
which colonial administration and the opportunistic transformation and exploitation of the economy created a number of ecological niches filled by various groups—Burmese, European,
Chinese, and Indian. Colonial rule destroyed native political institutions and organizations and eroded the various indigenous
forms of social ties based upon religion, custom, and personal
relations. In consequence, native social life was atomized. Nor
was it replaced by any new forms of "organic" community, for
the members of the various groups, though they had some sense
of membership in their subgroup, had no sense of membership
in an entity called Burmese society. They were reduced to mere
participants in economic roles and subjects of rational administration. Therefore, there was no political society for the effective
expression of what Furnivall called "social demands." In a plural society, the state operates only according to the dictates of
efficient economic administration in the short run; it is not subject to societal controls founded on an inner order of common
long-run interests and interdependence. In our terms, the state is
an instrumental social system. Again we see the possibilities
inherent in the ready expandability of social systems of the instrumental type.

The existence of such states has led some writers to insist
upon a totally political definition of society. A society must consist in a population within the territorial boundaries controlled
by a given government.[17] To insist upon a political definition,
because of the existence of plural societies or for any other reason,[18] is to ignore a very long intellectual tradition, a tradition

[15] E.g., J. S. Furnivall, *Netherlands India: A Study of Plural Economy* (Cambridge: Cambridge University Press, 1944) and M. G. Smith, *Plural Society*.

[16] J. S. Furnivall, "The Political Economy of the Tropical Far East," in *State and Society*, ed.
Bendix, pp. 460–474.

[17] See M. G. Smith, *Plural Society*, p. 79.

[18] E.g., Swanson, *Birth of the Gods*, p. 42.

founded in some instances on the actual existence of a society outside of the state. The idea of societal controls on political power did not originate as a mere figment of political imagination among critical intellectuals during the Enlightenment. The Jewish people as a solidary community, bound by worship of a common God and united by a sense of a God-given and distinct historic role, existed before the rise of a sovereign central state in Israel. The independence of the state from other forms of society continued to be manifested in the prophetic tradition as a long series of prophetic figures confronted the state and criticized regal authority whenever that authority appeared to abandon the Hebrew God. Further, the society survived its political destruction. Definitions are, of course, arbitrary, but the most useful definitions are not time bound. The most useful definitions of society should not be tied to those societies in which the most extensive social system consists in the jurisdiction of a coercive state.

EXPANSION AND THE INTEGRATION OF POLITICAL SYSTEMS

The Integrated Political System

The foregoing commentary on the dual use of the term *pluralism* brings us to what is by now a familiar theme in this book, the impact of societal expansion on the integration of social systems. Some use the term *pluralism* to refer to a societally regulated and institutionally integrated political system. Others use it to refer to a political system which is not integrated because it has expanded beyond the boundaries of any solidary community capable of exerting unified social control.

An integrated political system is a political system that includes all of its participants in a single "political community." A political community is a group of persons who:

1) recognize a common locus (or loci) of legitimate power;

2) do not use force unless empowered by the rules governing authority;

3) are included in political groups, that is, groups that formulate the demands and supports for political actions.

Nothing in this definition requires the concentration of power in the hands of the state. Power, including the use of force, may be widely diffused in various social groups (such as clans) as long as there is agreement on the locus of *legitimate* force and *de facto* control of illegitimate uses. Indeed, the definition supposes that a state of international peace represents an integrated political system of sorts as long as nations recognize the bounds of each other's sovereignty.

Malintegration and its Sources

This definition of an integrated political system implies two distinct types of failure of integration. The first type is violent war. The Vietnamese war represents this type of malintegration. Clearly, the inhabitants of South Vietnam do not recognize a common locus of legitimate authority, and combat each other over precisely this issue. To a lesser degree, the racial violence in American cities constitutes a breakdown of political integration. Some rioters clearly had political motivation; they hoped that deliberate confrontation and the disregard of police and law would improve the lot of black citizens. Such action is, in effect, a withdrawal from the political community on the grounds that its procedures do not provide adequate recognition of group interests.

The second type of malintegration occurs when persons and groups are not included in the political process. Noninclusion may or may not lead to violent activity as groups seek to force their recognition, but whether violence occurs or not, the exclusion of part of a population from the give and take of political demands and supports represents a lack of political community within the population. To return to Furnivall's Burmese example, the various laboring groups that emigrated to Colonial Burma did not form a part of the Burmese political community because they were mere objects of administration rather than participants in the process of aligning interests through the mediation of group demands.

The breakdown of political community and integration may occur in a variety of ways. The second type of malintegration, noninclusion, often leads to the first type, illegitimate violence, as excluded groups fight for position and recognition.

Failure to include the entire societal population within the political community is usually a consequence of societal expansion, either an immediate consequence of an ongoing process of expansion, or a heritage of earlier expansions that failed to completely incorporate new social groups. All of the familiar forms of expansion—conquest, territorial expansion, colonial rule, importation of a labor force, urbanization, and increasing mobility —can lead to expansion of the societal population relative to the political community. In some cases, expansion leads to a partial inclusion of a new group in the political community so that its members have some political privileges and influence, but the group remains burdened with political disadvantages, barriers, and incapacities of various kinds. Later, as social change in other institutional spheres makes tighter integration necessary, the barriers to full participation become more salient and conflict develops.

The history of the political inclusion of the American Negro illustrates several features of the dynamics of political community.[19] The black American was originally imported to the United States as a part of the expansion of plantation agriculture in the South. As a chattel, the black man was included in the political process only as an object, never as an actor. After emancipation, the members of the Southern political community took care to continue a variety of virtually complete political barriers, especially after the reconstruction period. At the same time, the continuing expansion of American society and the concomitant increase in the mobility of its population brought the descendants of the slaves to the cities of the West and North as urban workers. Away from the traditions and institutionalized social systems of the South, the Negro acquired more of a measure of formal citizenship at the level of legal political rights. But at the *de facto* level, the Negro was not effectively represented in the most powerful circles. Social prejudice and discrimination in education and employment, together with the internal social disorganization characteristic of poor immigrant groups, prevented the black community from developing an effective political base and entering into the higher political councils. Lack of power permits a continuing lack of responsiveness to Negro interests and contributes to the perpetuation of political incapacities.

In the long run, partial inclusion is not stable. Continuing economic development stimulates the need for development of economic and technical capacities and hence the need for greater economic participation for all groups. This in turn implies the expansion of educational opportunities, a higher level of economic rewards, and a broad range of incentives to bring the po-

[19] For a sensitive and enlightening treatment of the inclusion of the Negro American, see Talcott Parsons, "Full Citizenship for the Negro American?" in *Theory and Modern Society*, pp. 422–465.

tential contributions of minority workers into the economic system. These developments are inconsistent with the perpetuation of social stigma. Yet, within the established political arena, the black community cannot easily remove the residual stigma and the barriers of the past. Hence, the black militant is ready to reject the rules of the game and to seek a new game that can be played on more advantageous terms. Alternatively stated, each new breakthrough in the participation of Negro Americans in our social systems makes each remaining exclusion increasingly incongruous. In the face of increasingly salient social barriers, political exclusion becomes intolerable; and, in the eyes of blacks, constituted authority loses its legitimacy and violence gains acceptance. This represents a failure of political community. The militant is willing to use force to establish "institutions of incorporation" that will more fully include the Negro in the society. One example is the occurrence of sporadic violence in conjunction with the establishment of Black Studies programs in colleges and universities.

The problems of inclusion are not limited to the political integration of subgroups within a single sovereign political unit. The failure to achieve international political community is a serious problem in an expanding and increasingly interdependent world. The growth of communications and the consequent possibilities of economic penetration and expanded political influence have given us a world where large-scale political systems are unavoidable; nations and peoples are in constant contact. But these systems tend to be larger than any supporting infra-structures that might serve as a base for political community. And so it has been through history; man's *de facto* mobility has increased faster than his capacity to create political community, and war has been a dynamic factor in human society.

War

War is an especially dynamic factor in social systems for it inescapably links the power arrangements in one society to uncontrollable power factors in other societies. Further, war is inseparable from the founding of domestic political power by means of organized force. In consequence, war, whether waged successfully or unsuccessfully, upsets the domestic organization of power and stimulates the reorganization of domestic institutions.

Social-system theory might look at a nation's armed forces as a domestic boundary-maintaining mechanism, oriented to other societies, but functioning to maintain the stability of the society relative to external societies. Here is an excellent example of the weakness of an aspect of social-system theory that we have repeatedly mentioned. According to the foregoing account of the functions of the armed forces, winning a war would be interpreted as successful defense of the system's boundary and losing would be a case of unsuccessful functioning, that is, incapacity to control relations with an environment. In contrast, our analysis would view a nation's armed forces as participants in an intersocietal political system. Events in that system are transmitted quite directly to the inner order of a society because the internal social order is ultimately dependent on organized force. The impact of war is not limited to cataclysmic breakdowns of social systems when wars are lost. Winning a war may give new prestige to military leaders and lead to basic changes in a society's structure of leadership. Mere preparation for war produces a reallocation of economic and political priorities with wide ranging internal ramifications. This point has been one of the main themes of observers of the cold war "military-industrial complex" in post-war America. According to these critics, constant investment in a high level of military hardware has had an enormous impact on the structure of stratification in the United States, producing a military-industrial elite with convergent interests and near absolute power over the decisions that most influence our life and death.[20]

Losing a war does not necessarily lead to dissolution of the society through failure of boundary maintenance, but it does usually lead to fundamental changes in the domestic role of the military organization. This is illustrated by events in Germany after World War I. Germany had been in the forefront of the development of the theory and practice of civilian control of the military. The theory was represented by Clausewitz' classic theory of war as an extension of political aims by military means, which, in effect, asserts the supremacy of the state over its military foundation. The practice was represented by the professionalization of the German officer corps and its strict control by bureaucratic procedures and standards. But the vicissitudes of

[20] See C. W. Mills, *The Power Elite*, and Fred J. Cook, *The Warfare State* (New York: The Macmillan Company, 1962).

the First World War quickly overcame one-hundred years of tradition and social organization, and the German army took the reins of civil government.[21] Similarly, French difficulties in colonial wars in Algeria and Indochina following World War II led to the breakdown of civilian control during the Fourth Republic.[22] Again, we see an illustration of the difficulty of insulating social systems from events in other cross-cutting systems. During a long period of relative international tranquility, the internal organization of society may appear to be well protected from events in foreign systems. But, with the onset of war, members of the military arm of the society's political system begin to participate actively in an international action system. The action systems involved in international war are instrumental rather than institutional in character. They involve innovative activity, absence of traditional constraints, and the undermining of established arrangements, interests, and statuses. Once more, we see a vital feature of societal organization that violates the assumptions of social-system theory. Armies cannot be viewed as mere institutions for the control of the relations between societies and their environment. They represent a potentially independent basis of power, and, given their recurrent participation in instrumental intersocietal systems, the institutional controls designed to socially limit military power are often destroyed or radically transformed by external events. This phenomenon is increasingly important in the modern world because of the growth of world political organization—international alliances, international political movements, international associations, and foreign subsidization of domestic military apparatus.[23]

---

[21] Samuel P. Huntington, *The Soldier and the State* (Cambridge, Mass.: The Belknap Press of Harvard University Press, 1964), pp. 99–113.

[22] Raoul Girardet, "Civil and Military Power in the Fourth Republic," in *Changing Patterns of Military Politics*, ed. Samuel P. Huntington (New York: The Free Press, 1962), pp. 121–149.

[23] See in this connection Amatai Etzioni and Fredric L. Du Bow, "Some Workpoints for a Macrosociology," in *The Study of Total Societies* ed. Samuel Z. Klausner (Garden City, N.Y.: Doubleday and Co., Inc., Anchor Books, 1967), pp. 147–161, and their example of the link between the Dominican military and the American military, with its consequences for stability in the Dominican system. A series of such examples lead the authors to write," If one wishes to do a satisfactory systems analysis, it will be necessary to look beyond the boundaries of a particular society to the ties which link it to other societies" (p. 153), words which could stand as a motto for systems analysis.

The Political Market

Not all political breakdown derives from the failure to include all groups in the political community. Disturbance may follow internal failures in the "political market."[24] Social-system theory is more at home with this type of breakdown, for it begins with the concept of a well-organized political community that operates through the mechanism of a market-like exchange between citizens and political leaders. Moreover, in our terms, it assumes that social change occurs in the context of structural constraints. Social groups make demands upon political leaders. Leaders attempt to respond to these demands by exchanging acceptable political decisions for the support of political groups. In the process, the political leadership of a society attempts to mediate the demands of society's constituent groups and to make binding decisions on behalf of the whole society. These decisions involve adjustive changes to meet new challenges within the framework of an established constitutional order. Insofar as leaders are able to do this, the political energies within a society are collectively mobilized in the pursuit of national goals, and the political functions, as outlined earlier in this chapter, are successfully performed.

The advantage of this approach to political analysis is that it links a functional analysis of a society's collective political problems to the ongoing give and take of the concrete political process. We are able to see the juggling of political demands and supports as a process of integration. A president responds to the demands of workers by adopting a policy favoring legislative protection of union rights. Business cooperation is purchased by drafting legislation limiting the potential disruption of union activity by regulating union organization and tactics. Thus is a national labor policy born and disruptive conflict replaced by institutionally regulated bargaining; or so the political process works in theory.

The Breakdown of Political Markets

The theory of the political market also suggests sources of political breakdown. Political disruption occurs when leadership

[24] Political market analysis goes back to David Easton, "An Approach to the Analysis of Political Systems," *World Politics* (April 1957), pp. 383–408. The approach is elaborated in David Easton, *A Systems Analysis of Political Life* (New York: John Wiley & Sons, Inc., 1965), and is treated with great insight and sophistication in Talcott Parsons, "Voting and the Equilibrium of the American Political System," in *Theory and Modern Society*, pp. 223–263.

is unable to mediate the demands of a society's constituent groups, either because interests are irreconcilable, public demands misgauged, or compromise programs fail in practice.

The problem of equilibrating the demand-support market can even be analyzed in the language of economic theory. Because of the analogy to the concepts of supply and demand in economic theory, it is possible to utilize the metaphor of the political market to develop rather sophisticated theories of political breakdown modeled on the advanced theoretical apparatus of economics.[25] Just as the term inflation is used to refer to an excess of economic demand over productive capacity, so we may employ the term political inflation to refer to the analogous situation in political markets. If demands from political groups exceed the potential capacity of leadership to achieve the ends that groups desire, then political leaders are forced to pay off in promises. The currency of political discourse is cheapened. In economic markets, an excess of demand over supply results in bidding-up prices with consequent loss of faith in the value of the medium of exchange, i.e., money. Similarly, in the political market a high level of demand leads competitive leaders to bid-up the price they *claim* to be able to pay for political support. If it becomes clear that the leaders cannot deliver, then political groups come to lose confidence in the "currency" of political life, i.e., faith that group interests may be entrusted to leaders. In extreme cases, this can lead to the breakdown of the system. Just as in extreme inflation people refuse to accept money, but insist on holding goods, so in extreme political inflation people refuse to accept promises and insist on holding power in their own hands rather than entrusting it to the system. In other words, a high level of political inflation leads to a failure of legitimacy.

The social base of inflationary situations is most visible in a society where the emergence of the idea of modernity and nationhood has raised the aspirations of the people, but where the group is too heterogenous, conflict-ridden, and politically incompetent to permit effective mobilization of group energies in the establishment and pursuit of national policies.

A similar line of reasoning leads to the concept of a political depression. Again, following the analogy of an economic depression, in which the demand for goods is lower than the actual productive capacity of the economy, a political depression occurs

---

[25] Parsons, "Voting and the Equilibrium." For a well stated exposition of this idea, see Harry C. Bredemeier and Richard M. Stephenson, *The Analysis of Social Systems* (New York: Holt, Rinehart and Winston, Inc., 1962), pp. 381–392.

when a political system has the realistic capacity to move the society toward collective goals, but political groups fail to define interests, suggest policies, and demand action. They give their support away for nothing. In consequence, collective political action fails to be responsive to the actual needs of the constituent groups of the society because these needs are not expressed. The social base of political depression is widespread apathy, such as occurs in an advanced society when the major interests of the majority of the population are effectively met and the interests of political minorities are not well articulated. As minority interests become more insistently expressed, political depression can quickly change to inflation when new minority demands go beyond the system's capacity for easy adjustment. Thus, the process of inclusion in political community is often accompanied by political inflation.

The connection between inclusion and inflation suggests a weakness in the theory of the political market as it is usually expressed. The social-system theorist will usually describe the political exchange process (as we have here) as occurring within an established integrated political community. Political conflicts are pictured as disputes between essentially equal participants in the political system. In the language of this volume, the boundaries of the society are taken as coextensive with the boundaries of the political system. Participants within the system compete for the "services" of political leaders; out of this competition comes an allocation of political capacities to political tasks in a process essentially similar to the economic process whereby market competition allocates economic resources to competing uses. In an integrated system, there should be some correspondence between priorities of need and priorities of allocation — much will be bid for what is badly needed.

This view overlooks the fact that political conflict does not always take place within an integrated political community. The issues of political argument do not concern mere questions of allocation of resources between the goals of various participants; *they concern the terms of participation themselves.* The concern is who is to be included in the political community. Thus, the structural background of political inflation is not a high degree of political competition within a fixed system, but the expansion of the boundaries of political community. For an example we can turn again to our analysis of the process of inclusion of the black American in American society. Every increase in the participation of Negroes in American society involved an implied promise of inclusion in the American political community. Because the system lacks the flexibility to deliver promptly on these promises, which were regularly repeated by political leaders in America, an inflationary situation exists. Negroes are tempted to hoard power, to take it into their own hands. To exchange potential power for the promises of official leadership appears to be to exchange something real for a valueless symbol, an exchange comparable to the exchange of real goods for worthless money during a period of runaway economic inflation.

Political inflation is a chronic problem in societies facing the challenge of incorporation. When there is a low level of national solidarity, political leaders are prone to make extravagant promises of future gains in an attempt to purchase the allegiance of marginal or polarized groups. The fragility of political community in the face of ethnic, tribal, and regional divisions in many of the new nations is evident in the news that comes to us daily from Biafra, the Congo, Ghana, or Singapore.

POLITICAL INSTITUTIONS

Institutions of Authority

Authority, as the word has been used in this chapter, refers to the acceptance within a population of the right of those who occupy certain roles to make *binding decisions*, that is, decisions that commit the group to a certain course of action and require conformity to the orders of those in authority. Bodies of norms govern entry into positions of authority and the rights and obligations of incumbents. Following the usage established in chapter two, these bodies of norms may be referred to as *institutions* of authority. Concretely, institutions of authority include such things as kingship, the presidency, ministerial government, chieftanship, and so on indefinitely. Even more concretely, examples of institutions of authority would be the sacred kingship of Egypt or the American presidency in 1970. Human history has displayed a bewildering variety of institutions of authority, but sociological analysis has been less interested in studying the luxuriant variety of forms of authority than in establishing a historically relevant and enlightening scheme for delineating the major types of authority. Discussion of this issue has been dominated by the classificatory scheme of Max Weber. Weber's types of authority differ in the basis of the leader's claim to legitimacy. *Traditional authority* rests on "established belief in the sanctity of immemorial traditions and the legitimacy of those exercising authority under them." Charismatic authority rests on "devotion to the specific and exceptional sanctity, heroism, or exemplary character of an individual person, and of the normative patterns or order revealed or ordained by him." *Rational or legal authority* rests on "a belief in the 'legality' of patterns of normative rules and the right of those elevated to authority under such rules to issue commands."[26] Both charismatic and traditional authority lead to loyalty to a person. Legal authority involves loyalty not to the person but to the impersonal order, the structure of offices established by law. Thus, legal authority is rational in two senses: First, impersonal order is not fixed by tradition; it is an instrumental order, adapted to the exigencies of effective administration. Second, the radical differentiation between person and office prevents the incumbent from having any claims to the office that might interfere with the strict and rational performance of his duties.

Each of the types of authority is associated with a characteristic mode of organization of administration. Traditional authority is associated with feudal or patrimonial administration. The ruler either relies on a group of *personally* dependent officials who are personally attached to him, or he exercises power through a set of personal alliances with other men of power. In either event, administration is relatively stably organized around the political and economic vested interests of the dominant men of the realm. In contrast, charismatic administrative organization is founded upon the labor of a small group of devoted followers or disciples whose interest in political and material rewards is secondary.

Legal authority is implemented in bureaucratic organization. There are a number of elements of bureaucratic organization in Weber's ideal type,[27] all of which represent an elaboration of the basic idea of an impersonal order of offices within which the incumbents are radically subordinate to the offices themselves and to the explicit written rules governing performance of official duties. The bureaucrat does not own his office and is not personally dependent upon the ruler. He receives a salary in money, and both incumbency and advancement depend upon

---

[26] Weber, *Social and Economic Organization*, p. 328.

[27] Ibid., pp. 329–336.

his technical qualifications and his strict performance of official duties according to the legal rules and in compliance with the orders of his superiors within the hierarchy of bureaucratic offices. For Weber, bureaucratic organization is the true instrument of rational public administration. Bureaucratic administration is the subordination of political effort to controlled policies and rational means. Political leaders need not bargain with subordinates; subordinates need not compromise principle with political reality in the performance of their duties. In other words, politics and administration are separated. Bureaucratic organization is essential to modern political organization because it is the means by which collective energies can be mobilized in the efficient pursuit of deliberately chosen collective goals.

Bureaucratization, Modernization, and Westernization

As this exposition might suggest, Weber's typology of authority is intended as a dynamic model of the emergence of modernity. The implied query is: How did modern, that is, legal-bureaucratic, authority emerge from its traditional precursor? According to Weber, charismatic authority represents a transitional stage. Charismatic leaders can be critical of an established order and contemptuous of its rewards. In our terms, the order created by a charismatic leader is instrumental rather than institutional; a charismatic order breaks through, or at least disregards, traditional means, traditional values, and the patrimonial conditions of loyal service. The disciples and assistants of a charismatic leader follow an idealistic vision of a better world and disregard the practical and mundane side of securing their own means of livelihood. The charismatic order is instrumental, but it is instrumental in the pursuit of high values rather than mere survival. In this sense, charismatic authority is unstable, for it is careless of its own physical and political survival. A new generation of leaders will be more interested in organizing and routinizing their access to financial resources and their positions of power. At this point, the charismatic order must either revert back to a traditional form of organization or progress to legal-bureaucratic techniques. The direction of movement is determined by the character of the larger social order: If social arrangements are becoming more tightly organized, rational, and utilitarian, then successful adaptation to this emergent order

must follow the lines of rational bureaucratic technique. In Weber's view, this was precisely the trend in the Western world,
which moved to more and more rational organization of every
sector of social life.[28]
From this perspective, the expansion of Western social systems takes on a new dimension. As charismatic leaders move
nations from their traditional past, they also confront the problem
of adapting to the conditions of the modern world. If that world
involves complex rational markets of international scope,
intense international political competition, and participation in
bureaucratically organized international organizations, then
successful stabilization of national authority at a high level of
responsiveness to political demands will require the bureaucratization of authority. Internal political authority becomes
rationalized not merely in response to changing internal conditions, but because of increased contact with global social systems.
Again we see the importance of intersocietal systems in societal
analysis.

Weber's analysis does not exhaust the possibilities of the
functions and consequences of bureaucracy. "Rational authority" and "bureaucratic organization" are two of Weber's famous
"ideal type" constructs, and as such are not intended to represent historical reality exactly but to isolate the fundamental dynamic in the rationalization of authority in Western history.
Even so, there is some evidence that Weber's exclusive emphasis
on the modernizing efficiency of bureaucratic technique creates
a somewhat limiting perspective.

In the first place, Weber's image of bureaucracy as a subordinate entity, devoted merely to implementing the programs of
higher authority in the most efficient way, neglects the politically
active role of bureaucracy, even in Western history. Although
the force of bureaucratic "politics" is most often conservative,
working to maintain the status quo and sometimes even undermining radical reforms,[29] it is nonetheless political.[30] In this
sense, bureaucracy can neutralize rather than implement political power.

S. N. Eisenstadt has suggested that the maintenance of bu-

[28] Ibid., pp. 363–373.

[29] Seymour Lipset, *Agrarian Socialism* (Berkeley: University of California Press, 1950).

[30] Fritz Morstein Marx, "The Higher Civil Service as an Action Group in Western Political
Development," in *Bureaucracy and Political Development*, ed. Joseph La Polombara (Princeton: Princeton University Press, 1963), pp. 62–95.

reaucracies approximating Weber's ideal type is dependent on a fragile equilibrium between the professional autonomy of bureaucrats and their control by representatives of other centers of power in society. In the absence of this balance, bureaucratic organization changes in one of two directions. The bureaucracy can progressively increase its power and increasingly regiment social life in its own interest or in the interest of some special power group. Or "debureaucratization" can take place: The bureaucracy becomes penetrated and subverted by a number of the groups it purports to serve and regulate, leading to lower levels of bureaucratic coherence and power.[31]

The position of the bureaucracy in developing nations is especially ambiguous. Historically, the bureaucratic class was a Westernized native elite, often working to implement the policies of a foreign colonial power. With the casting off of foreign colonial authority, the trained native bureaucracy comes to occupy an awkward and ambivalent position. Native bureaucrats initially tend to lack the wholehearted national identification, the close touch with the people, and the activist political style of the leaders who were in the forefront of the fight for independence. As the latter elite penetrates the bureaucracy, both the social role and the daily life of the bureaucrats become politicized. Such politicization, though it is anti-Weberian in the sense of violating the image of a technically oriented, politically neutral bureaucracy, may nonetheless support the cause of modernization. If major social policies are to be changed and the leadership is to be open to new segments of the emerging nation, then political penetration of the bureaucracy might be necessary.[32]

The development of a powerful bureaucracy isolated from the give and take of political life may actually prevent the development of viable political institutions for articulating demands. Fred Riggs has even suggested that the precarious bases of French political life may be a consequence of the notoriously highly-developed French bureaucracy. Ironically, the very institutions that are said to provide underlying stability to the French government, despite its chequered career at the higher political

---

[31] S. N. Eisenstadt, "Bureaucracy, Bureaucratization, and Debureaucratization," *Administrative Sciences Quarterly* 4 (1959), pp. 302–320.

[32] S. C. Dube, "Bureaucracy and Nation Building in Transitional Societies," in *International Social Science Journal* 16 (1964), pp. 229–236.

levels, may be one source of the political instability for which it is supposed to compensate.[33]

Paradoxically, it may even be that an intensively *politicized* administration will be a functional equivalent of an intensively *neutralized* administration. Where traditional forms of administration are deeply entrenched in politics and those politics are in turn embedded in vested networks of traditional status and corruption, the development of the separation of politics and administration along Western bureaucratic lines may be impossible.[34] A functional equivalent may be the penetration of the bureaucracy by an intensely ideological political cadre, charged with a responsibility for policing administration from within. A number of revolutionary regimes have experimented with variations of this theme, and one form has been thoroughly institutionalized in Soviet society: this form is the system of dual control of every governmental unit by operational managers and communist-party representatives.

Institutions of Participation

The foregoing account of the problem of authority in developing nations suggests that institutions of authority do not develop in isolation from institutions of participation. Just as there are bodies of institutional norms for organizing and regulating political domination, so are there institutions for organizing and stabilizing the framing, aggregation, and combining of demands—the lobby, the political party, the legislative body, the citizen's advisory board, the political press, etc.

In traditional political organization, this political process takes place within the administrative machinery. Official factions, great men of the realm, and official representatives of various sectors of the state carry on disputes and jockey for political position. With the rise of the modern state, we see the emergence of new private, or at least only semi-public, organs for the formulation, representation, and reconciliation of demands. The mod-

---

[33] Fred W. Riggs, "Bureaucrats and Political Development: A Paradoxical View," in *Bureaucracy and Development*, ed. La Polombara, p. 127. See also Stanley Hoffman, "Heroic Leadership: The Case of Modern France," in *Political Leadership in Industrialized Societies*, ed Lewis J. Edinger (New York: John Wiley & Sons, Inc., 1967), pp. 108–154.

[34] W. F. Wertheim, "Sociological Aspects of Corruption in Southeast Asia," in *State and Society*, ed. Bendix, pp. 561–580.

ern state is founded upon the institution of citizenship, and the history of the increasing inclusiveness of the nation-state is a history of the extension of citizenship. More and more of the population become defined as legal participants in the political community.[35]

The more the public at large is brought into the political process, the more necessary becomes institutional apparatus for regulating the expression of public demands. Political parties can perform this function and can also provide a structure for recruiting political leadership.

Political Parties

According to two recent analysts, the modern political party must be distinguished from the clique, the political club, and other quasi-parties. The full-fledged political party is distinguished by four criteria: (1) organizational continuity longer than the life span of members; (2) organization at the local level with regularized communication between local and national levels; (3) self-conscious determination to capture and hold decision-making power; (4) a concern on the part of the organization for electoral or some other form of popular support. By these criteria the authors distinguish the political party from the temporary faction that seeks in some ad hoc instrumental way to influence public decisions; the political party operates within an institutionalized framework.[36]

The party in this sense is a recent phenomenon, not appearing in Europe or America until the mid-nineteenth century. Maurice Duverger traces the original emergence of the modern party to the attempt of committees within parliamentary bodies to organize on behalf of their own electoral support. Later parties formed when groups outside of legislatures sought to participate in the parliamentary process.[37] Thus, the modern party is a

[35] Reinhard Bendix, *Nation Building and Citizenship* (New York: John Wiley & Sons, Inc., 1964).

[36] Joseph La Palombara and Myron Weiner, "The Origin and Development of Political Parties," in *Political Parties and Political Development*, ed. La Palombara and Weiner (Princeton: Princeton University Press, 1966), p. 8.

[37] Maurice Duverger, *Political Parties: Their Organization and Activity in the Modern State*, 2d ed., trans. Barbara and Robert North (London: Methuen and Co., Ltd., 1959), pp. xxiii–xxxvii.

product of the emergence of democratic structures of authority — parliaments and the electoral process.

The strict definition of the political party raises the question of the theoretical status of the party in the one-party system. Although the political party originally emerged from the setting of parliamentary democracy, party-like apparatus is often assembled in noncompetitive political systems. Such parties not only call themselves parties, but appear to function in a manner similar to classic political parties. They are a source of recruitment to political leadership and provide an arena for political discourse. The difference is that, in the absence of realistic political competition, the party penetrates the state and becomes inseparable from institutions of authority. It may be that the domination of a single political party is a source of political stability in many of the new nations that have emerged in the aftermath of political expansion. In the absence of a tradition of legitimate opposition, in the absence of political experience, and, most important, in the absence of political community, a single dominant party can link the government to the public, politically socialize the plural groups in society, and carry on the process of political bargaining within its own regulated boundaries.

Fritz von der Mehden, in a study of political process within eighty-three developing nations,[38] found that the majority (50) had either no parties at all (17), only one effective party (21), or one dominant party (12). Only eleven nations had two parties, and four of these were actually undemocratic nations. The remainder (22) had multi-party systems. Significantly, political instability in the form of coups or attempted coups is more prevalent in systems without political parties (83 percent) and in multi-party systems (68 percent) than in one-party and one-party-dominant nations (18 percent). It appears that an arena for political expression cannot be provided in the absence of political parties and that multiple political parties fail to canalize the many sources of disunity and heterogeneity in the plural society. Single parties appear to be able to stimulate and yet control a national political life in an emergent political community.

On the other hand, multi-party systems have operated successfully for long periods of time in some stable European nations such as Belgium, Sweden, Norway, Holland, Denmark, and Switzerland. Given an established political community, it is pos-

[38] Fritz von der Mehden, *Politics of the Developing Nations* (Englewood Cliffs, N. J.: Prentice-Hall, Inc., 1964), pp. 53–76, 142–143.

sible to organize stable democratic government around a number of relatively specialized parties. Such systems tend to be associated with electoral institutions based upon some form of proportional representation.[39] A winner-take-all system discourages minority parties since it is difficult to translate moderate amounts of support at the polls into actual representation in governmental bodies.

In the multi-party system, the process of political bargaining and compromise tends to be located within the councils of government. The two-party system tends to enclose political process within the parties themselves; the parties must, if the system is to be effective, balance and reconcile interests within their own councils. For this reason, some commentators have seen the two-party system as an important integrative device in a society containing a wide variety of status, religious, regional, and ethnic cleavages. More generally, the number of actual cleavages in any society is greater than the number of political parties. Accordingly, every political party tends to follow some cleavages and to cross-cut others. The study of the relations between societal cleavages and party alignments has become one of the principle objects of attention in political sociology[40] and rightly so, for the structure of conflict and accommodation is implicit in the grouping of social interests into the active political groups of society. To illustrate: Much of the stability of the American political system from 1932 to 1968 was a consequence of the compromise political coalition, within the Democratic Party, of many of the most potentially disruptive groups in American society—workers, farmers, Southerners, and minorities. The apparent collapse of this coalition may well presage a major reorientation of American politics.

Political Development

The discourse of contemporary political sociology is filled with references to "political development," a phrase that often implies the existence of a logic of political modernization, a discernible common trend in the movement of political systems

---

[39] Duverger, *Political Parties*, pp. 245–255. See also Seymour M. Lipset, *The First New Nation* (New York: Basic Books, Publishers, Inc., 1963), pp. 286–317.

[40] See Lipset, ibid., and the excellent collection of essays edited by Lipset and Rokkan, *Party Systems and Voter Alignments*.

throughout the world. The term "development" can be used in a variety of ways, and many usages are subject to the criticism that they imply a Western bias. To define political development by explicit reference to democratic forms or Western legal ideas is to beg the question of the position of the West in evolutionary history, if, indeed, there is such a history. Accordingly, scholars have sought a more abstract, general definition of political development and have found it in the concept of political capacity. Gabriel Almond's definition may be taken as typical and illustrative: "The criterion of political change (development) . . . is the acquisition of a new capability, in the sense of a specialized role structure and differentiated orientations which together give a political system the possibility of responding efficiently, and more or less autonomously, to a new range of problems."[41] Almond has in mind the capacity to perform the various political functions that he has posited, which we have outlined at the beginning of this chapter.

According to Lucian Pye, there are three central elements in the process of political development.[42] Capacity in the execution of public policy is certainly one aspect, but increased political participation of the citizenry, "equality" in some sense of the word, is also a part of development, and (as Almond's definition suggests) so is the differentiation and specialization of political structures. There is fairly high consensus among political analysts that these are the three main facets of political development. Human history, at least recent history, has exhibited a number of forces leading to the development of increased political capacity through citizen participation and the creation of specialized political organs. At this point, observers part company. Some argue that the variety of cultural backgrounds, of organizational problems, and of historical experience insures that each nation will build its own institutional and organizational forms for development; there is no strict logic of development. Others argue for a convergence of institutional organization across nations on the grounds that particular organizational forms have more intrinsic functional capacity. From this perspective, political development can be defined not in mere general terms but in terms of specific political institutions. For example, Parsons has suggested that bureaucratic organization in

---

[41] Almond, "Political Systems and Political Change," p. 8.

[42] Lucian W. Pye, "The Concept of Political Development," *Annals of the American Academy of Political and Social Science* 358 (March 1965), pp. 1–13.

the Weberian sense, universalistic normative order such as is embodied in an autonomous legal system of the Western type, and the democratic association are "evolutionary universals" in human society.[43] The democratic association[44] can be further specified as an association with elective leadership and fully enfranchised membership. The franchise involves formal procedural rules governing voting and the counting of votes and, following the research of Stein Rokkan into the development of the franchise in Western political systems,[45] three other universal features: universal suffrage, an equal vote for each voter, and the secret ballot. According to Parsons, the democratic association is "notoriously difficult to institutionalize,"[46] but that difficulty notwithstanding, it stands as a relatively specific institutional pattern toward which social organization evolves. It is not a historical accident of Western political development but an intrinsically effective form of political organization; in the last analysis, it is a condition of the development of very high levels of political capacity. Parsons is even willing to conjecture that evolutionary pressures will lead the Soviet Union in this direction.[47]

The Nation-State

It is easy to dismiss this view and others like it as sheer ethnocentric glorification of the ways of the West, but on second glance there is a line of argument that can lend weight to the theory that there is a degree of convergence in political development. After all, there does seem to be one complex of political institutions that has been universally adopted throughout the world, the *nation-state*. With the exception of a few pockets of dependent colonial territories, the entire world is divided into territorial states (usually, with a few exceptions such as Pakistan, territorially coherent and contiguous) whose governments claim to have ultimate sovereignty within their territories and seek to

[43] Talcott Parsons, "Evolutionary Universals in Society."

[44] Ibid., pp. 514–519.

[45] Stein Rokkan, "Mass Suffrage, Secret Voting, and Political Participation," *The European Journal of Sociology* 2 (1961), pp. 132–152.

[46] Parsons, "Evolutionary Universals," p. 517.

[47] Ibid., pp. 518–519.

control the flow of persons and goods across their boundaries. The emergence of a world organized into nation-states is founded on the ideology of nationalism. Nationalism is the doctrine that there exist (1) bodies of culture, historical experience, tradition, or common purpose that (2) bind persons into united communities that (3) should be further united by possession of a sovereign state because (4) this is necessary to the welfare and prosperity of the people.

Nationalism spurred the destruction of European empires, and the fight for independence among former colonial peoples continues today to motivate the struggle for unity and political capacity in the new states. Is this the consequence of the fortuitous diffusion of a Western ideal to Asia and Africa, or does its worldwide acceptance reflect something about the intrinsic political capacity of the nationalistic ideology? A high level of political capacity requires a closely knit political community capable of defining a collective goal and enjoying the willing cooperation of citizens in the pursuit of such goals. A nation, being a unit of solidarity, can meet this requirement in ways that the dynastic or imperial state cannot. Added to the universality of the thrust toward a nation-state are the constraints on political organization that stem from participation in the international political arena. Some of the paraphernalia of the modern state is a condition of carrying on diplomatic relations and participating in international projects. Given these fixed contexts for political development, we should not be surprised to discover some convergence in development. The nationalistic form of development implies the existence of some mechanisms for aligning the interests of varied groups with the goals of the total collectivity, and it may well be that the institutionalization of some form of competitive politics is a condition of successful alignment. It is in the context of discussion of public policy that the sense of the existence of a common public emerges. The democratic association as it developed in the West may be too historically specific to serve as a model for development in the rest of the world, but we ought to be sensitive to other forms of competitive politics and to the possibility that functional equivalents to the democratic association may universally develop as nations increase their political capacity. Further work on this problem awaits the development of methodological and theoretical tools equal to the task of separating the dual elements of party organization. Parties socialize political participants by placing their political activities in the context of a nationally regulated system. At the same time, parties are agents for making political demands. Both processes occur side by side, sometimes subtly intertwined in the same interaction and usually hidden from public scrutiny. In consequence, the relation between modernization and democratization is a thorny problem indeed.

Correlates of Political Modernity: Expansion of the Political Community

Another reason for suspecting some convergences in political development is that political modernization tends to be accompanied by parallel changes in other sectors of the society, changes that should be reflected in political institutions.

Phillips Cutright, drawing on and extending other related studies, examined the correlates of competitive politics in seventy-seven nations.[48] Using a composite index that included democratic attributes in the legislative and executive branches of the government and political stability, Cutright produced a multiple correlation of .82 between this index and educational development, participation in a nonagricultural labor force, urbanization, and communications development. Cutright's index was intended as a measure of political modernity, of the degree of development of complex and specialized national political institutions. It is interesting, in view of our previous discussion, to note that the index depended upon the presence or absence of specific institutional apparatus — parliaments, parties, elected chief executives, etc.

This study and other similar studies suggest that competitive political organization may in fact accompany the rise of modernity. Cutright's findings describe only statistical tendencies, so it is easy to point to exceptions. However, his overall findings suggest that with the growth of urbanization, mobility, and intense communication — in our terms, with the growth of society in the population — comes a high level of pressure to accommodate and implement the interests and demands of the citizenry. The highest level of government can no longer rest its power on various forms of social indifference. As long as the interests and concerns of the population are largely contained within the horizons of the traditional work group, the local

---

[48] Phillips Cutright, "National Political Development: Measurement and Analysis," *American Sociological Review* 28 (April 1963), pp. 253–264.

community, and the plural ethnic or religious segment, national politics can remain a matter of competition within segments of the national elite. When a population becomes involved in large-scale work organizations, moves to national centers, and enters into the national discourse of mass communications, new institutions of incorporation must develop, institutions as broadly based as the breadth of emergent political community.

Nevertheless, American social scientists have been taken to task for introducing a democratic bias into their concepts of modernization.[49] Marvin E. Olsen has attempted to reduce the "democratic bias" in multivariate cross-national studies of political development by considering five aspects of development separately—executive functioning, legislative functioning, party organization, power diversification, and citizen influence. These variables were correlated across 115 nations with fourteen socioeconomic background measures of economic, educational, and communications development. The multiple correlations obtained between socioeconomic development and political development ranged between .75 and .98 for the various aspects of political development.[50] Olsen's findings (though they must be treated very cautiously, for they compare nations at a given point in time rather than longitudinally over time) suggest that there is an empirical referent for the concept of political modernization. Olsen suggests that such development is caused by what Karl Deutsch calls "social mobilization," that is, the process of involving individuals in new, nontraditional patterns of collective activities.[51] An increase in mobility within a population, what we have called more technically an increase in its "societal" character, leads to the expansion of the political community, to growth in the number of persons and associations who, in Deutsch's terms, must be taken into account in politics.[52]

Convergence in Leadership

The expansion of political community, the mobility of populations in modern society, their relative emancipation from tra-

[49] See, notably, Charles C. Moskos, Jr., and Wendell Bell, "Emerging Nations and Ideologies of American Social Scientists," *American Sociologist* 2 (May 1967), pp. 67–72.

[50] Marvin E. Olsen, "Multivariate Analysis of National Political Development," *American Sociological Review* 33 (October 1968), pp. 699–711.

[51] Ibid., pp. 704–710.

[52] Ibid., p. 710.

ditional moorings, and their entry into a more open political market have led political scientists to wonder whether modern society also leads to a convergence of styles and techniques of leadership.[53] If mass support becomes the main locus of the resources of leadership, it follows that only those with charismatic qualities can achieve the highest levels of leadership. In this vein, Erwin Hargrove has argued that in all the Anglo-American democracies, successful leaders have been able to transcend the inner conflicts of the society by their capacity to dramatically appeal to a popular sense of a formula for the good society.[54] On the other hand, Stanley Hoffman has argued that leadership must always be understood in its special cultural context. In France, the dramatic leader is put down as a threat to the stagnant entrenched bureaucracy and the French parliamentary stalemate. Only when that stalemate exhibits its political incapacity in crisis situations do the French respond to the "heroic formula" for leadership.[55] Again, the separation of the generically modern and the uniquely historical presents a difficult problem, a problem we must necessarily meet again under the heading "societal evolution."

A Technical Note on Political Boundary Maintenance

With the emergence of the modern nation-state with high political capacity, we begin to see a society which resembles the self-sufficient social system of social-system theory. Such a system is not closed; it carries on interchanges with other systems. But it has the capacity to control these interchanges and thus to maintain its boundaries. A high level of political capacity and a high level of national identity permit a relatively well-demarcated social system. Even though such a system contains subsystems (e.g., the national economy) that are closely linked with larger transnational systems (e.g., the international economy), the system can clearly make the boundaries of its internal systems congruent with the boundaries of the nation. This is possible because the society can use its political apparatus to organize

[53] For several discussions of this problem and a bibliography, see Edinger, ed., *Political Leadership.*

[54] Erwin C. Hargrove, "Popular Leadership in the Anglo-American Democracies," in *Political Leadership,* ed. Edinger.

[55] Hoffman, "Heroic Leadership."

the internal system and to restrict movement across national frontiers through tariffs, immigration restrictions, information embargoes, import and export prohibitions, and the like. The American economy is deeply involved in a larger international economy but, through internal organization and external barriers, it is possible to draw a boundary around the American economy that has a close correspondence to the boundaries of the state. Because of this boundary and the machinery for maintaining it, American society can become *relatively* insulated from events and movements in the international economy. If this were not the case, there would be no such thing as an American economy since it would have no lines of demarcation from the larger network of international transactions. The criterion of independence in a system is its capacity to control relations with an environment in such a way as to protect the stability and continuity of its own internal structure. Placing a sufficient tariff on foreign-made cameras to keep imports at a low enough level to prevent the bankruptcy of the domestic camera industry would be an example of such control. A large series of such controls will produce a number of indices of boundaries to the economy, such as higher wages within the domestic economy, more output per man-hour, etc.

Nevertheless, boundary maintenance is a relative thing, and to stress the independence of an internal system is to exaggerate its isolation from external influences. This is so because boundary-maintaining mechanisms lack the capacity to successfully predict what inputs threaten the continuity and stability of the system. Hence, cumulative, unexpected structural change can occur despite a high level of regulation of the interchanges with an environment. For example, a nation may have a carefully regulated immigration policy, one that seeks to maintain a constant ratio in the size of the constituent ethnic groups of the society. Yet, new arrivals carry with them new ideas, adopt new occupations, live in new regions, and otherwise fail to reproduce the exact behavior and position of the immigrants who preceeded them. In sum, even when discernible boundaries separate a domestic subsystem from its corresponding larger intersocietal system, the effects of external participation are not to be dismissed.

7

Culture and Cultural Systems

THE NATURE OF CULTURE AND CULTURAL SYSTEMS

Definition

In defining "culture," we encounter a problem parallel to the problem of delimiting a less than all-encompassing definition of society. Just as society is sometimes defined as the sum total of all the relationships of men, so "culture" is sometimes used as a term to describe all the ways that man is a product of "cultivation." Since man's behavior is not fixed by a set of specific instincts, but is learned in diverse human associations and shaped by the varied ways of living devised by his groups, we sometimes rely on the word "culture" as a shorthand reminder of man's social and plastic nature. A. L. Kroeber and Clyde Kluckhohn, after an exhaustive review and analysis of various concepts of culture, hazard a composite definition that illustrates definitions of the global, summary type:

Culture consists of patterns, explicit and implicit, of and for behavior, acquired and transmitted by symbols, constituting the distinctive achievement of human groups, including their embodiments in artifacts; the essential core of culture consists of traditional (i.e., historically derived and selected) ideas and their attached values.[1]

The composite definition is valuable and does suggest the essential features of the phenomenon of culture, but we have in mind a somewhat more specific element of human action.

T. S. Eliot, in his provocative *Notes Towards the Definition of Culture*, begins with what appears to be an omnibus definition of culture:

> It includes all the characteristic activities and interests of a people: Derby Day, Henley Regatta, Cowes, the twelfth of August, a cup final, the dog races, the pin table, the dart board, Wensleydale cheese, boiled cabbage cut into sections, beetroot in vinegar, nineteenth-century Gothic churches and the music of Elgar.[2]

A few American equivalents of Eliot's English examples might include the Indianapolis "500," horseshoes, hamburgers, ranch houses, and the music of MacDowell.

Eliot is here, of course, opposing the traditional humanist notion that culture includes only "high culture": *haut cuisine*, the poetry of Milton, and perhaps no English music at all. However, a few pages earlier Eliot had commented:

> Culture may even be described simply as "that which makes life worth living." And it is what justifies other peoples and other generations in saying, when they contemplate the remains and the influence of an extinct civilization, that it was worthwhile for that civilization to have existed.[3]

Further, Eliot emphasizes the centrality of the religious component in culture, for it is religion that "gives an apparent meaning to life, provides the framework for a culture, and pro-

---

[1] A. L. Kroeber and Clyde Kluckhohn, *Culture: A Critical Review of Concepts and Definitions* (Cambridge, Mass.: Harvard University, Peabody Museum of American Archeology and Ethnology Papers, Vol. 47, No. 1, 1952), p. 181.

[2] T. S. Eliot, *Notes Towards the Definition of Culture* (New York: Harcourt Brace Jovanovich, Inc., 1949), p. 30.

[3] Ibid., p. 26.

tects the mass of humanity from boredom and despair."[4] In other words, culture is a repository of meaning and value. We adopt here this more specialized sense of culture. It is not all of the learned patterns of and for behavior. Rather, it is a body of collective definitions, concepts, values, knowledge, myth, artistic symbols, and philosophies that impart intelligibility and value to the world and its participants. It provides a storehouse of shared meanings and values that individuals can use to make sense of their experiences.

This approach to culture closely parallels the "normative theory of culture" of Gertrude Jaeger and Philip Selznick, who argue that the psychic source of culture is the quest for "person-centered meanings," and that symbolic elaboration is both source and product for this quest. Following their own adage that "an effective symbol combines economy of statement with richness of expression,"[5] the authors state that "men create symbols in order to continue and sustain meaningful experience,"[6] and quite economically conclude that "culture consists of everything that is produced by and is capable of sustaining shared symbolic experience."[7] They further argue that there is in culture a "strain toward the esthetic," an important reminder of the centrality of the esthetic in human experience.[8] However, we must not forget that some culture is instrumental and cognitive. Some cultural symbols are oriented to the manipulability of reality, and these definitions are effective in accordance with their approximation of scientific accuracy. As instrumental symbols they have great power and are relatively easily diffused across societal boundaries, with profound consequences to the societies that receive them.

In chapter two we described every action system as having a cultural component, that is, a body of symbols and ideas that facilitate communication and define the concepts and meanings involved in the system. To some extent this chapter will be concerned with the cultural level of all of these process systems, the

---

[4] Ibid., p. 32.

[5] Gertrude Jaeger and Philip Selznick, "A Normative Theory of Culture," *American Sociological Review* 29 (October 1964), p. 664.

[6] Ibid., p. 662.

[7] Ibid., p. 663.

[8] Ibid., pp. 663–666.

total culture of a society. In what sense then is it possible to speak of cultural systems as a special type of action system in society? In this respect, cultural systems are no different from the other types of systems we have examined. Political systems have an economic aspect; they must have access to and allocate resources. Economic systems have political aspects; they require leadership and mechanisms for the resolution of conflict. We must remember that the process systems of society are analytical constructs. When an action system makes a primary contribution of a given sort to the organization of a societal population, then we classify it accordingly as a solidary, an economic, or a political system, even though it contains within its own organization a variety of elements—solidary, economic, and political. By analogy, when a system of social process is organized around cultural functions for a population, we may speak of a *cultural system*. Cultural systems are organized around creating, elaborating, disseminating, reaffirming, intensifying, enhancing, and teaching collective meanings and values. In referring to the functions of cultural systems in teaching and enhancing cultural meanings, no restriction to *established* traditional meanings is intended; the creative element must not be overlooked. Raymond Williams, seeking to interpret the British fiction of the 1840's, found a creative and critical undercurrent even in the conventional and popular forms:

> We find some art expressing feeling which the society, in its general character, could not express. These may be the creative response which bring new feelings to light. They may be also the simple record of omissions: the nourishment or attempted nourishment of human needs unsatisfied.[9]

The collective and institutional organization of cultural systems centers around such phenomena as families, churches, schools, museums, learned societies, artistic communities, the press, and other media of communication. Note that this definition of a cultural system does not refer merely to cultural objects themselves, either in their concrete manifestation as books, statues, or monuments, or as abstract meanings or definitions. A cultural system (more technically a system of cultural process) is an action system; it consists in organized human conduct that cre-

---

[9] Raymond Williams, *The Long Revolution* (New York: Columbia University Press, 1961), p. 70.

ates and sustains meaning.[10] In order to avoid confusion, we will refer to the former systems as *systems of cultural form.* We will have reason to refer to such systems because one of the interesting features of cultural systems is their potential for moving according to an inner logic or dynamic that causes cultural forms to change or develop independently of the dynamics of the action systems that sustain them. All cultural symbols are not mere reflections of the events in society; the culture of a society may be driven according to a logic inherent in its own forms.

Solidary Systems and Cultural Systems

In analytically distinguishing the types of action systems, the most difficult distinction is between solidary and cultural systems. They are closely associated in popular thought, in many of the ideologies of intellectuals, in much sociological theory, and, in some cases, in national policies. Does not the solidarity of any society derive from its shared culture, its common meanings and values—the shared national experience as it has become manifest in a cultural tradition? Conversely, can culture be born and nurtured in any but a solidary community? From this perspective, culture is but the means, or perhaps the symbol, of solidarity.

To return to our illustrative vehicle, T. S. Eliot's essay on culture, Eliot believed that culture can survive only in solidary contexts. The major theme of Eliot's essay is that a national culture can only maintain its vitality in a society composed of a variety of smaller solidary groups, groups with a vital collective life and a distinctive culture—elites and social classes, religions, sects and cults, political groups. If such groups can operate within the general boundaries of a national cultural tradition, then a rich complementarity and mutual influence can maintain a viable culture. A mass culture on the other hand, is a contradiction in terms. Persons united only by their professional interests will have no social cohesion, no social continuity, none of the prerequisites for the creation and transmission of culture.[11]

Without denying the empirical relations between solidary systems and cultural systems, we can nevertheless assert their analytical independence. There is a difference between liking

[10] Parsons, et al., *Theories of Society*, pp. 963–964.

[11] Eliot, *Notes*, p. 46.

someone and sharing his appreciation for Bach or the Beatles. We can distinguish between feeling a solidary bond with a student and the activities involved in explaining to him the intricacies of the Pythagorean theorem. Similarly, at the societal level, it is possible to distinguish a network of solidary bonds from a system of higher education. Moreover, it is my thesis that the practice of absolutely identifying solidary and cultural institutions is yet another example of a form of ideology very familiar to us by now, the search for a standard of value in some external and collective reality.

Culture and the Collective

According to one extremely prevalent ideology, the nation or people is a natural organic unit. Its unity lies in its historic national experience and is manifest in such things as language, religion, literature, and race. Its culture is the foundation of its nationhood. The culture defines not only the current situation of a people but their destiny as well. This type of ideology attributes the unity, the truly collective character of a population, to its common participation in a cultural heritage. The cultural heritage is neither arbitrary nor accidental, but real, and is a source of a standard of value, a guide to national policy.

In its original classic form, German Idealism found in the developmental movements of the human *Geist* (a culture-like entity) the true source of progressive change in the history of social organization. The culture of each civilization was, in Hegel's thought, a manifestation of the level of development of the world-spirit at that point in human history; and the logical sequence implicit in this developmental process was a guide to and a standard for the policies of a nation.[12] This style of argument became very prominent in nineteenth-century German political discourse. For example, the proponents and opponents of the codification of a pan-German legal system were perpetually arguing about whether this or that proposed codification was in tune with the essential spirit of German history.[13] A great deal of social thought, including schools of thought with contemporary

---

[12] Hegel, *Philosophy of History.*

[13] For an account of the relevant controversies and legal philosophies, see Julius Stone, *The Province and Function of Law* (Cambridge, Mass.: Harvard University Press, 1950), pp. 421–448.

descendents, was born in the context of this argument and others like it. Anthropologists and sociologists search for means of depicting the unique cultural patterns or themes of various societies and communities. In the modern ideological version of this school, the actions and programs of one's political enemies are characterized as "un-American" or out of tune with "the spirit of the times." The implication of this type of attack is that the cultural incongruity of one's opponents' ideas or proposals are a threat to the solidarity of the group, as if the group had no source of unity, cohesion, or coherence outside of the realm of cultural consensus. Without denying the role of common culture as a unifying device, it is still possible to object to the complete identification of culture and solidarity because the assumption that the continuation of social integration depends upon the maintenance of *specific cultural content* is unwarranted. Cultural forms and cultural systems are capable of independent and adaptive variation, change, and development without destroying the solidary base of group life. Consider, for example, the stable multilingual society. Linguistic variation and change coexist with a stable national life. To assert a given cultural tradition as the one true source of group unity is but one more episode in the attempt to establish some concept of society as a standard for evaluating social attitudes and programs.

Cultural Efflorescence and Decline

An especially prominent variant of this fallacy has been one of the main contexts for the discussion of the sociology of cultural life. In the opinion of many students of cultural forms, the decline of societal solidarity, or, alternatively stated, the rise of the mass society, dooms high culture. The mass society cheapens, commercializes, and vulgarizes the cultural tradition. If the artist, the writer, the intellectual, the priest, or the secular pundit must serve a massified audience, he must appeal to the lowest common denominator of their cultural needs, which will be low in quality and, since the recipient of culture has been torn from any vital communal memberships, will be superficial and dehumanized.[14] The proponents of this view can point to the vulgarity of the popular media, the mechanization of religion (e.g., dial-

[14] For a collection with many readings on this topic, see Bernard Rosenberg and David M. White, eds., *Mass Culture* (Glencoe, Ill.: The Free Press, 1957).

a-prayer), the subordination of art to advertising, and numerous other examples of the penetration of cultural systems by essentially commercial, political, or other utilitarian interests.

On the other hand, by focusing on these selected aspects of modern culture, the critic may overlook another very important concomitant of social differentiation, the efflorescence of culture in specialized autonomous cultural systems. The process of social differentiation involves the emergence of specialized cultural systems, collectively and institutionally organized around specialized full-time cultural roles, groups, and institutions. The proliferation of such groups increases the number of cultural systems that are relatively isolated and insulated from the immediate pressures of other spheres of social life. This development at the level of cultural systems has a great impact on development at the level of cultural forms. It is my premise that *the more specialized and isolated a cultural system, the more its associated cultural forms begin to develop according to their own autonomous logic.* Thus, if painters can become emancipated from the requirements of religious symbolization or the desires of a social class of patrons, they can become more interested in the aesthetic potential of paint itself; they become concerned that their works are "painterly." They explore in their work the logic of paint on canvas and produce a revolutionary efflorescence of new styles and forms. Cultural content is enriched.

Similarly, at an earlier stage in cultural history, the development of a specialized priesthood leads the way to the systematization of religious doctrine as an autonomous system of cultural forms. The logic of the system of meaning implicit in systems of myth and ritual becomes problematic, and religious specialists can concern themselves with explicitly developing this logic.

This is one of the processes that Weber had in mind in his classic discussions of logical rationalization. Symbolic rationalization occurs when the creators of cultural symbols go beyond the mere representation of society to the development of a logically systematic body of symbols and meaning. Such logical development can lead to a stage where systems of symbols, rather than reflecting an underlying social reality, are actually in tension with established social arrangements. The rationalizer follows his logic to its bitter conclusions, without reference to its impact on society or, indeed, with a deliberate commitment to radical transformation of the established order in accordance with the dictates of his own system of thought. Thus, in an early manifestation of this process, the Hebrew prophet, emancipated in important ways from both political involvement and the established priesthood, interpreted the tradition of the will of Yahweh and "established a religion of faith that subjected man's daily life to the imperatives of a divinely ordained moral law . . . (helping to) create the moral rationalism of Western civilization."[15]

Some students are troubled with the idea of immanent development of cultural forms. The concept seems to imply that ideas can act on their own; for this reason, the concept appears animistic, or at least appears to reify ideas. This objection is based upon an elementary misunderstanding. Nothing in the concept of immanent development implies that ideas are anything more than figments of the imagination of actors. The argument merely asserts that actors, when they work with ideas, can be guided by a logic of transformation implicit in the ideas themselves. There is no reification in assuming that those who operate within a cultural system are influenced by its forms and meanings.

The idea of the immanent development of cultural forms by a group of differentiated intellectual specialists has peculiarly revolutionary implications in the realm of science. Science, as a developing system of cultural forms, implies and permits technological innovations that, by increasing man's potential control over energy, allow for radical reformations of social life. The increased productivity of scientific technology permits a very high degree of elaboration of social life. Moreover, its effective utilization has led to a variety of radical changes in the collective and institutional organization of activity, e.g., the factory system, modern medical organization, and modern forms of war.

Cultural Diffusion

The foregoing point is rather obvious and, having been remarked myriad times, does not bear repeating. However, in the present context it provides an excellent illustration of one more motif in our theme of the differential expansion of action systems: Cultural forms diffuse from system to system and from society to society with relative ease. Their very separation from social contexts makes their movement across societal boundaries

---

particularly easy. Moreover, the underlying social organization of a differentiated cultural system is especially easy to establish across a societal boundary. Minimally, cultural transmission requires only two interacting persons whose contact is not even cultural in character, or who need not even maintain direct contact. Trading partners may exchange information by long-distance correspondence. Add to the basic ease of transmission of cultural items the relatively autonomous character of some cultural systems, and the dynamic potential of cultural life becomes plain. Scientific and learned societies, artistic circles, international cultural programs, the international movement of students, universal churches, and universal associations devoted to the dissemination of ideological propoganda represent intersocietal social systems of considerable importance.

This is not to say that the transmission of culture across social-system boundaries is not problematic. New cultural meanings compete with old, and, as Parsons has convincingly argued, there are always vested interests in the retention of old cultural meanings. Even physical science, with its relatively cross-cultural empirical validity "may remain undeveloped unless the cultural pattern element comes into the proper articulation with the institutional structure of the social system."[16]

The internal resistance of social systems to new cultural concepts with obvious practical validity helps to account for one of the principal centrifugal movements of human history: the decline of dominant centers of civilization and their replacement by conquering peoples located on the peripheries of the old order. New military technologies develop, technologies that the old social system, with its established political and military arrangements founded upon vested interests, is unable to incorporate effectively into its military apparatus.[17]

Nevertheless, the resistance to external cultural innovation is not sufficient to justify the notion that societies, considered as self-maintaining social systems, can fully control the movement of cultural forms across their boundaries or easily equilibrate the social impact of cultural innovation. Intersocietal cultural systems are too easily established. Deliberate policies of absolute international isolation, such as were attempted by Japan from 1600 to 1850, ultimately break down in the face of confrontation

---

[16] Parsons, Social System, p. 345.

[17] McNeill, Rise of the West, pp. 116–118. See also Arnold J. Toynbee, A Study of History, vol. 8 (London: Oxford University Press, 1954), pp. 16–31.

with cultural forms with superior potential power. It is noteworthy that, within fifteen years after contact with the West was established, the feudal social structure of Japan broke down in favor of the centralization of imperial power in Tokyo, an event which testifies to the profound internal rearrangements that can follow breaches in the boundaries of social systems.

THE INTEGRATION OF CULTURAL SYSTEMS

The Integrated Cultural System

In view of the diffusibility of cultural forms, the prominence of cross -societal cultural organization, the proliferation of autonomous cultural systems, and the conglomerate character of many modern societies, we might expect cultural integration to be a relatively rare phenomenon on the world scene. If a population has an integrated cultural system only when all its members participate in associations which transmit and reinforce a consistent and common cultural heritage, then cultural integration must be considered a rare phenomenon. Some anthropologists have described relatively homogenous isolated societies which appear, at least in the anthropologists' accounts, to be culturally integrated. The culture is consistent and self-contained—its population is homogenous and of relatively equal status. There is relatively little role differentiation and no differentiated cultural institutions. Thus, as each member grows up in a kinship system, participates in a common religious tradition, and learns to perform economic roles, he automatically comes to learn and share a common culture.

Let us look at a model of an integrated cultural system for the population of a modern society in order to more fully appreciate the cultural tensions and problems endemic in modern life. The societal population will be said to participate in an integrated cultural system when four criteria are met:

1) *The integration of cultural forms.* This phrase refers to what Sorokin calls the "logico-meaningful" integration of a culture.[18] Since, when we consider cultural forms, we are not referring to action but to symbols and meanings, integration does not refer to causal or functional connections between items. At the

[18] Sorokin, *Social and Cultural Dynamics,* vol. 1, pp. 3–53.

formal level, cultural integration refers to the logical consistency and meaningful coherence within a system of cultural symbols. The integration of cultural forms is a difficult criterion to assess empirically. Concern for this level of cultural integration derives from older attempts to summarize the overall style or themes of a culture. Some would abjure this task altogether on the grounds that it is intrinsically impossible or, at least, so abstract and subjective as to lack scientific utility. For example, some would characterize Parsons' description of American values, which he considers ultimately based upon the concept of "instrumental activism," as so abstract as to be virtually devoid of any concrete referent. Or, to state the problem more directly, how would we assess the logico-meaningful integration between, say, Huckleberry Finn and the music of Edward MacDowell?

The first problem is to isolate more specific meanings for terms describing cultural integration. Donald Levine has distinguished seven separate forms of cultural integration.[19]

a) *Configurational or thematic integration.* To what extent do different cultural items conform to a common theme? To cite Ruth Benedict's classic example, the various themes of Zuni culture are said to be permeated by an "Apollonian theme" of sobriety, moderation, and ceremoniousness.

b) *Connective integration.* To what extent are cultural items linked in the daily activities of life? In this sense, the music of Mozart and Tchaikovsky are connectively integrated because they are often played on the same program, despite their vastly different stylistic ingredients.

c) *Logical integration.* To what extent are the items of a culture logically deducible from each other or from some common premises? This form is especially characteristic of the various rationalized bodies of culture in philosophical, scientific, or legal systems.

d) *Adaptive or functional integration.* To what extent are cultural items mutually compatible relative to social functions or goals?

e) *Stylistic integration.* To what extent are the parts of cultural experience so meaningfully related as to produce in the actor an intense feeling of an emotionally gratifying whole? Style refers not only to the arts but to speaking, eating, dressing, playing games, walking, and all the activities of daily life.

[19] Donald Levine, "Cultural Integration," *International Encyclopedia of the Social Sciences,* vol. 7, pp. 372–380.

f) *Regulative integration.* To what extent is the total complex of culture capable of regulating conduct so as to prevent social conflict?

g) *Subcultural consistency.* Cross-cutting each of the previous types of cultural integration is the question of whether any of these types of integration apply across the various cultural subgroups of society. For example, are the themes of French Canadian culture consistent with the themes of the culture of English Canada?

It would be tempting for the student of societal integration to try to limit his concept of cultural integration to those types whose import is obviously social, i.e., connective, adaptive, and regulative integration. To submit to this temptation would be an error, for the other types clearly have social implications. The study of logical integration is very important in the light of Weber's concerns for the rationalization of life. If rationality is valued, cultural contradictions become problematic for actors. Moreover, if the premises of the cultures of different spheres of life are in tension, then the rationalization of those spheres heightens that tension. Thematic and stylistic integration are also important because of the significance of expressive symbolism in social conflict. Acute conflict can turn on matters of style, as in the case of the frequent Afro-American complaint that an institutional regulation deprives the black man of "soul."

Given the complexity of formal cultural integration, its many meanings, and its resistance to easy measurement, it may well be impossible to assess the degree of cultural integration of a total society or to depict its essence in terms of a few summary themes. Heroic efforts have been made along these lines. Witness Sorokin's immense undertaking—a vast set of numerical indices seeking to assess the dominant "culture mentality" in the painting, architecture, music, literature, and thought of an era.[20] Such ambitious schemes may have dubious validity and value, but that should not be allowed to obscure the fact that cultural tensions can be located and that they have profound social implications. The tension between science and religion in the Western tradition is one example of such a tension, but this is only one aspect of the tensions inherent in the development of rationalism in a cultural pattern. The rational, systematic, self-conscious development of cultural premises leads to the isolation and confrontation of various potentially contradictory elements in value

[20] Sorokin, *Social and Cultural Dynamics,* vol. 1.

patterns. Thus, Lipset has written of the tensions between equality and achievement in the American value system,[21] and, in a similar vein, Mayhew has shown that the conflict between the value of economic rationality and the value of equality of opportunity had a detrimental effect on a program designed to reduce discrimination.[22]

2) *Cultural consensus.* Here we refer not to the internal consistency of a given self-contained cultural tradition, but to the agreement on basic cultural premises and values within and across social strata, regions, ethnic groups, and religious and political groups. The requirement of consensus does not rule out a degree of cultural pluralism; it does not imply that every member of the society agrees with every other member on every cultural item. It only means that there must be sufficient common agreement on the basic character, meaning, and value of the world to permit communication across groups and effective participation in the associational life of society. Remember that associational life is institutionally regulated, that institutions are formed of norms, and that norms imply values. It follows that effective participation in associational life, the ability to arrange social life, and the capacity to resolve conflicts within and between associations requires some consensus on a variety of symbols, values, perspectives, and definitions.

3) *Effective cultural associations.* In a relatively undifferentiated society, cultural learning can occur in the context of the family and ordinary daily life. But as the technical complexity of culture increases and the incorporation of members from diverse backgrounds becomes a crucial problem, more specialized cultural systems emerge. Although cultural learning tends to lodge in educational associations, the contribution of the media of communication and art should not be overlooked. Other associations, not exclusively cultural, such as the political party, can also play a part in the process of teaching, reinforcing, intensifying, and enhancing cultural forms.

4) *Participation in cultural associations.* The final criterion of cultural integration involves the reach of cultural associations. To what extent do these associations include as participants the complete range of compositional categories in the population? Do cultural associations transcend the division of a

[21] Lipset, *First New Nation*, pp. 1–2, passim.

[22] Leon H. Mayhew, *Law and Equal Opportunity* (Cambridge, Mass.: Harvard University Press, 1968), especially pp. 56–74.

population into rural and urban sectors, into regions, strata, and ethnic and religious groups?

Barriers to Integration

By now, the barriers to integration should be familiar. Our discussions of the integration of solidary, economic, and political systems have stressed the consequences of expansion, mobility, and growth. The expansion of Western society, its intrusion on the societies of the rest of the world, and the accompanying movements of peoples thrust persons of diverse heritage into common territorial areas. The growth of mobility and urbanization within a territorial area also brings about the confrontation of people of culturally diverse backgrounds. These general sources of institutional malintegration do not require further explanation in speaking of cultural integration in particular beyond some reemphasis of the point that cultural integration is not inconsistent with cultural diversity. The question is whether cultural forms that transcend cultural diversity develop, permitting communication, joint action, and institutional participation among the various cultural sections of a population. Suffice it to say that where cultural diversity is deeply rooted in historic traditions among solidary groups, the emergence of such transcendent cultural forms is problematic. It is clear that enough forms do develop to permit a wide variety of international transactions, especially of the instrumental type. On the other hand, cultural consensus of the sort posited by social-system theory, consensus deep enough to provide a common framework for political legitimacy and the setting of national goals, is far more difficult to create.

The "constraints" model of social change, which assumes a set of common values from which integrative cultural institutions can be derived, seems not to apply to this problem, or if it is relevant, it seems to imply a solution through the assimilation of all segments to the dominant culture. The model of assimilation is not absurd, for one can point to any number of examples of at least partial assimilation of cultural groups to the standards of a dominant group. Successive waves of immigrants from various sections of Europe have become Americanized, and other nations of North and South America have had similar experiences, at least within elite groups. An analogous process occurs when a cultural tradition expands outward from a center during a process of expansion. Processes of assimilation were at work when all of the great nation-states of Europe were formed.

Nevertheless, the degree of cultural pluralism to be found in many new states seems to require the emergence of new formulas of unity that were not implicit in the traditions of any of the cultural sections of the new nation.

Cultural Integration, Cultural Autonomy, and Diffusion

Cultural malintegration has sources other than the forces we have stressed in previous chapters, sources relating to the special prominence of the formal symbolic level in cultural systems. Formal culture is subject to elaboration and development within each of the social systems in which it is embedded. The possibility of formal malintegration and dissension increases in proportion to the number of culture-bearing groups in the society — professional groups, leisure groups, youth groups, religions, mass movements, etc. The problem is compounded when some of these groups are specialized cultural groups devoted to elaborating, developing, and innovating within cultural systems; and it is further compounded when these associations and systems are intersocietal in character, thus promoting the flow of new symbols, meanings, and ideas across the boundaries of societal populations. The growth of science, of technical knowledge, and of systems of social thought and ideology implies the possibility of cultural tensions.

One of the prominent themes in this discussion is the problem of cultural lag, a phrase associated with the name William F. Ogburn. According to Ogburn's definition, "a cultural lag occurs when one of two parts of culture which are correlated changes before or in greater degree than the other part does, thereby causing less adjustment between the two parts than existed previously."[23] Ogburn takes pains to point out that cultural lag is not merely a name for an observation; it is a theory. It asserts the interconnection of parts of culture, that they may change independently of one another, that if they so change, strain and malintegration occur, and that malintegration is a social force leading various sectors of culture to "catch up" by readjusting. In

[23] William F. Ogburn, "Cultural Lag as Theory," *Sociology and Social Research* 41 (January-February 1957), p. 167.

short, the theory of cultural lag is a theory of malintegration. Ogburn did not believe that all cultural lags are caused by changes in the technological sector of modern culture, but he did believe that in the modern world the rate of technological invention is increasing so rapidly as to have become the major cause. Cultural lag is a problem even in a society built around modern technology and committed to adapting to technological improvement. But the problem is compounded in traditional societies in the process of receiving advanced technologies and their associated cultural forms and organizational devices from Western societies. Different techniques and ideologies are accepted by or imposed upon different sectors of the society. In consequence, rural and urban differences are intensified and political cleavages reinforced. The theory of cultural lag, as applied to the problems of world development, is a particularly telling example of the significance of the differential boundaries of social systems. Cultural action systems have little respect for political boundaries. Traditional value systems may have boundaries closely correlated with the traditional boundaries of peoples, but in the total cultural realm, the boundaries of cultural systems vary from too limited to bring consensus to nations to too broad to prevent the reception within nations of disruptive, divisive, and unassimilable ideas.

In sum, the record of cultural history is clear. The great systems of cultural forms, religious and scientific, have cut across societal boundaries and have even encompassed multiple sets of societies or "civilizations." Toynbee attempted to isolate nineteen civilizations and treat them as units, but, in the end, he came to focus upon their contacts and upon the great world religions that emerged in areas where civilizations overlapped.[24] Any historically relevant theory of society must recognize the cross-societal character of cultural systems and their development.

CULTURAL INSTITUTIONS

Cultural Differentiation and Solidarity

The cultural institutions of modern society present a paradox. Of the types of societal subsystems, cultural systems are at

[24] Toynbee, *Study of History*, vol. 8, and criticism by Marshall G. S. Hodgson, "The Interrelations of Societies in History," *Comparative Studies in Society and History* 5 (January 1963), pp. 227–239.

the same time the most and least differentiated. On the one hand, the progressive specialization of roles and groups in modern life produce a variety of specialized cultures. On the other hand, culture remains deeply embedded in the family and in other solidary settings.

The order of presentation of the institutional spheres of society in this volume has been a reflection of aspects of the logic of differentiation. Solidary systems were discussed first on the assumption that they have an evolutionary primacy in the sense that primitive social organization can be largely founded around the solidary ties defined by kin and community. Economic systems were then presented as a direct contrast to solidary systems in that, because of the instrumental character of economic activity, economic systems easily outrun the boundaries of solidarity and create far-flung networks of interdependence. It then becomes problematic whether the differentiated economic order becomes subject to political controls. With the introduction of the realm of the political, our attention turned to the penetration of society by the differentiated institutions of the modern state. The rise of state power raises the question of the penetration of less powerful by more powerful states, and the consequences of intersocietal penetration on political integration.

In a sense, the cultural realm becomes the most differentiated sector in modern societies. The heterogeneity of modern society, its tremendous variety of specialized roles and groups, and the explosive proliferation of symbols accompanying the rise of science, secular thought, leisure, and education are all conducive to the development of differentiated and diverse cultural institutions.

Robert Bellah has posited a sequence of developmental steps in the evolution of religion from a primitive stage through archaic and historic stages to modernity.[25] Religious evolution involves the progressive elaboration of systems of religious symbols and the development of specialized religious associations. Not only do the symbols themselves become more differentiated, they come to assert a more and more distinct differentiation between the social world and the realm of the sacred. In consequence, religious symbolism and organization provide more and more leverage on the established social world, and, as religious attention turns toward man himself, they clearly distinguish

---

[25] Robert N. Bellah, "Religious Evolution," *American Sociological Review* 29 (June 1964), pp. 358–374.

man's intrinsic possibilities from his actual state. Thus, differentiation has dynamic potential, for it creates the possibility for continuing elaboration of the goals and values of human life.

If Bellah is right, and if other cultural systems develop according to a parallel logic, then cultural modernization means the progressive separation and enhancement of cultural life; it means the emancipation of culture from playing the part of merely reinforcing the established order.

Having said that the cultural sphere becomes the most differentiated in modern society, it is necessary to say that culture also remains the most deeply embedded in solidary settings. The family remains a focal point for cultural socialization; and other solidary groupings, religious and ethnic, remain the bearers of distinctive cultural traditions. In consequence, a high level of tension emerges around control over cultural socialization. On the one hand, cultural integration requires the maximum participation of the societal population in associations sustaining a common national culture. On the other hand, solidary groups wish to maintain control over the cultural socialization of their own members. Emergent national cultures may run counter to the special cultural values of subgroups in the society. Further, because of the dynamic potential of specialized cultural systems, participation in the specialized life of modern cultural associations leads in (what seem to solidary groups) unknown and perhaps dangerous directions. Out of this tension many of the conflicts of modern society emerge. Who shall control the educational apparatus? What will it teach? Who may or must participate? How much autonomy should its leaders be given to follow what seems to them the logic of educational development?

Differentiation and Homogeneity

There is another paradox of cultural development. Despite the fact that the differentiation and specialization of society are clearly proceeding and that this obviously involves the creation of new and diverse cultural forms, we regularly hear that mass man is becoming increasingly homogenized. Mass education and the mass media lead to a mass culture. Regional and other subcultural variations die, the high cultural traditions are diluted, and modern man becomes mass man, each like every other. To some extent this is true; indeed it is the announced function of the associations of cultural integration to create and perpetuate enough of a common stock of symbols and values to enable all citizens to participate in a common national life. And yet, beneath the surface of successful integrative homogenization, there is a layer of variegated cultural life corresponding to both the historic diversity within a societal population and its intense role specialization. Harold Wilensky has suggested that the apparent homogeneity of cultural life, which is implied by some data on the mass media and their use, may be somewhat illusory. It is a spurious product of weak concepts and measures of social organization. If we pin down the "groups and events that grip men in the daily round," we begin to see cultural diversity that such gross concepts as age, sex, education, and occupation do not distinguish.[26] The implication of Wilensky's observation bears explicit statement in the light of the strategy of societal study advocated in this volume; if we want to understand society, we must ultimately descend to the level of the actual conduct of actors in groups—in Wilensky's terms, "return to the study of group life."[27]

Of course this is a counsel of perfection. Close observation of the cultural life of a total society reveals a staggering array of diverse cultural activity and forms, so diverse that in this chapter we will be forced to radically neglect most of the cultural institutions of modern society. Only two topics in the sociology of cultural institutions can be treated—the process of secularization and the development of mass education. These topics are chosen because of their special relevance to previous themes—growth, mobilization, integration, and development.

Secularization and Differentiation

Secularization at the organizational level refers to the progressive elimination of sacred controls over social life. If people come to disbelieve in supernatural sanctions, if they refuse to accept the legitimacy of authority based upon claims of supernatural endowments, or if they refuse to accept sacred interpretations of natural or social events, they are exhibiting secular attitudes.

At the cultural level, secularization refers to the decline in

---

[26] Harold L. Wilensky, "Mass Society and Mass Culture: Interdependence or Independence?" *American Sociological Review* 29 (April 1964), pp. 173–197, see especially p. 183.

[27] Ibid., p. 195.

the influence of sacred symbols, whether they be symbols of the supernatural world, or supernatural interpretations of the natural and social world. At the institutional level, secularization refers to the progressive elimination of the grounding of institutional norms on sacred symbols, supernatural premises, or religious authority. At the level of collective organization, secularization means, concretely, the decline in the control by religious associations over political and economic life and other forms of cultural life—educational, artistic, philosophical, and technical.

Note that the previous definitions quite closely identify the sacred with the realm of the supernatural and with religious life. In this respect the present usage, though hardly neologistic, parts company with the theory developed by Howard P. Becker, the sociologist who most completely constructed his social theory on the distinction between the sacred and the secular. For Becker, a sacred society is a society with a value system that "imparts to its members evaluations that can be altered, if at all, only in the face of definite emotionalized reluctance."[28] In other words, the sacred society is the society resistant to change. On this basis, Becker attempted to construct a sacred-secular continuum ranging from "holy" sacredness at one extreme, through the sacredness of loyalty, intimacy, morality, and appropriateness, to various degrees of intensity of secularity—the secularity of principle, of ad hoc rationalization, of expediency, and, at the extreme, of the comfortable and the thrilling. Becker attributes secularization primarily to mobility, that is, to the decline of geographic, social, and mental isolation. Accessibility brings on "the mutually destructive clash of value systems."[29]

In its details, Becker's work illuminates problems of secularization, but his basic definition suffers from a serious fault, the inclusion of the problematic propositions of the theory in the definition itself. It may well be that sacred attitudes and institutions founded on sacred values *are* more resistant to change, but that is a question for investigation and not a definition of the sacred in any conventional sense. It is easy to find counterexamples. By any reasonable definition, Polynesian religion, with its emphasis on the sacred power of *mana*, a supernatural ema-

[28] Howard P. Becker, "Current Sacred-Secular Theory and its Development," in *Modern Sociological Theory*, ed. Howard Becker and Alvin Boskoff (New York: Holt, Rinehart and Winston, Inc., 1957), pp. 141–142. See also Howard Becker, *Through Values to Social Interpretation* (Durham, N. C.: Duke University Press, 1950), pp. 248–280.

[29] Becker, "Current Sacred-Secular Theory," p. 171.

nation so powerful as to kill those who intrude upon it by breaking taboos, is sacred. And yet, ancient Polynesian attitudes toward religion were quite instrumental and flexible. If this god has shown a lack of power, then try that one instead. In Hawaii, the whole system broke down quite quickly when Western contact and other forces demonstrated the inefficacy of traditional religious entities.[30] The Hawaiians were quite willing to try Jehovah for a while. At a less primitive level of development, what are we to do with the prophet who claims to have a special connection to the sacred world and calls upon the people and the realm to change their ways, in some cases to destroy sacred objects in the name of a higher God? In some cases, this higher God is the individual whose sacred inviolability must be protected from violation by the established order. The relations between the sacred and change are complicated, to say the least. In view of this complication, it is better to rely upon a less neologistic definition of the sacred, a definition that will clearly comprehend such obvious examples of secularization as the separation of church and state and the rise of secular education.

Let us then say, with Durkheim, that the sacred is that which is set apart from the profane ordinary world and treated with awe and respect.[31] This meaning for the sacred, though drawn from Durkheim, is not far removed from the etymology of the word and its dictionary definition.

Given this rather concrete definition, a secular trend in Western history is indisputable. It is implicit in a variety of symbolic and structural developments in social life—the rise of secular thought, including science and technology, the emergence of economic rationality, and the declining political power of religious associations. From a structural point of view, these phenomena can be seen as a series of differentiations. Systems of secular symbols develop as cultural associations separate from the church or the sacred state. These symbols may be purely cultural associations, as in the case of the rise of scientific and learned societies, or they may be cultural symbols within other types of associations. Thus, ideologies of secular authority develop within political associations. In this sense, political slogans as different as "reason of state" (i.e., the state may do what it must) and "popular will" are alike in being secular symbols of

---

[30] A. L. Kroeber, *Anthropology* (New York: Harcourt Brace Jovanovich, Inc., 1948), pp. 403–405.

[31] Durkheim, *Elementary Forms*, pp. 31–38.

legitimacy, removed from religious contexts. As secular symbols arise and secular associations obtain more power, alternatives to sacred interpretations and sacred authority emerge.

The causes of secularization are obscure. Becker, as we have seen, attributed the phenomenon to the clash of mutually destructive value systems brought together by increases in mobility or societalization. In this interpretation, he is within an important intellectual tradition that stresses the fragility of any set of sacred symbols, its inability to withstand detached criticism. Opposed to Becker's view is the view that areas of the clash of separate traditions are the fermenting vats of novel and more universal religions.[32] Perhaps the views can be reconciled, for in some cases religions become more universal by limiting the reach of their claim to ultimate authority: "Render unto Caesar the things that are Caesar's." In this sense, the universal religion can be seen as a differentiating force.

An evolutionary theory of secularization would stress the functional capacity of secularization as a form of differentiation. To free economics, politics, and knowledge from sacred constraints is to increase the capacity of specialized systems to deal with special functional problems in their own terms. This argument is related to Becker's, for it attributes secularization to the power of secular systems to comprehend and deal with the variety and change in the world, a power they hold because they are freed from the constraints of a fixed religious tradition. The capacity of secular science to develop when freed from sacred preconceptions is a clear example of this argument.

The evolutionary theory of secularization has an interesting corollary. If secularization has the function of freeing each specialized system to do its own job according to the exigencies of its own problems, then it might be that the sacred has a job of its own. If this is true, then secularization does not mean the elimination of the sacred, but its differentiation around its special function—elaboration of problems of the ultimate grounds or premises of cultural meaning. Bellah takes this tack in tracing the movement of religious concern towards exploration of the ultimate potentialities of man. At this point I can do no better than to quote Bellah's own succinct statement:

It is not that life has become again a "one possibility thing" but that it has become an infinite possibility thing. The analysis of man as secular, materialistic, dehumanized, and in the deepest sense areligious seems to me fundamentally misguided, for such a judgement is based on standards that cannot gauge the modern temper.[33]

Mass Education

Mass education is unquestionably a correlate of modernity. The percentage of the school-age population enrolled in primary and secondary schools varies from well under 20 percent in many of the underdeveloped nations of Asia and Africa to well over 80 percent in most of the developed nations. Olsen reports a correlation of .85 between energy production per capita and the percent of the population that have completed a primary education, in a sample of 115 nations. High correlations between primary education and other indices were also reported: .85 with gross national product per capita; .78 with a measure of labor diversity; and other high correlations with various measures of communications development, transportation development, and political modernization.[34]

National development requires mass education. As social mobility increases and the population is brought together to participate in modern economic organization, to become involved in national political life, and to extend their loyalties to the nation, the problem of cultural integration becomes very salient to national leaders. Cultural integration, as it has been defined here, requires extensive participation in associations that effectively transmit a national culture, which includes both elements specific to the nation and the modern technical culture that is the foundation of economic development. The associational foundation of this form of cultural development is in a system of mass education.

Although the intellectual roots of the idea of mass education lie in the Enlightenment, the idea of mass education as national education by the state was most clearly established by Fichte in

---

[33] Bellah, "Religious Evolution," p. 374.

[34] Olsen, "National Political Development." For international statistics on mass education, see United Nations Educational Scientific and Cultural Organization, *Statistical Yearbook, 1966* (Louvaine, Belgium, 1968), pp. 59–78.

his *Addresses to the German Nation* of 1807–1808.[35] For Fichte, a proper educational system is nationalistic in content, provided for all, and operated by the state. Its purposes are national political and economic development through instilling technical competence and national loyalty. The echoes of Fichte's addresses are still heard around the world. This conception of education took firm root in the West in the nineteenth century, and is universally accepted by nationalistic, modernizing elites in the underdeveloped world today.

The ideal of mass education as both means and expression of national identity and aspiration is embodied in the fundamental law of the developing states, often in explicit national symbols. To cite but one example, the basic education law of Indonesia announces that a system of mass compulsory education is an expression of the fundamental formula of Indonesian nationhood, the *Pantja Sila*, five philosophic principles on which Indonesia is said to be based—divine omnipotence, humaneness, national consciousness, faith in democracy, and social justice for all.[36]

Why should mass education require such a high level of persuasive symbolic justification? Any system of state-supported mass education brings to the fore the latent tensions between national differentiated cultural systems and the traditional culture embedded in solidary contexts. The question of who shall control the socialization of the young is raised. Shall the family, the ethnic group, and the religious association be deprived of their right to educate their own? In underdeveloped areas there is also the economic question: Shall the family be deprived of the child's labor?

So deep were these tensions in European history that Lipset and Rokkan take the issue of control of emergent mass education as one of the four issues that formed the four basic dimensions of cleavage in European political systems.[37] At this point, we can see that problems of mass education and of secularization are closely intertwined. The first cleavage point in modern European states came during the Reformation over the question of church and state. Out of this struggle, two types of society emerged. In

---

[35] Johann Gottlieb Fichte, *Addresses to the German Nation*, trans. R. F. Jones and G. H. Turnbull (Chicago: The Open Court Publishing Company, 1922).

[36] M. Hutasoit, *Compulsory Education in Indonesia* (Louvaine: UNESCO, 1954).

[37] Lipset and Rokkan, *Party Systems and Voter Alignments*, pp. 33–50.

one type, the state controlled a national church, and in the other, the state was closely allied to the Roman Catholic Church. These two types of structures formed a backdrop to the issue of control over mass education as the educational apparatus burgeoned in the wake of the democratic revolutions of the nineteenth century. In Southern and Central Europe the Counter-Reformation strengthened the position of the church and its alliance with traditional authority. In consequence, the progressive drive for national education was a battle against the church and the *ancien regime*, leading to a polarized division between a national-radical-secular coalition and a religious-traditional coalition. In contrast, in Northwest Europe, Britain, and Scandinavia, the established churches were national and did not oppose nation-building. The nationalist position was not driven to the left, and a different type of left-wing alliance was formed, drawing its support from nonconformist religious opponents of the established church and the rising urban strata.[38] This type of leftist alliance is not in a position to demand a system of compulsory secular education. Rather, it favors the development of a dual system of proprietary and free secular schools and the maintenance of pluralism.

Cognate problems exist in the developing nations. To return to our Indonesian example, this nation is culturally diverse, geographically fragmented, abounding in religions and sects, and divided into thirty major language groups. The higher schools have played a major role in creating and disseminating a national culture; but, at the same time, many conflicts exist within the educational system, and these conflicts are manifest in a number of particularistic schools, especially at the primary level. The central government has never been able to penetrate and organize the national educational system in a purposeful and effective way.[39]

Conflict over education is exacerbated by the close relation between educational organizations and the distribution of elite status. Despite national aspirations, universal education is never achieved. Schooling is distributed and diffused within a societal population through a set of structural channels.[40] Elite status is

[38] Ibid., p. 38.

[39] Joseph Fischer, "Indonesia," *Education and Political Development*, ed. James S. Coleman (Princeton: Princeton University Press, 1965), pp. 92–122.

[40] C. Arnold Anderson, "Patterns and Variability in the Distribution and Diffusion of Schooling," in *Education and Economic Development*, ed. C. Arnold Anderson and Mary Jane Bowman (Chicago: Aldine Publishing Company, 1965), pp. 314–344.

associated with a high degree of education, particularly in nations where higher education is difficult to obtain. Under such circumstances, various elites seek to maintain access to and control over educational opportunities and to link other opportunities to education. Conversely, subgroups who feel that they have been deprived of status also seek greater access to and control over education.[41]

This is true in modern and transitional societies alike. In the United States the conflict between solidary and state authority over schools was "solved" (as in the other Anglo-American democracies) by a dual system of state and proprietary education and a high degree of local control. Hence, the school became a center of local political controversy, and we are now witnessing another act in the drama of solidary conflict over education, — an attempt by the black community to assert direct control over a portion of the educational system of America.

The implications of the foregoing materials are clear. There is a general relationship between national solidarity, political development, economic growth, and the extension of education. But this is not to say that we can treat the relationship between solidary systems, economic systems, political systems, and cultural systems as a set of mutually beneficial facilitations. The dynamics of social action within concrete societies involve complex relations between a variety of solidary and cultural systems, some limited in extent and some broad, even international, in scope. The tensions implied by these incongruous and overlapping boundaries are translated into issues and cleavages in political life which, in turn, react back on cultural and solidary systems as divisive issues and animating concerns. This illustration of the varied and dynamic interconnections between the types of societal systems forms a backdrop for the next chapter. Having analyzed solidary, economic, political, and cultural systems in turn, how do we put them together to form a society?

---

[41] Ibid., and Coleman, *Educational and Political Development*, pp. 353–371.

8

The Total Society: Relations Between Systems

INTRODUCTION

Having defined society with reference to a certain type of population in chapter three, we went on to describe some of the kinds of systems in which the life of such populations is organized. How are actors bound together in systems of solidarity? How are they organized to produce and distribute wealth? How are they organized to clarify collective purposes and mobilize energies in the pursuit of collective goals? How are the members engaged in systems that create and perpetuate a cultural life? But so far we seem not to have described *a society*; society appears to be a set of disparate systems, not a unified entity. We have analytically separated aspects of the activities of human populations in order to illuminate some of the organizational devices for bringing coherence to the varied conduct within human society. But how do these aspects of activity fit together—how does activity cohere into a unit called a society?

According to the theory of the social system (the theory that society is the largest self-sufficient social system), the best way to obtain an overview of the whole is to see society as a set of relations between constituent subsystems. A modern society contains an economy, a political system, an integrative system, etc., and we can view the whole society as the interconnections between these separate systems. The social-system approach proposes that these systems become separated; it is because they become separated that we can analyze society as the interconnections between them, their contributions to each other, or the inputs and outputs between one system and another. This idea has some merit, especially as it applies to highly differentiated societies that have developed a number of highly specialized systems. Thus, the idea has led to the development of some of the most imaginative, powerful, and sophisticated concepts yet proposed for the analysis of society.

At the same time, the basic premises of this book imply that the problem of intersystem connections must be approached with great caution. We must remember that the isolation of special types of functional systems—solidary, economic, political, and cultural—was an act of analytical abstraction. Systems of conduct in the real world hang together in ways that cross-cut our analytical distinctions. To speak of "inputs" from one analytically defined system to another compounds the abstraction and tends to remove our language from concrete process to a metaphorical level. We are in danger of overlooking firmer and more direct connections between the sectors of activity.

The first premise of this volume is that human society consists in activity. Without denying the value of abstraction in isolating types of functional problems and institutional responses to functional problems, it is nonetheless necessary to return to action itself in our discussion of the interconnections of human affairs in society as a whole. It would be well to generalize the advice of Raymond Williams, who, in speaking of the relation of art and society, said, "We do not now compare the art with the society; we compare both with the whole complex of human actions and feelings."[1]

It is my contention that if this advice is to be taken seriously, it demands a fundamental canon for all attempts to study the relations between the sectors of society: Never forget that (even in the most highly differentiated societies) the subsystems of society are embedded in networks of interaction and relationships that cross-cut and transcend differentiated functional institutions. Solidary systems, economic systems, political systems, and cultural systems, *and the links between them,* are always

[1] Williams, *Long Revolution,* p. 69.

deeply involved in cross-cutting channels of communication, in systems of stratification, in networks of interest, and in morphological arrangements.[2]

The foregoing discussion suggests several approaches to the study of the total society, and the following sections of this book are organized under headings appropriate to these approaches. The total society may be seen as a set of relationships between differentiated sectors, as a system of communication, as a system of stratification, as a network of interests, and as a structured population. Finally, we will return to the problem of overlapping boundaries in social systems.

RELATIONS BETWEEN SYSTEMS: EXCHANGE OF RESOURCES

Integrated Subsystems as Resources

The conception of integrated systems of solidarity, economy, polity, and culture provide one possible starting point for the study of intersystem relations. Any given set of types of action systems that is integrated within an entire societal population constitutes a resource for the other systems of society. Hence, we can view the operation of one integrated system as making a set of contributions to the functioning of other integrated systems.

For example, if the cultural systems of a societal population form an integrated cultural system for the total society, other social systems are provided with the following resources: (1) *solidary systems* with common values and symbols to unite the total society; (2) *political systems* with common values, symbols, and formulas to legitimize authority over all groups in the society and to draw upon in creating cooperative arrangements and compromises between competing political groups; (3) *economic systems* with willingness and capacity to adopt economic roles, and a common cultural framework for organizing economic enterprise.

This list could be extended to include the contributions of other integrated systems, but the whole procedure is question-

---

[2] This issue is treated within the specific framework of Parsonian theory in Mayhew, "Ascription in Modern Society," pp. 105–120.

able, for in many instances the resulting propositions about the contribution of one system to another border on the tautologous. What is described as a "contribution" of an economy to a polity can also be seen as a mere redescription of economic events in political terms. If we take seriously the point that the separation of society into different types of systems is an analytical act, it is, in a sense, more appropriate to view the preceeding four chapters not as chapters about different *parts* of society, but as discussions of *the total society from four different points of view*.

The validity of treating intersocietal relations as "outputs" from one system to another depends on two factors: the extent of concrete structural differentiation of society and the extent to which differentiated institutional spheres are not embedded in larger social networks that incorporate both systems. The remainder of this chapter will examine these two problems.

The Parsonian Paradigm: Introduction

One paradigm for viewing society as a set of interchanges between functionally differentiated sectors, the scheme devised by Talcott Parsons, deserves more detailed attention because of its sophistication and influence. It should be emphasized that Parsons does not allege that all societies exhibit these types of interchanges; his model is specifically intended to apply to *modern* societies. By a modern society, Parsons means a society that is highly differentiated on a functional basis, one in which separate and systematic structures exist to deal with analytically separate types of social functions. In a more primitive society, social functions are fused in unitary structures, as in the case of a lineage of kin with economic, political, and solidary functions. This condition is sometimes referred to as ascription. In societies characterized by a high degree of ascription, the sociologist's task is to show how unitary structures perform quite diverse functions; but as differentiated spheres of life emerge, the sociologist must be concerned with what holds the disparate elements of the total society together. For Parsons, the answer lies in the emergence of institutions of exchange.[3]

---

[3] See Parsons, *Societies; "Outline of the Social System"; Theory and Modern Society*, pp. 347–354; and "On the Concept of Value Commitments," *Sociological Inquiry* 35 (Spring 1968), pp. 137–140.

Functional Differentiation and Exchange Processes

The first step in the Parsonian paradigm is to find concrete structures in the modern society that seem to be relatively specialized around serving the particular system functions outlined in chapter two. *The crucial assumption is that structural differentiation occurs along functional lines.* Given the definitions of the functions, the main outlines of the argument should not surprise us. Specialized economic systems develop around the production of wealth, the generalized resource which any society must have in order to pursue its more specific policies and goals. Hence, the economy is identified with the adaptive function. The goal attainment function is quite obviously centered in the polity, with its emphasis on mobilizing capacities in the pursuit of collective goals. The "integrative system" is a bit more difficult to locate concretely, but Parsons believes that it is centered in the legal system and in other institutions of social control. Finally, the institutional focus of pattern maintenance is in the family, and in religion and other cultural systems.

Once structural differentiation has occurred, the reintegration of the specialized parts into a societal whole is problematic. Parsons posits that the reintegration takes place through the development of a set of exchanges between the structural sectors. These exchanges are very complicated, for they do not consist in mere barter of concrete resources between one system and another, say an agreement by businessmen to pay taxes to government if government will agree to provide roads and other public means of commerce; rather, generalized types of activity are exchanged by means of *symbolic media.*

The prototypical example of an exchange process is provided by economic theory in its treatment of the exchange of labor for goods, using money as symbolic medium. Wage earners contribute labor to the productive process and in return are given the results of productive labor in the form of consumer goods. But the exchange is indirect; it is mediated by money and hence has a symbolic level — wage income flowing from business to the worker and consumer spending flowing from workers to business enterprise. It is because of the symbolic level of the interchange that imbalances in the relation of real to money transactions — inflation and deflation — can occur. By the simple expedient of identifying the wage earner as representative of a *family* household and, thus, the structural locus of pattern maintenance, and business firms as the *economy* or adaptive subsector. Parsons finds in this interchange a prototype for other institutional exchanges. He is not without historical justification in treating the household-economy exchange as an interchange between differentiated sectors, for it is possible to trace the historical development of a mobile labor force that sells its labor to business; in earlier forms of economic life, the family *is* the productive enterprise, or the worker is bound to familially organized aristocratic estates. In this sense, family and economy are not differentiated.

Having established a model interchange between the pattern maintenance and adaptive subsectors, Parsons proceeds to develop analogous symbolically mediated interchanges between other subsectors. Treating the public as a structural instance of an integrative subsystem (the population in their *legal* roles as citizens, as it were) and the polity as the structural locus of goal attainment, Parsons develops a model of a political market along lines already adumbrated in chapter six.[4] The public exchanges their generalized support for constituted authority in return for a set of binding decisions about public goals. Because authoritative decisions are binding on all citizens, they ensure that public support will be "rewarded" with collective cooperation in the implementation of public policy. But again the interchange is mediated by a higher level symbolic exchange. In this case, *influence,* in the sense of generalized capacity to persuade, is the media. The public advocates a variety of policies, and the polity supplies effective leadership by responsibly aligning and consolidating support for consensual policies. Both advocacy and leadership are forms of influence. As suggested in chapter six, this type of analysis opens the way for applying the concepts of economic discourse to events in other social spheres, an idea which, to say the least, ought to produce interesting insights and novel formulations of problems.

The paradigm contemplates six such double interchanges between four functionally differentiated sectors.[5] The exchanges are mediated by four generalized media: money or generalized capacity to buy, power or generalized capacity to coerce, influence or generalized capacity to persuade, and commitment or generalized capacity to invoke moral sanctions. These are somewhat vulgar definitions of media that Parsons has defined with a

---

[4] Parsons, "Voting and the Equilibrium."

[5] For a map of the six double interchanges see Parsons, *Theory and Modern Society,* p. 350, and "Value Commitments," p. 138.

great deal more analytical rigor. Our purpose here is to communicate his basic idea: That the coordination of highly differentiated and varied activity in a complex society is possible only because systems can transcend the limitations inherent in meeting every coordinative problem through a set of concrete deals between each actor and every other actor. Actors are given generalized resources. Money allows us to buy at a supermarket instead of looking for someone who will exchange turnips for shoes. Common value commitments make it possible to invoke and to activate moral commitments in a large number of actors instead of dealing with each one separately in terms of his unique conscience.

Critique

Without denigrating this insight or its potential power, it is possible to remain skeptical of the attempt to structurally locate all of the functional systems and their symbolically mediated interchanges. As we move from the economy to the political realm, and from there to the integrative and pattern maintenance systems, the referents of the systematic categories become progressively vague and amorphous, the concrete structural loci more obscure. The terms themselves become more abstract and metaphorical. One can easily understand, indeed measure, flows of goods and services as they are mediated by money. Even the political market, though based upon an analogy, can be given a fairly concrete locus. But what are we to make of the idea that the pattern maintenance system sends to the goal attainment system "legality of powers of office" in exchange for "operative responsibility," and that this exchange is mediated at the level of generalized commitments by an output from the polity of "moral responsibility for collective interest" in return for "legitimation of authority."[6] We cannot say that the idea is without content, for it refers to some fundamental sociological ideas that have a long history: The apparatus of political control cannot operate without legitimacy; such legitimacy is gained by taking moral responsibility for the collective interest; the polity cannot attain this form of legitimacy unless political leaders and the society at large share generalized commitments to common values. Nevertheless, it is difficult to visualize this interdependency as an ac-

---

[6] Parsons, "Value Commitments," pp. 138, 150–152.

tual flow between structurally differentiated social sectors, and much more difficult to locate this flow in a set of transactions in any way comparable to a market. Parsons sometimes emphasizes that he is speaking analytically about aspects of society rather than about concrete structures, but it is hard to reconcile this disclaimer with the theory that *structural* differentiation *does* take place around the analytically separate functions.

In the context of the argument of the present volume, my criticism can be restated in this way: Parsons is not always able to locate the structure of human society in the concrete flow of human action. When he states that "the output from the polity to the pattern maintenance system of 'moral responsibility for the collective interest' comprises the obverse aspect of the sharing of values by ego and alter,'"[7] he seems to be attempting to transform a structural category,"sharing of values," to a processual category, "output," without precisely locating that process in human conduct.

It is very difficult to locate analytically pure social functions in the concrete institutional sectors of a society, and, because of the involvement of every institutional sector in an interconnected social structure, it is difficult to depict the process we call society as a set of exchanges between sectors.

ALTERNATIVE APPROACHES TO THE TOTAL SOCIETY

Cross-Sectorial Models

There is no irrefutable argument to compel the student of total societies to concern himself with institutional subsectors as such. We think about the relation between economic and political systems because a long tradition of thought separates the two spheres, and, to some extent, in some societies, the two realms are in fact separated. On the other hand, it is possible to construct a model of society that ignores the distinction.

If a long tradition of thought on the methods of social and historical analysis has taught us anything, it is that we cannot describe any event, let alone any society, in exhaustive detail. We cannot, to borrow a recent pithy phrasing of the point, study

---

[7] Ibid., p. 150.

the total society totally.[8] Every conceptualization of society is an abstract selection of a few features that are thought to be strategic relative to some goal of analysis. Hence, it is possible to depict a total society in terms of a radically simplified model whose elements cross-cut or embrace all institutional spheres. These elements or variables can be chosen for their relevance to the most important sociological problems or human concerns in order to maximize the strategic focus of the model. Logically, the simplest model of a society is one that relates two components of the total society. Thus, in a somewhat Durkheimian manner, we can posit that the entire population of a society is involved in a division of labor and in a regulative order. We then hypothesize that the greater the rate of increase in the intensity of the division of labor, the greater the disintegration of the moral order. The former can be measured by the number of specialized roles in the population and the latter by some index of deviance—suicide rate, crime rate, rate of participation in deviant cults, etc. It may be objected that the above is a statement of relations between two institutional spheres, the economy and the integrative system, but that would be an arbitrary interpretation of the relationship. The division of labor is not, properly speaking, the economy, nor does the model posit any specialized organs of integration. The hypothesis merely asserts that the greater the rate of increase in the specialization of roles, the greater the deviance from role expectations. This simple two-variable model encompasses a great deal of the historic concern of sociological thought. Moreover, a study of these variables across societal populations would truly be a comparative study of total societies.

With the addition of other cross-sectorial variables, this type of model can be made increasingly elaborate. Some movement in the direction of such cross-sectorial models of society can be detected. One reason for this movement lies in the capacity of digital computers to analyze and simulate very complex processes if the fundamental components in a system can be isolated.[9]

Intersectorial Links

We have approached the total society through looking at analytically separate types of sectors. We did so for a number of

[8] Ithiel de Sola Pool, "Computer Simulations of Total Societies," in *Total Societies*, ed. Klausner, p. 45.

[9] Ibid., pp. 45–65.

reasons. First, this approach gives a variety of perspectives on the total society, perspectives closely related to basic functional problems in human organizations. Second, thought about society has evolved in the context of concerns about whether a given sector of society can be controlled by a "larger" society or can be a source for such control. Third, it simplified the job of testing the adequacy of the model of society as a social system. Finally, social systems of various types do come to develop boundaries, to expand at different rates, to become structurally differentiated. We live much of our lives within specialized associations and are constantly wondering how these associations and communities can be linked in the service of human goals. How can government control the economy? How can the economy be tapped to provide more income for deprived ethnic (solidary) groups? How can home and school be linked?

Despite the existence of specialized spheres of action, and despite the importance of relations between them, it is possible to view society as a total set of links within the total societal population, links that cross-cut or transcend institutional boundaries. Accordingly, we will now view the total society as a complex of communication, a system of stratification, a network of interests, and a structured population.

Society as Structured Population

Society as structured population will be discussed first and very briefly, for it has already been treated at length in chapter three. In the present context, it is only necessary to indicate that differentiated institutional spheres within the same society are inseparably connected because they are all sustained by the same population, a population with a size, a composition, and patterns of location and movement in space. Causal effects flow along these links.

De facto segregation is a familiar example of this phenomenon. *De facto* school segregation arises from links between housing and education. When school districts are drawn along neighborhood lines, the patterns of segregation that appear in housing will be reproduced in education. If such segregation is truly *de facto*, it is not deliberate; it is a structural consequence of the presence of spatially defined norms in the institution education, namely, the concept of the neighborhood school. In consequence, the educational process is influenced by all other institutional spheres in which spatial arrangement is a structural element, and that means *all* institutional spheres.

Similar examples can be found in other spheres. Studies of voting behavior show that in highly homogeneous neighborhoods the effect of socioeconomic status on voting is accentuated by the strengthening of the pressures of majority opinion.[10] Hence, residential segregation by socioeconomic status increases the impact of status on the political process. It can also be shown that political parties adapt their strategies of choice of local leaders to the party's degree of dominance within a precinct, which in turn reflects residential homogeneity.[11] Again, spatial elements in the institutional organization of political life incorporate another spatial phenomenon, residential social segregation, into the political process.

SOCIETY AS COMMUNICATION

Every social act involves communication: Whether it be an act of solidarity, an economic transaction, an exercise of power, or a reaffirmation of cultural meaning, a social act involves communication. Hence, human society as an ongoing process of activity can also be depicted as a network of communication. The pioneer in conceptualizing society as communication is Karl Deutsch. Deutsch, in his very influential work, *Nationalism and Social Communication*, states the idea of society as communication very effectively, and builds upon it to develop a theory of the rise and integration of the nation-state.[12] Deutsch starts, as we do, by looking at the variety and types of human activities as they are spread about the globe. Whether we view human activity as patterns of settlement, networks of transport, areas of culture and language, markets, or levels of development, we see not uniformity but highly uneven clusters of distributions. These distributions permit us to isolate centers of influence and boundaries. Centers of influence are centers of communication, and boundaries are barriers to communication. The boundaries of

[10] Bernard Berelson, et al., *Voting* (Chicago: University of Chicago Press, 1954), pp. 98–101.

[11] Samuel Eldersveld, *Political Parties* (Chicago: Rand McNally & Company, 1964), p. 70.

[12] Karl W. Deutsch, *Nationalism and Social Communication* (Cambridge, Mass.: M.I.T. Press, 1953). See also Daniel Lerner, "Communication Systems and Social Systems," *Behavioral Science* 2 (October 1957), pp. 206–275; and Lucian W. Pye, ed., *Communications and Political Development* (Princeton, N.J.: Princeton University Press, 1963).

various systems are diverse and overlapping, and it is for this reason that national integration is problematic. But, by the same token, it is because systems overlay each other and their centers congregate that political power arises, because power is based upon *intense* communication. National development occurs whenever a well-organized elite, based upon intensive communication, can extend its communication outward. This occurs when industrialization and other forms of large-scale organization offer opportunities for those who are isolated by their traditional moorings to secure social advancement by "cutting loose" and participating in communication networks expanding outward from the elite.

Deutsch's pathbreaking work has led to a number of significant studies on the impact of communications development. One of the outstanding features of the concept of society as communication is its susceptibility to operational definition in research. We have cited two of these studies already, the cross-national studies of political development by Cutright and Olsen (see chapter six). Olsen, for example, shows correlations between various measures of communications development—daily newspaper circulation, radios per 1000 population—and various aspects of political development or capacity.[13] The strongest multiple correlation between a combined set of indices of communications development and an index of a type of political capacity was the association between communication and executive functioning,[14] indicating (as Deutsch might predict) an association between communications development and the ability to radiate power outward from a center.

In a sense, Parsons' theory of society is in a similar stream of thought, for, in his emphasis on media of influence, he is explicitly emphasizing the importance of institutionalizing the means of communication. Money, power, influence, and commitment are all specialized media for generalizing the capacity to communicate in the face of the complexity of modern integrative problems.

In this respect there is a common theme in Parsons' work, in some of Deutsch's work, and in the empirical work on communications development, namely an emphasis on the development of the specialized means of general communication, means for the expansion of communication beyond the face-to-face setting.

[13] Olsen, "National Political Development," p. 708.

[14] Ibid., p. 706.

Students of communication have been interested in the development of specialized institutions for increasing the breadth of cultural transmission, especially mass education and the mass media, and rightly so, for this type of development is clearly a part of the process of modernization. Nevertheless, overemphasis on mass communications, on the increase of social capacity through the specialization of institutions of communication, is comparable to any other overemphasis on differentiation; it overlooks the embedding of all specialization in encompassing social networks.

Mass communication does not do away with face-to-face communication; it merely supplements it. Indeed, students of mass communication, in discovering the "two-step flow" of mass communication, have shown that the messages of mass communication are interpreted and diffused in the context of small face-to-face groups.[15] I would go further and argue that social development depends not only on the growth of means of transcending the limitations of face-to-face encounters, but on means for extending direct communication. One possible interpretation of Olsen's findings lends support to this idea. Olsen used a system of partial correlations to determine which of his fourteen socioeconomic variables was the best predictor of political development when the other thirteen were held constant. In all but one instance, the number of motor vehicles per 1000 population manifested the highest partial correlation with political development.[16] The present author suspects that this finding indicates that the capacity to physically move persons from one point to another to bring them into common participation in group life may be the most important form of social mobilization.

Be that as it may, the importance of networks of face-to-face communication should not be slighted because influences often flow from one institutional sector to another in the context of direct communication.

The Structure of Primary Communication

Direct face-to-face communication may be called *primary communication* for it is primary in several senses:

1) Most of the communication between persons is direct, even in a modern society.

[15] Berelson and Steiner, *Human Behavior*, p. 550.

[16] Olsen, "National Political Development," p. 709.

2) The communication by which the individual is socialized in the family and in later life is primarily direct.

3) Personal communication is more influential than indirect communication via the mass media.

The third of these three assumptions is the most problematic. Berelson and Steiner, in their inventory of the findings of social science, summarize the relevant literature in this proposition: "Word of mouth or personal communication from an immediate and trusted source is typically more influential than media communication from a remote and trusted source, despite the prestige of the latter."[17] This proposition should be linked to our previous reference to the two-step flow of communication. When media communication is successful in influencing conduct, it tends to operate through the intermediate effect of opinion leaders who interpret and pass on the message to members of their primary groups.

Thus, the study of communication brings us back to the subject of solidarity. A large portion of all acts of communication, especially influential acts, occur between persons linked by ties of solidarity, within family and kin groups, among friends, and in informal groups within larger associations and communities.

The point may be made in more general terms: By definition, face-to-face communication must take place between persons who are physically close to one another. Most of the structural forces that bring people into physical contact with each other have solidary elements. Apart from the fact that people choose to communicate with solidary associates, actors with solidary ties are pushed together by the structural force of segregation. Choice of mate, of friend, or work-partner, and of neighbor is affected by ascriptive criteria. The structure defines who may associate with whom in terms of a set of presumed or possible solidary connections.

Because of the segregation of communication, barriers develop in the pattern of channels of primary communication in the societal population. Primary messages are more likely to flow within the boundaries established by solidary systems than across those boundaries. Because information and influence within society flow through solidary channels and are obstructed at the boundaries of solidarity, the structure of the solidary system penetrates all of the other spheres of society. All social systems involve communication, and, insofar as this communica-

---

[17] Berelson and Steiner, *Human Behavior*, p. 550.

tion is shaped by solidary networks, a solidary element is included in the structure of all the process systems. It is incorrect to conceptualize this as an "output" from the solidary system to another system. It is a direct incorporation of solidary structure as a part of the structure of the system; it is an *absence* of differentiation. Furthermore, because the economic, political, and cultural realms all incorporate these networks of communication, they are directly linked to each other through sharing a common structural element.

A good example of the impact of solidary relations on a differentiated subsystem is the power of racial segregation to maintain itself in patterns of employment, even when employers utilize the criterion of economic rationality and do not actively discriminate on the basis of race. Consider a complex modern business firm faced with the problem of recruiting and maintaining a labor force. For some types of positions there may be chronic shortages of qualified manpower, while for other positions there is only relatively slow normal attrition. The problems of shortages will be more salient, and a great deal of time and energy will be devoted to specialized techniques for expanding the firm's range of purview over potential labor in these categories. News media will be used, special recruitment programs undertaken, and internal training programs may be adopted. Such special efforts may involve special efforts to integrate new ethnic groups into the labor force.

On the other hand, for those positions subject only to normal replacements, it will be easier to rely on natural flows of labor input. The ordinary process of recruitment is tied to networks of primary group affiliation and informal contacts. Information and recommendations about job openings pass by word of mouth, from relative to relative, neighbor to neighbor, friend to friend, in networks with racial or ethnic boundaries. This process reproduces the established structure of solidarity within the community in the labor force of the business firm, despite the firm's economic specialization and rational economic standards.

Such examples can be multiplied indefinitely for even the most differentiated societies, and the argument holds with even more power for societies characterized by deep cleavages of solidarity. Cleavages in solidarity have an impact on other societal systems. Our definitions of integration for economic, political, and cultural systems all included elements implying a free flow of information and a high level of participation in associational life. Whenever solidary boundaries exist, they act as barriers to communication and influence; in consequence we may assert as a general principle of societal analysis that *the greater the malintegration of a societal system of solidarity, the greater the malintegration of that society's economic, political, and cultural systems.*

SOCIETY AS A SYSTEM OF STRATIFICATION

In chapter three, a social stratum was defined as a "subpopulation of actors with more or less equal status on any of the dimensions along which persons may be arranged hierarchically." Every member of a societal population may be placed along these hierarchies, and hence a total society can be viewed as consisting in a stratified population.

According to one theory, the most important dimension of stratification is prestige, and the differential allocation of prestige is a product of the joint action of two factors, the division of labor and systems of social values.[18] Because in every society there are a set of values, varied activity is valued differentially, or, to put the matter more plainly, various roles are granted more or less prestige.

Some would designate this approach as a form of the "functional theory of stratification."[19] The functional theory alleges that stratification serves an integrative function for society in several ways. When more value and prestige is placed on an important role, the best talent is drawn to the role. Further, those responsible for leadership are granted the resource of prestige to help them carry out their responsibilities. Finally, as in Plato's utopian republic, those who do the necessary but lower level work are taught to understand their place; recognizing the limited social value of their social roles, the lower strata are willing to recognize and accept their low social standing. Because of this alleged set of functional contributions, social stratification is considered an integrative subsystem of the society.

---

[18] Talcott Parsons, "A Revised Analytical Approach to the Theory of Social Stratification," in *Essays in Sociological Theory*, rev. ed. (Glencoe, Ill.: The Free Press, 1954) pp. 386–439; Bernard Barber, *Social Stratification* (New York: Harcourt Brace Jovanovich, Inc., 1957)

[19] See Kingsley Davis and Wilbert E. Moore, "Some Principles of Stratification," *American Sociological Review* 10 (April 1945), pp. 242–249.

The functional theory of stratification undoubtedly underplays the malintegrative forces of stratification, its capacity to create tension and conflict even in such highly institutionalized and "accepted" settings as the caste system of traditional India, and even more in the face of egalitarian ideologies in modern nations. Moreover, it is easy to demonstrate, by minor extensions of the premises of the theory of differential prestige, that *stratification is not a specialized integrative subsystem, but a system that permeates the total society and all of its differentiated subsectors.*

In the first place, even adherents of the functional theory admit that it is not roles that are valued, but groups. In admitting that the family, rather than the individual, is the unit of stratification,[20] one recognizes that group membership confers status for some actors (wives and children) apart from their functional contributions. By extension, it should not be too difficult to recognize that other types of group memberships confer status.[21] Second, it is clear that prestige is granted not only on the basis of a person's activity, but on the basis of the resources he controls — wealth, power, knowledge, etc.[22] Hence, the members of groups that control resources are accorded prestige. Moreover, the allocation and control of resources is in large measure a product of the operation of the several process systems of the total society. A variety of economic and political exigencies contribute to the allocation of resources, and in this sense it is difficult to imagine a stratification system as a separate and differentiated mechanism for allocating prestige.

For these reasons, the type of group we have called a social stratum can be defined more adequately as *a subpopulation of a society accorded more or less prestige by virtue of the valued resources that are controlled by the members individually and through their group memberships.* Such a definition does not exclude the possibility that stratification can contribute to integration by allocating prestige in effective ways. Neither does it assume the effective allocation of prestige. In insisting that systems of stratification do not merely value activities directly, it

---

[20] Parsons, "Revised Analytical Approach," p. 422.

[21] Arthur L. Stinchcombe, "Social Structure and Organizations," in *Handbook of Organizations,* ed. James G. March (Chicago: Rand McNally & Company, 1965), pp. 171–176.

[22] Parsons at one point explicitly recognized this. See Talcott Parsons, "An Analytical Approach to the Theory of Social Stratification," in *Essays,* pp. 75–76.

becomes more difficult to make the inferential leap to the functional theory.

Stratification as Activity

True to the assumptions of our approach, we must not lose sight of the fact that, though the concept of a stratum is a structural concept, a system of stratification is a system of activity. Four types of process are involved in stratification:

1) *Evaluation.* Stratification requires a continuous process of evaluation. Actors must assess, in the context of concrete activities, the status of other actors.

2) *Control of resources.* The control of resources by a stratum, or the failure to control resources, is not a given; it is an ongoing process of seeking, obtaining, wielding, and being deprived of valued resources. A system of stratification is maintained because the members of higher strata do not freely disburse their resources of wealth and power, but manipulate the social systems of society to protect and invest them.

3) *Organization.* The crucial element in the capacity of a stratum to protect its resources and continue their control is its internal organization. Stratification is not a matter of each member of a stratum holding and wielding his resources of status. The stratum as a unit, and its constituent groups, engage in an ongoing process of organizing their control over resources. When a stratum develops cultural styles, schools, and other socializing techniques for inculcating symbols and life styles within the stratum, the identity and boundaries of the stratum are protected. If the stratum develops associations and alliances for maintaining its position, its status is similarly protected.

Strata vary in their organization. The gentry in traditional China was a very well-organized stratum. Its members were organized through an extensive system of kinship groups and ties, and those ties were actively mobilized to further the careers of members. Advancement depended on mandarin learning, and, more generally, on learning a life style. Solidary units within the gentry subsidized some members of their group as they learned the life style, and, if these members were successful, they were expected to further the careers of other members.[23] In this way, the

---

[23] Wolfram Eberhard, *A History of China* (Berkeley: University of California Press, 1960), pp. 71–86.

gentry organized their activity in a far-flung network of class ties to further their control of the resources of status. Lower strata tend not to be as well and broadly organized to try to capture the resources of status as are the higher strata to retain them. On the other hand, revolutionary parties do develop to speak for and advance the interests of lower strata in a prolocutory way, and, in more routine settings, labor unions, farmers associations, and the like operate as organizing groups within the lower strata. Marx's theory of the transformation of the proletariat from a class-in-itself to a class-for-itself is, in effect, a theory of the emergent organization of the class interests of the lower strata.

One of the most persistent arguments about American society concerns the degree of organization of the upper strata. The argument that there is a "power elite" or a "military-industrial complex" is an argument that there are upper strata, bound by ties of common interest and well-organized (at both the institutional and collective levels) to maintain and use their position. This problem is closely linked to the problem of the degree of differentiation of institutional spheres and will bear reexamination when we arrive at the problem of the embedding of differentiated institutions in the common matrix of stratification.

4) *Recruitment.* Like any other population, a stratum is maintained by a continuing process of recruitment; old members die, or leave the population for other reasons, and new members are recruited. The focal question in sociological analysis is whether recruitment is by birth or by achievement (or, in the case of downward mobility, by the lack of achievement). If the ultimate unit of stratification is the family, then, in a sense, initial recruitment is always by birth; the child inherits, temporarily at least, membership in the strata of his parents. Since parents have a great deal of control over early socialization, they can train the child early to the values and life styles that will either help him to maintain his class position or prevent him from changing it. In this sense, birth (or what is often called ascription) is an element in recruitment within all systems of stratification. The question is whether birth absolutely determines status, as in a *caste* system, or whether there is a degree of intergenerational mobility.

There has probably never been a completely ascriptive status system. All systems must adapt to a variety of contingencies, and the omnipresence of change insures that alterations of population size, occupational structure, and political organization will force some horizontal movement from stratum to stratum.

On the other hand, some structures appear to be more open than others. In a modern industrial society, status is strongly associated with occupational role, and occupational roles involve technical qualifications. These facts, in conjunction with internal transformations of the occupational structure (such as the elimination of agricultural employment and the rise of white-collar employment), create a relatively open stratification system. A father cannot pass his status on to his son directly; he can only pass it on indirectly through early training and investments in education. Studies of occupational mobility in industrial societies, and especially studies of the occupational structure of American society, show that, at least within the white population, moderately high rates of mobility exist and that education is the main link along which status transmission takes place.[24]

On the other hand, when a status system is shrouded in sacred symbols and uses them as criteria of evaluation, when elites are well-organized to monopolize control over resources, including education, and when a social structure is relatively static, birth can dominate the system.

Finally, it should be stressed that the set of strata that are produced by the processes of stratification have systematic relations with each other. Stratification forms a system, which engulfs all of the process systems of society. One of the reasons that it is inappropriate to view society as a set of separate, functionally differentiated institutions, connected only by exchanges, is that systems of solidarity, economy, polity, and culture are all deeply embedded in a common system of stratification.

Stratification and the Differentiation of Institutions

One of the debatable questions in social thought concerns whether systems of stratification undergo a parallel differentiation when social institutions differentiate from each other. This question has been treated primarily as a problem in *elite* theory. At the higher levels in every system of stratification, there is at least one elite—a stratum that has high prestige and controls important resources. The question is: Are there sometimes *multiple* elites? According to one of the "founding fathers" of elite theory, Gaetano Mosca, multiple elites are the foundation of the

[24] Otis Dudley Duncan and Robert W. Hodge, "Education and Occupational Mobility, *American Journal of Sociology* 68 (May 1963), pp. 629–644.

rule of law.[25] Pure democracy is always a fiction, for every society has elites. But as plural resources of power arise, multiple elites develop, each based upon a different resource. The rule of law has its origin in compromises between competing elites. It is the countervailing power of differentiated elites that leads to those ground rules for elite competition that we call constitutions; ordinary people obtain legal protection only because elites regularize their own power struggle in legal forms.

Mosca's theory has some support in European history. Magna Carta, a fundamental document in English constitutional history, had its origins in struggles between royal authority and the landed nobility. Certainly, domestic European politics during the age of democratic revolution involved intense competition between a set of old elites—dynastic central authorities, landed aristocracy, and the church—and new elites—capitalists, popular leaders, and secular intellectuals. These groups formed a variety of alliances, and the shape of contemporary domestic politics in European nations depends on the kinds of alliance combinations that were formed in earlier days.

If differentiated elites develop around differentiated types of social systems, then the argument that all of the sectors of society are embedded in a common system of stratification would be weakened. But if the interests of variegated elites merge and elites are bound in networks of interlocking ties, then these webs of ties form direct links between institutional sectors. When critics speak of a "military-industrial complex" or a "power elite," they are referring to interlocks of this sort. If university presidents or retired generals sit on the boards of directors of large corporations, if large churches invest their money in these corporations, if corporation presidents sit on university boards of regents and contribute large sums of money to political campaigns, if labor leaders invest union pension funds in real estate developments, then elites, though differentiated in function, are welded into one well-integrated system of power.

It may be that a system of competing elites is a fragile and temporary phenomenon that occurs only when a number of new elites are in the process of emerging. The emergence of new elites and the decline of old elites may be a common concomitant of social change. But once born, an emergent elite struggles for recognition in the system and, to that end, enters into and alters

[25] Gaetano Mosca, *The Ruling Class*, ed. Arthur Livingston, trans. Hannah D. Mahn (New York: McGraw-Hill Book Company, 1939), pp. 120–152, 360–429.

established structures of alliance. Elites seek *establishment;* they seek to protect their prestigous position by guaranteeing the stability of their control of resources. Stability is guaranteed by investing in an established order, by forming as many cross-cutting links with the holders of other resources as possible. The more a set of elites becomes integrated by a set of cross-cutting ties, the more they come to form a single well-defined class. When elites are so merged, then the specialized spheres of society are quite directly linked by the ties between their elite participants.

Influences flow along these links. For example, the capacity of an elite to press its ideological demands depends upon its investments in other systems, a phenomenon well-illustrated in the collapse of pacifism in the international labor movement at the beginning of World War I. National labor leaders had opposed war as contrary to the interests of the working man. They had said that a new war would be met by an international general strike. But when war was declared, labor leaders fell into line. Why? Labor leaders had entered into party politics in ministerial electoral systems. They had made investments in political position in national government.[26] Thus, a set of events in the economic sphere was influenced by events in the political sphere, not through the operation of a political market, but because of the direct integration of the two sectors at the elite level of the stratification system.

Karl Mannheim has suggested a distinction between political, organizing elites, concerned with integrating and guiding the society, and intellectual, aesthetic, moral-religious elites, concerned with problems of cultural interpretation and expression. This distinction raises the question of whether these two types of elites become differentiated in the course of social modernization. Do the conditions of modern life, especially the creation of specialized cultural institutions, the rise of mass media, and the emergence of a mobile intelligentsia who congregate in great cities, lead to the differentiation of a relatively autonomous cultural elite? Is such an elite likely to engage in running criticism of established institutions? Thought is more flexible than social arrangements, and established political elites are always vulnerable to criticism from the premises of pure ideology. Hence, given an independent social base, conflict between political and cultural elites would seem to be a probable concomitant of modernization. Under these conditions, the members of cultural elites can become spokesmen for and mobilizers of a variety

---

[26] Barbara Tuchman, *The Proud Tower* (London: Hamish Hamilton, 1966), pp. 407–462.

of publics, thus contributing to pluralistic, democratic social life. On the other hand, intellectuals can be tamed by the same devices that incorporate other groups, namely giving them a stake in the established order. Further, as a later section on elites in modernizing nations will suggest, the differentiation of autonomous, critical cultural elites is a historic variable, not an evolutionary universal.[27]

Stratification and Democracy

If, at the upper strata, systems of stratification link institutional spheres, even more are they linked at the lower strata. The absence of resources is an undifferentiated state; those who lack resources lack all kinds of resources. Thus, low economic status is tied to low political power. The rise of democratic electoral procedures may be seen as a differentiating device since, in theory, it bestows political resources on strata that lack other kinds of resources. There is a serious question as to whether the franchise can bestow power in the absence of effective political organization in the lower strata. Organization requires resources. Effective organization also implies leadership, and this raises the question of whether leaders maintain allegiance to their strata, or become captured by the elite classes that they enter once they become established leaders. The crucial question is whether the institutionalization of the franchise creates a continuing sequence of opportunities for leadership based upon democratic resources, so that as one group of leaders is captured by an establishment another group arises to take over new opportunities. This is the sort of dynamic implied by Alvin Gouldner's concept of an "iron law of democracy,"[28] but as yet we lack the close empirical studies that would substantiate this theory.

Elites and Modernizing Nations

The theory that modernization is a matter of structural differentiation and that structural differentiation follows functional lines receives a severe test in contemporary processes of modernization in the new nations. It is impossible to establish universal

---

[27] On this problem, see Karl Mannheim, *Man and Society in an Age of Reconstruction*, trans. Edward Shils (London: Kegan Paul, Trench, Trubner and Co., Ltd., 1940), pp. 79–114. See also Edward Shils, "Centre and Periphery," in *The Logic of Personal Knowledge: Essays Presented to Michael Polanyi* (London: Routledge and Kegan Paul, Ltd., 1961), pp. 117–130.

[28] Alvin W. Gouldner, "Metaphysical Pathos and the Theory of Bureaucracy," *American Political Science Review* 49 (1955), pp. 496–507.

generalizations about the new nations in a few words, but Edward Shils' analysis of the role of intellectuals in the politics of new nations suggests an outline of developments common to a number of such societies.[29] Education, particularly education in the cross-national cultural system of the West, was a route to upward mobility for a relatively small elite in colonial days. As often as not, even this small elite was unable to find satisfying employment within the colonial regime. Many were educated in law and, disgruntled with colonial theory and practice, turned to intensely political careers. These were the small elites who led the revolutionary overthrow of colonial governments and became heirs to governmental authority when the colonial power departed. Deeply imbued with nationalistic ideology (because of both their Western contacts and their marginal position with respect to their indigenous heritage) these elites turned their attention to nation-building by political techniques. The struggle for independence tends to undermine traditional elites and to discredit economic elites, who are usually of foreign origin. The field is left to the small, indigenous, intensely political elites who, through extension of the apparatus of state and party, attempt to build an economy, extend popular loyalties, and educate the populace. In consequence, all institutional spheres are merged in the political.

Wherever the dynamic suggested by Shils is at work, the separation of traditional, foreign, and indigenous modernizing sectors, and the parallel differentiation of elites, is stronger than the separation of functional institutional spheres. The push to modernization does not come from the functional incapacities and tensions within a functionally undifferentiated society. The important conflicts are between nationally oriented indigenous elites (who also participate in an intersocietal cultural system), foreign-dominated economic elites, and traditional locally oriented national populations. In studying institutional connections in modernizing societies, it is more reasonable to study the expansion of the modern system and the creation of new links to the traditional sector than to look for differentiating tendencies within the modern sector. What tensions exist within the elite seem more attributable to politicized factionalism, a heritage of the spirit of opposition as it developed during the colonial era, than to any tensions deriving from the merger of functions in a monolithic structure.

[29] Edward Shils, "The Intellectuals in the Political Development of the New States," *World Politics* 12 (April 1960), pp. 329–368.

9

Society as Organization and Process

SOCIETY AS A NETWORK OF ORGANIZATIONAL INTERESTS

Interests and Institutions

There is a long sociological tradition that views society as a network of interdependent interests. According to the utilitarian tradition, a system of interdependent interests is the other side of the coin of the division of labor. The division of labor, by specializing each man's contributions, makes him dependent on the contributions of others and, accordingly, gives him an interest in cooperating with others through exchange. Spencer used this argument as foundation for his notion that modern society is a "regime of contract." Parsons, in considering the relations between institutional spheres to be a network of exchanges reflecting the interdependence of specialized spheres (see chapter eight), is merely extending Spencer's argument (which posited individuals as units) to a society made up of institutional sectors. However, Parsons (like Durkheim before him) insists that relationships of exchange must be "institutionalized"; there must be a framework of institutional order outside of the network of interests to ensure stability in the face of a rapidly changing pattern of interests. For Durkheim, a contract does not merely express a temporary identity of interests; it binds the parties even after interests change to a stable framework of normative order that establishes contract as a social institution addressed to problems of coordination.

The imagery of this approach suggests two levels of society: first, a level of interest-driven activity—mobile, ever changing, and unstable—and second, a level of institutions—stable and integrative. Such imagery leaves out other levels and sources of stability, structural sources that lie behind the patterning of interests, and organizational forces that stabilize interests at the collective level. More concretely stated, it leaves out the stability found in a layer of organization sometimes referred to as *vested interests*. In economic exchange, for example, partners maintain their relationship through the ups and downs of short-term variations in interests because they have made investments in each other. It would cost resources to seek and establish a new partner. To change partners is to lose all the investments built up in good will and influence, in communications habits, in the mutual adjustment of routines, in the predictability that comes from knowledge of one another, and also in unrecoverable material items that the partner may be holding.

The brunt of the foregoing argument is that the analysis of society as a network of interests must not be confined to analysis at the institutional level. We must also begin to develop (as several capable scholars already have) the study of relations between organizations at other levels.

For example, J. D. Thompson and W. J. McEwen have made an important contribution to the study of interorganizational relationships by distinguishing four types of relationships, which they arrange in order of increasing support of organizations for each other and decreasing separation of the organizations.[1] The types range from *competition*, where there is no direct contact, through *bargaining*, where contact is in the form of limited short-term agreements, to *cooptation* and, finally, *coalition formation*. Cooptation refers to incorporating the leaders of another organization into an organization's leadership structure, and coalition formation refers to a commitment to joint decisions. From the present perspective, this typology has the advantage of call-

---

[1] James D. Thompson and William McEwen, "Organizational Goals and Their Environment," *American Sociological Review* 23 (February 1958), pp. 23–31.

ing attention to the various levels of investment that groups make in each other. Nevertheless, the scheme fails to adequately suggest the wealth and variety of interorganizational forms in modern society and the networks of interests that flow from these forms. How do we interpret such complex forms as the contract of franchise, sponsorship, or the interlocking directorate?

A Scheme of Interorganizational Relations and Interests

Several strategic assumptions form the basis of the scheme of interorganizational relations and interests:

1) The division of labor and the differentiation of control over resources makes groups interested in forming stable relationships. These relationships may be complementary, founded on interdependent interests, or supplementary, founded on a desire to increase access to a resource or goal by forming an alliance.

2) Organizations are linked in a variety of ways. Their memberships overlap, they form alliances, they have power over each other, etc.

3) When organizations, in order to further complementary and supplementary interests, make investments in links to other organizations, the interest in stabilizing relationships is reinforced. The resulting pattern of interorganizational links is a *network of vested interests.*

4) When vested interests become vested in a second sense, that is legitimized by a normative and legal order, the resulting structure becomes particularly resistant to change, for it is supported at three levels, the level of first order interests, the level of vested interests, and the level of institutional legitimacy.

Links fall into two main classes, links between separate organizations and links resulting from overlapping memberships. Let us take the former class first. Links between separate organizations are of two types. Either groups form an *alliance* for the pursuit of common or mutually beneficial ends, or one group *borrows* the facilities of another group in order to indirectly increase access to a target population. The contract of exchange, the political alliance, and the joint authorship are diverse examples of alliances.

The interorganizational borrowing of facilities occurs when a centrally located organization tries to increase access to an ultimate clientele by using the facilities of locally based associations. When the Boy Scouts of America organizes through local church-sponsored scouting groups, or when Kentucky Fried Chicken obtains outlets by selling franchises to local dealers, we have examples of this type of link. In both cases, sponsorship and the franchise, one organization "borrows" the facilities of a local organization to gain indirect access to a clientele.[2]

The links that derive from overlapping membership can also be divided into two subclasses according to whether the overlap involves purposive penetration or a given pattern of common membership. A pattern of common membership derives from the established social structure rather than from deliberate attempts to link organizations. It is exemplified by overlapping affiliations to traditional groupings. The Irish subgroup in American society is so linked to the Catholic church, and there are countless similar examples.

Purposive penetration, on the other hand, involves the deliberate attempt to utilize overlapping memberships for integrative purposes, either to consolidate control over or to come to terms with organizations whose aims are potentially competitive or disruptive. Such links have many forms.

Cooptation is one classic example. As defined by Philip Selznick, cooptation refers to "the process of absorbing new elements into the leadership or policy-determining structure of an organization as a means of averting threats to its stability or existence."[3] Cooptation is a common form of relationship between economic and governmental organizations. When governmental agencies have precarious political support, they frequently adjust their regulative policies to suggestions made by regulatees who are either formally or informally brought into the decision-making process. One subtle form of cooptation deserves special mention, for it illustrates an intermediate form of organizational link. Sometimes organizations do not have overlapping memberships at a given point in time, but they are linked because there is an established pattern of mobility from one organization to another. Thus, if industry makes a habit of recruiting executives from amongst officials of regulatory agencies, we have, in effect, a form of latent cooptation. If the chairman of the Michigan Civil Rights Commission is given a position with the personnel department of the Ford Motor Company, it implies nothing about the

---

[2] Phillip Kunz, "Sponsorship as an Organizational Device: The Case of the Boy Scouts of America" (Unpublished doctoral dissertation, The University of Michigan, 1967).

[3] Philip Selznick, *TVA and the Grass Roots* (Berkeley: University of California Press, 1953), p. 13.

honesty of the official, but it does alert civil rights officials everywhere to the possibility of such mobility and subtly affects the working relationships of industrial and administrative officials. Penetration is used not only by weak agencies but by powerful governments desiring to consolidate their control over a far-flung and varied bureaucratic apparatus. The dual system of Soviet bureaucratic organization, where each technical unit manager has an opposite number in the form of a party official, who supervises activity from the point of view of party policy, is another example of penetration.

Organizational Relationships and Links Between Sectors

The foregoing forms of interorganizational links and the network of vested interests established by these links form connections between the institutional spheres of societies. In abstract terms, every institutional sphere is linked to other spheres not only by a common normative order and a flow of exchange, but also by a pattern of connections at the level of collective organization. This pattern gives rise to a network of established interests binding the spheres of society into a web of interconnections. To fail to consider this web is to overestimate the differentiation of society and to fail to understand the proper theoretical foundations of such concepts as "the power elite."

The web of organizational links also occurs at levels far below the power elite. Consider the relations between solidary systems and cultural systems stemming from the link of sponsorship. Let us consider the Boy Scouts of America to be a cultural (educational) organization. Insofar as the scouting movement uses solidary organizations as a means of sponsoring scouting activity at the local level, then solidary inclusions, exclusions, and segregations will be introduced into the movement. If segregation exists in a sponsoring church, it will be reproduced in the sponsored scouting activity. Thus, features of the structure of the solidary system are transmitted to the cultural system by virtue of the character of the organizational link between them.

The Incongruence of System Boundaries

In previous chapters we have repeatedly noted the incongruity of the boundaries of the various subsystems of society. Economic systems expand beyond the range of solidary systems and political controls. Political control expands beyond the range of political community. Some cultural systems, deeply embedded in solidary institutions, fail to extend to the boundaries of the nation, and other cultural systems totally transcend national boundaries. Intersocietal contact and penetration have been a vital element of history; economic and political expansion have repeatedly increased the territorial scope of action systems. Despite the rise of the nation-state as a system with relatively controlled boundaries, the incidence of cross-societal contact continues to grow. By one recent reckoning, contacts between citizens of different nations are increasing at a rate of between 5 and 10 percent per year.[4]

At this point, the positive strength of social-system theory deserves recognition. The various social functions *are* interdependent, and, for this reason, the incongruity of system boundaries creates malintegration and tensions. These tensions are dynamic forces in social life. For example, the integration of a political system implies political community, and, in the absence of the extension of solidary loyalties to the boundaries of the nation, political community is difficult to achieve. Wider systems tend to be unstable when the other systems that they depend upon are integrated only over a narrower population.

At the same time, the present analysis rejects the idea that integrative strains are always solved by increased functional differentiation and institutionalized exchanges between differentiated sectors. Problems of incongruence of boundaries are met by a variety of types of interpenetration, which sometimes lead to specialization and sometimes to new forms of the structural merger of functions. In some cases, when the tensions between two incongruously bounded systems are met, the boundaries of a third system are further extended. Some of the varied dynamics of response to incongruity can be clarified by examining some common types of integrative process. These are, of course, only analytically distinct types. Concrete processes of integration usually involve a mixture of processes:

1) *Institutional penetration* occurs when a wider system obtains the required support of a narrower system by penetrating organizational life within the narrower system.

2) *Parallel organizational development* occurs when the

[4] Robert C. Angell, "The Growth of Transnational Participation," *Journal of Social Issues* 23 (January 1967), pp. 108–129.

wider system meets functional problems that are not met by narrower systems by developing, within its own boundaries, parallel organizations for that purpose.

3) *Cross-cutting organizational development* occurs when the wider system obtains support by creating organizations that include members from the various fragmented sectors of the narrower system.

4) *Extension* occurs when actors in the wider system, because sufficient support cannot be obtained from narrower systems, turn to even broader intersocietal systems to create resources, thereby enhancing the organizational life of these intersocietal systems.

Each of the four processes can be illustrated with reference to a crucial problem of incongruence, the development of a political system at the level of the nation-state in the absence of the extension of national loyalties in the population. This situation occurs when the political process produces a state whose territorial sovereignty embraces a population divided into solidary ethnic subdivisions whose horizons and loyalties do not extend to the total population. This problem is often referred to as the problem of "mobilization," on the assumption that it is solved by moving members of the population out of an isolated daily round, completely encapsulated by a local traditional group, and into an organizational life that transcends traditional group memberships. It is also referred to as the problem of the development of societal community.

Institutional Penetration

Arthur L. Stinchcombe, following a long line of studies on the small primary group, has argued that solidarity exists within large communities only when the "communal group is a group whose writ runs in the primary groups and smaller communities of which it is composed."[5] The culture of the community forms a part of the culture of the smaller groups, overriding anticommunal interests and inculcating communal loyalties. Stinchcombe further argues that the solidarity of the community depends on the richness of its organizational life, because it is within associations that primary groups become accessible to the culture of the larger group. Communal symbols are transmitted to primary groups as their members participate in intermediate

[5] Stinchcombe, "Social Structure and Organizations," p. 186.

level organizations.[6] Without necessarily accepting the idea that these communal symbols are symbols of consensus and solidarity, I would make a parallel argument that the penetration of the solidary life of large solidary subgroups by the nation-state depends on the richness of associational life within the subgroup. It is difficult for the nation-state to penetrate the primary group directly, but, if ethnic groups or other large solidary groups carry on group activity at an intermediate level, these groups are subject to penetration by the political system.

An example of this is the politicization of the Indian caste. Caste-based political associations have become party-like units within the Indian political arena.[7] In the process, caste members are brought within the orbit of broad-scale politics, not by elimination of solidary subunits, but by penetration of these units by a larger political system. In Stinchcombe's terms, the "writ" of the nation comes to run in the caste system. Ethnic politics in Western nations (whenever it is not separatist in character) constitutes a similar example. Of course, penetration can be more deliberate, as in the case of a national political party that deliberately attempts to infiltrate solidary life by planting party cadre in villages and ethnic associations. In any event, penetration is not a form of differentiation of institutional spheres; it is a response to incongruence that increases the interpenetration and merger of the two incongruous systems.

Nevertheless, penetration does not guarantee that penetrated groups will themselves be integrated, cohesive, or peaceful. The more the writ of the nation runs in its smaller units, the more the cleavages and conflicts of the nation become focal issues within these units. Witness the playing out of current American racial conflicts within local associations and especially within local communities. The pervasiveness of the conflict is an indication of the breadth and depth of the cleavage of solidarity; at the same time, its similarity from community to community is an indication that the writ of the nation, however confused, permeates community life.[8]

[6] Ibid., p. 187.

[7] For example, see Lloyd and Suzanne Rudolph, "The Political Role of India's Caste Associations," *Pacific Affairs* 33 (March 1960), pp. 5–22; M. N. Srinivas, *Caste in Modern India* (Bombay: Asia Publishing House, 1962); Robert L. Hardgrave, *The Nadars of Tamiland* (Berkeley: University of California Press, 1969).

[8] See Albert J. Reiss, Jr., "Some Sociological Issues About American Communities," in *American Sociology*, ed. Talcott Parsons (New York: Basic Books, Inc. Publishers, 1968), pp. 66–74.

Parallel Organizational Development

A national political system may come to extend the loyalties of subgroups through a state takeover of a part of the socializing function. This involves building a parallel set of socializing associations, e.g., a set of national primary schools, within the state itself as a part of the official governmental apparatus. In this case, integration is not a matter of penetrating ongoing solidary life, but of creating new organizations for building national solidarity by teaching national symbols and loyalties under the aegis of the state. Again we see not differentiation but the specialization and incorporation of cultural institutions within the political system.

Cross-cutting Organizational Development

Even within a national educational system, individual schools may include only members of a solidary subgroup, especially at the primary level; but at the level of higher education, a national educational system, by drawing talented persons from a widely dispersed territory, brings together persons of diverse solidary identities. This is an example of cross-cutting organization.

The development of political and economic organization also incorporates the members of solidary groups into relationships outside the group. Stinchcombe has noted that the incorporation of smaller groups into the nation depends on the degree to which the smaller groups are not "institutionally complete."[9] If the smaller groups do not contain within themselves self-sufficient economic and political apparatus, their members are drawn into the organizational life of a larger group, one with more extended membership. John H. Kunkel, in a survey of the degree of participation of Mexican villages in a national culture, showed that the main explanatory variable was the strength of the ties of the village to the national economy.[10]

In the case of cross-cutting organizational development, the development of congruence between the boundaries of the solidary and the political system is enhanced by differentiation. The elaboration of specialized political and economic institutions

[9] Stinchcombe, "Social Structure and Social Organizations," p. 188.

[10] John H. Kunkel, "Economic Autonomy and Social Change in Mexican Villages," *Economic Development and Cultural Change* 10 (October 1961), pp. 51–63.

draws the population into new cross-cutting groups that can sustain a sense of participation in national life.

Extension

The foregoing arguments have presumed the existence of a national culture to form a foundation for national solidarity. According to the model of social change that we have referred to as the "constraints model," such national cultures exist. According to the constraints model, it is only necessary to develop an associational life to teach and sustain national culture and to adapt it to concrete problems of modernization as they arise. In fact, in an ethnically diverse "plural" society, such a cultural tradition may not exist. It must be created by an intellectual elite who, drawing on both particularistic traditions and modern ideologies, create a set of national symbols of history, identity, aspiration, and destiny. Insofar as such elites draw upon modern ideologies, they draw upon intersocietal cultural systems and movements. Nationalist elites in developing nations were exposed to Western ideologies of nationalism, socialism, progress, Marxism, etc. As students they had contact with each other in Western universities, and they continue to interact as they jointly build the ideologies of development. Thus, the search for national identity has as a latent consequence the further development of intersocietal cultural systems.

The concept of extension, and our example of it, can, in a sense, be fitted into the framework of the theory of constraints. The example presumes a body of cultural premises on which problem-solving actors can draw; it is just that this body of culture extends even beyond the nation. But some processes of extension are more instrumental and, as such, are validated more by their de facto efficacy than by any historic cultural justification. Thus, even though Germany had a common cultural heritage, the "Bismarckian" unification of Germany as a nation was largely a product of the successful prosecution of three wars and the annexation of French territory, which served as symbol of a supposed common German need to protect the Fatherland from French aggression. Bismarck, despite his domestic unpopularity, was able to activate the international political system in such a way as to involve the traditional German states in a common international political enterprise. National commitments were activated by extending the de facto political system.[11]

LAW: A SUMMARY EXAMPLE OF
INSTITUTIONAL INTERPENETRATION

At several points, the word "law" has entered the discussion. The institutional organization of the economy involves a wide array of legal forms for stabilizing joint activity. A bureaucratically organized polity is ordered by a set of legal norms defining the rights, powers, and limitations of office. Given the complexity of modern financial and bureaucratic arrangements, modernity implies a high degree of legal development, that is, the elaboration and specification of a set of legal norms. Because of the breadth and variety of the normative order in a modern society and the complexity of the integrative and regulative problems involved, it is not surprising that modernization entails the growth of legal specialization. Specialized roles and organizations emerge to deal with integrative and normative issues, to cope with the problems involved in constructing, elaborating, disseminating, and interpreting legal norms. Courts, administrative agencies, the legal profession, and law schools involve actors in a continuing process of constructing and interpreting legal norms and adapting them to the complicated ordering problems presented by modern activity and institutions. The interdependent activity involved in this interpretive process can be termed a legal system.

Because of the importance of the function of institutional integration in legal systems, Parsons treats the legal system as the integrative subsystem of the social system in a modern society. The differentiation of a legal system so that integrative problems can be met in their own terms (without arbitrary and constricting religious or political interference) increases the functional capacity of the social system and is a hallmark of modernity, indeed, an evolutionary universal. Such institutional phenomena as specialized techniques of legal argument and rule-making, a specialized and autonomous legal profession, and a system of independent courts constitute the differentiation of a legal system.

This conception of the legal system puts the concept of modern society as a differentiated social system to a severe test and provides an illustration of the characteristic weakness of this theoretical standpoint. The placement of law in the integrative

---

[11] See Emil Ludwig, *Bismarck*, trans. Eden and Cedar Paul (Boston: Little, Brown and Company, 1928), especially p. 359.

system of the social system rests on an analytical distinction between law as a process of elaborating, constructing, and interpreting norms and law as a process of enforcing norms. The latter is then alleged to be a political function. Concretely, it is the function of the court to decide questions of the meanings of legal norms and their applicability to specific questions; it is the function of the political system to enforce those decisions. The placement of law in the integrative system also rests on an analytical distinction between policy-making and the incorporation of policy into specifically legal norms. The former involves the general setting of social goals and is political in character; the latter involves the construction of legally binding norms to implement the policy and the articulation of these norms with the total complex of legal norms.

As analytical distinctions, these separations between law and policy are useful; they offer a good antidote to the popular concept of law as a process of enforcing norms. These distinctions turn our attention to some of the distinctive qualities of legal activity—its orientation to the elaboration of argument, its concern for internal consistency, its creative impulse. But law is not law if it is not articulated with the political system. The difference between law and legal interpretation and other normative processes is that the outcomes of the former are *enforceable.* The close connection between law and the political sphere creates so much interpenetration between them that the distinction between them is only analytical; it does not refer to two separate and structurally distinct institutional realms.

Insofar as such institutions as judicial independence *do* create real separations between the realm of the legal and the realm of the political, the problem of integration of the two spheres exists. In the United States, the problem is especially crucial at the level of the higher appelate courts, where the legal process often turns on matters of normative interpretation. It then becomes quite important to study the relation between legal and political processes conceived as structurally separate entities. How has the political realm reacted to legal decisions calling for desegregation of schools, and how will the legal realm respond to new interests in the political arena calling for forms of black separatism? How will police and prosecutors respond to changes in constitutional standards governing criminal law? Such questions might profitably be treated in terms of inputs and outputs between interdependent systems, and proposals for such analysis have been made.[12] But to look at the relation between law and other parts of society exclusively in these terms is to overlook not only the often noted political elements and connotations of political decisions, but also, more crucially, to overlook the deep embedding of the legal process in the structure of society.

The American legal system provides an excellent example of this problem. In a sense, it is highly autonomous and differentiated. There are a set of independent appelate courts, an organized legal profession, and a set of law schools that produce not only professional lawyers but a voluminous body of specialized legal writing. And yet the legal process as an ongoing process of concrete activity is linked to the polity, to the economy, to systems of solidarity and stratification, and to cultural systems in a variety of direct, organized, and structured ways. The legal profession is highly stratified, and high-status lawyers tend to come from the higher strata of society, to be trained in high-status educational institutions, and to serve high-status clients and the more important economic interests.[13] The lower level metropolitan courts are highly politicized, and the low-status lawyers who actively participate in them are forced to ignore standards of conduct established by the higher strata of the bar.[14]

The more we focus on the rarefied atmosphere of the highest level of appelate courts and of academic discussion, the more we can see law as a differentiated system concerned with constructing and interpreting a normative order. The more we look at the day-to-day ordering process as it occurs at lower levels in the legal hierarchy, the more inescapable the conclusion that law is structurally linked to the general organizational life of society.

In analytical theory, the police are an enforcing rather than an interpretive body, but the police cannot avoid interpreting the law as they engage in their daily rounds. Moreover, the police are brought into the daily life of the community. The most routine police activity is reactive; it is in response to calls from the community. As the police operate in answering these calls, they are responsive to and interpret the cultural norms of the subgroups that call upon their services—here breaking up a fight,

---

[12] Parsons, *Theory and Modern Society*, p. 350; Harry C. Bredemeir, "Law as an Integrative Mechanism," in *Law and Sociology*, ed. William M. Evan (Glencoe, Ill.: The Free Press, 1962), pp. 73–90.

[13] Erwin O. Smigel, *The Wall Street Lawyer* (New York: The Free Press, 1964).

[14] Jerome Carlin, *Lawyers' Ethics* (New York: Russell Sage Foundation, 1966), pp. 87–93.

here giving a "dutch uncle" lecture in a domestic dispute, there deciding to let events run their natural course.[15]

This responsive and reactive character of the legal process is crucial to an understanding of the sense in which it is not differentiated. Even the highly specialized agency, set up to be a reordering force on the established social order, can, by simply acting as a reactive agency responding to the pressures and disputes that confront it, reproduce in its own activity the same conditions it was designed to change.

This author's study of the Massachusetts Commission Against Discrimination (MCAD) demonstrates in concrete detail the embedding of the legal process in the structures of society and serves to illustrate the main theme of this chapter.[16] Massachusetts' law provides that any person who feels that he has been a target of discrimination may bring a complaint to the MCAD. The agency has the responsibility for investigating such allegations and, if they find probable cause for believing them to be true, the commission must attempt to eliminate discriminatory practices. The private complaint of the aggrieved individual is the key that unlocks the door of the firm and legitimates MCAD investigation of the entire range of the firm's policies and practices. What more effective means of discovering discrimination than to allow the targets of discrimination to activate the legal machinery? Those who are most hurt will have the most reason to complain, and this should lead to efficient use of the limited resources available for investigation.

The facts do not support this theory of enforcement. Investigation unearthed the fact that the mean percentage of Negroes employed at firms that had been targets of complaints was twice the percentage of Negroes in the labor force of the community. Further, most of the jobs in question were of the sort that were already readily available to Negroes. There was a noticeable lack of the pioneering, strategic complaints that could give the commission access to significant targets.[17] The pattern of complaints seemed to reflect not a differentiated legal purpose—the elimination of discrimination—but the established structure of discrimination.

---

[15] Donald J. Black, "Police Encounters and Social Organization: An Observation Study" (Unpublished doctoral dissertation, The University of Michigan, 1968).

[16] Leon Mayhew, Law and Equal Opportunity.

[17] Ibid., pp. 152–198.

These findings, though ironic, were neither inexplicable or unexpected. The private complaints of individuals reflect everyday life, which in turn is structured by an established set of social arrangements. The Negro citizen, as he looks for employment, goes to firms where he thinks work might be available. He follows leads given by friends, relatives, and neighbors. The information network in which he participates is itself racially structured. Hence, the pattern of complaints reflects the very structure that is being attacked. The pattern of routine complaints reflects the established boundaries of community life; it does not extend to the sectors of associational life in which the potential complainant does not participate. What we see here is a subtle form of *de facto* segregation. The social segregation and isolation of the Negro community is reproduced in all patterns of Negro activity, even in the pattern of complaints to an antidiscrimination agency! In the meantime, MCAD officials acquired a vested interest in this strategy of enforcement, for it helped to establish their political position by keeping them in contact with those business firms that were easiest to deal with rather than those who, because they *did* discriminate, might make political trouble for the agency if they were pushed. On the other hand, middle-class Negroes, supported by civil rights groups, were able to push the MCAD into a more militant position in their enforcement of a similar law forbidding discrimination in housing.[18] In sum, the activities of a very specialized legal agency could only be understood in the context of the location of these activities in a structure of segregated information networks, residential patterns of segregation, stratification, and organizational interests.

SOME COMPARATIVE AND EVOLUTIONARY PERSPECTIVES

Evolution and Comparative Analysis

The approach and concepts of this book have been critical of the conception of society as a social system undergoing a process of evolutionary functional differentiation. These criticisms have implications for several underlying issues of comparative analysis. The failures of the evolutionary theory of the social system stem from the same intractable social facts that create many of

[18] Ibid., pp. 278–283.

the most formidable problems of comparative analysis, the facts of societal overlap and institutional interpenetration.

Orthodox evolutionary theory, as it has been developed by Parsons and various others, makes two strategic working assumptions:

1) Incongruent boundaries among the subsystems of neighboring societies are unstable. Hence, there is a long-run evolutionary tendency toward boundaries congruent with the territorial jurisdiction of the nation-state. Thus, the process of evolution will make concrete societies more closely resemble the self-sufficient social systems of analytical theory.

2) Analytically pure functional subsystems cross-cut the concrete institutions of society. However, since the functional capacity of any society is increased by structural differentiation along functional lines, the process of evolution will produce societies made up of functionally separate structural spheres.

Were these assumptions correct, sociological analysis would be simplified by the process of social evolution since, in the long run, two crucial problems of comparative analysis will be solved. First, we will come to have a large number of independent societal units to form a universe of comparison; second, the societal units will be made up of comparable structural components. In the meantime, we are not so fortunate and must try to study societies as they are.

The Problem of Comparable Structural Units

One of the classic problems of comparative analysis stems from the incomparability of superficially similar structural elements. Roles, groups, and institutions that appear to be similar (because they are called by the same name or are similar in some other inconsequential way) are found, upon closer examination, to be profoundly different in the concrete activities and functions performed and in their place in a larger structure. Richard E. Neustadt has pointed out that the United States has counterparts to the cabinet ministers in the United Kingdom, but not mainly in the president's cabinet. Our equivalent of cabinet ministers are, for the most part, the various congressional leaders and other men of independent influence who represent *political interests in the inner circles* of presidential power.[19] As Neustadt

---

[19] Richard E. Neustadt, "White House and Whitehall," *The Public Interest* 2 (Winter 1966), pp. 55–69.

emphasizes, activity, not nomenclature, is the key to locating counterparts.

The example underlines the difficulties in undertaking comparative analysis when similar functional activities are embodied in variable structures. What is performed in one system within a differentiated structure by actors who are specifically assigned the relevant duties is performed in another system informally, as an aspect of other apparently quite different activity, beneath the surface of public life, even under the cloak of deliberate secrecy. As long as our categories are analytical in character (and they must be if they are to have precision and cross-societal applicability), the identification of equivalent activities in various systems will present serious difficulties.

The Problem of a Universe of Independent Societal Units

The usual mode of testing sociological hypotheses with statistical rigor is to look for associations between variables across an array of "independent" units. The more a relation holds across a set of independent examples, the more confident we become that it is not an accident. But as any neophyte statistician knows, the assumption of independence is logically essential. If the boundaries of the constituent systems of a number of societies overlap, it is difficult to assert that these societies are independent. Francis Galton originally raised this problem in 1889 when Edward Tylor first introduced the cross-cultural method.[20] The problem of distinguishing "historical" from "functional" associations in cross-cultural societies has since been known as "Galton's problem."[21]

The problem can be illuminated by comparing two studies of "the birth of the Gods." E. O. James, in *The Ancient Gods*, arguing that the ancient Near East and Eastern Mediterranean comprised a single vast culture complex,[22] traces the develop-

[20] Report of Galton's comments on Edward B. Tylor's first reading of his classic paper "On a Method of Investigating the Development of Institutions." Tylor's paper and Galton's objection are reprinted in Frank W. Moore, ed., *Readings in Cross-Cultural Methodology* (New Haven, Conn.: Human Relations Area Files Press, 1961), pp. 1–25.

[21] Raoul Naroll, "Two Solutions to Galton's Problem," in *Cross-Cultural Methodology*, ed. Frank Moore, pp. 221–245.

[22] E. O. James, *The Ancient Gods* (New York: Capricorn Books, 1964).

ment and diffusion of religious ideas within this entire region, considering local differences to be but variations on a common theme. Such themes as the marriage of the fertility goddess to the young divine consort, the annual death and resurrection of this young god, and the ritual dramatic reenactment of the annual cycle in a set of seasonal festivals are considered to be symbolic representations of the seasonal changes. The beliefs and rituals are traced to common sources, their diffusion and adaptation is examined, and new versions are observed in later religious developments. Unfortunately, want of comparative evidence makes it impossible for such an approach to demonstrate any causal or functional relations. James can only say, "Aha! I have found another example."

By contrast, Guy E. Swanson, in the *Birth of the Gods*, takes a sample of fifty "societies," primitive and historical, and tests several hypotheses about the relation between social structure and sacred symbols on the assumption that each "society" is an independent unit.[23] In this way, Swanson is able to show, to cite but one example, an association between the presence of belief in supernatural sanctions for sin and the presence of the institution of debt.[24] His causal argument is that debt increases the tensions in social relationships, making additional supernatural support necessary to maintain the social order. Swanson also shows that this relationship is not a spurious product of the involvement of societies with debt in the common culture of the civilized world. Belief in supernatural sanctions shows no association with societal complexity as such. As compared with James, Swanson appears to have the advantage of having explained something. Since Swanson, in selecting his sample, employed procedures specifically designed to avoid choosing societies with close historical connections, and since there is no reason to suppose that the relationship that he unearthed is a product of some more-remote connections (such as participation in the cultural orbit of civilization), his statistical evidence is *relatively* immune to the strictures we are discussing.

Suppose, on the other hand, that a hypothetical sociologist told me that he had found an association between the myth of a dying and resurrected God and the presence of full-time religious specialists. No matter how plausible his causal argument, I would be quite skeptical of his evidence, on the grounds that

---

[23] Swanson, *Birth of the Gods.*

[24] Ibid., pp. 153–174, esp. pp. 166–167.

James has shown that this myth was a part of the general culture of the ancient civilized world and is also, of course, part of the religious symbolism of Christianity.

Unfortunately, many cross-societal studies are subject to precisely this criticism, or to some variant of it. Contemporary cross-polity studies of modernization usually include each nation-state in the world for which data are available, apparently on the patently false assumption that each society is an independent unit. Modernization is clearly a process within an international system. Certain features of modernity have been forcibly imposed upon non-Western nations; others have been accepted voluntarily. Still others have been incorporated into the structure of non-Western societies because participation in the international system requires adaptation to the characteristics of that system. Studies of the social correlates of modernity among a cross section of nation-states at a given point in time clearly capitalize on historical connections between societies, and on similarities between societies that entered the world system of modernization at given points in time and must therefore be used only with great caution. It is very difficult to assess the strength of the evidence they present. Investigators clearly take some cross-national correlations seriously only because they are plausible in terms of prior theoretical assumptions. Others would certainly be interpreted as historically accidental rather than causal or functional in character. A correlation between political modernity and railroad mileage is taken as reflecting something inevitable about modernity; the mobilization of a population requires facilities to move members around. On the other hand, one need only consider what to make of a correlation between an index of modernity and the percentage of the population speaking an Indo-European language to see that a correlation itself proves nothing about causal and functional correlates of modernity. There is obviously nothing intrinsically more modern about European languages. What, beyond surface plausibility, would make us think railroads are any different in this respect? Indeed, the specific correlation between development and railroads is probably closely related to the prominence of railway transportation during the development of societies that entered early into the intersocietal systems of modernization. Modern communications devices might even make it increasingly possible to substitute communications for transportation. Hence, the current correlation between modernity and transportation might become attenuated over time. To lift a phrase, present associations may not hold in the future because "in the future nations will become modern in modern times."[25]

Apart from the pros and cons of this particular issue, the abstract problem should be clear: If the units of a universe are units within a single system, then correlations between attributes of the units are poor evidence for causal or functional relations between these attributes. Such correlations may reflect similarities between units that entered a changing system at a given point in time. Or, they may reflect similarities between units that play a similar role within a differentiated system. They may reflect similarities within groups of units that are relatively closely integrated with each other by regional or historic ties. In any event, one cannot, in the absence of rigorous precautions, assume that given societies manifest independent instances of the relations between items of social organization.

It is a mistake to identify this problem exclusively with "Galton's problem." Galton was worried about whether societies were not independent units because of the diffusion of cultural items across societal boundaries, and this particular problem can be attacked in a number of ways. The cultural link of diffusion is only one form of link between societies. Systematic political and economic connections pose parallel and even more challenging difficulties.

Societal Typologies

One device for reducing the variety and complexity found in human societies to manageable proportions is the societal typology. The concept of a type is one of the most controversial notions in sociological literature.[26] For some sociologists, typological construction is an unavoidable task, for others, a cardinal sin. To argue against all typological classification on the grounds that it fails to deal with the world in all of its concrete variety and detail is to argue against abstraction. In this sense, a variable, or

[25] Jonathan Mayhew, personal communication, in response to the question, Do you think that railroads will be as important in the future in making new countries modern as they were in making countries modern in the past? My eight year old son appears to understand these things even if a few sociologists do not.

[26] For a bibliography on this subject, see John C. McKinney, Constructive Typology and Social Theory (New York: Appleton-Century-Crofts, 1966). See also Edward A. Tiryakian, "Typologies," International Encyclopedia of the Social Sciences 16: 177–186.

indeed any analytical tool, is a "type," and to argue against typologies is to argue against science. But the opponents of typology usually mean the word in a more limited sense. They are thinking of classificatory systems of types of society (or of personality, institutions, or roles), that list combinations of discrete attributes or traits in order to define a type and thereby facilitate comparative analysis.

Properly used, societal typologies may be a guide to theory construction or a prod to the sociological imagination. On the other hand typologies are dangerous when they come to be seen as empirical descriptions of actual classes of concrete societies. It can even be argued that societal typologies by their very nature obscure the most essential characteristics of societies as social organizations. Societies exist precisely because they are not types.

At this point, some previous themes should be reemphasized. The emphasis on society as a process of human action, the depiction of that action as flexible, instrumental, and adaptive in character, the argument for a tendency for system boundaries to break or expand in the face of instrumental human conduct — all of these themes reflect a certain image of society. Societies as human organizations must not only meet conditions of continuity and integration, they must also meet the problem of adaptation. They must come to terms with the variety and complexity of the environment[27] and with the varied range of human and social problems. The autonomy of individual behavior, its adaptive movement across established boundaries, *its processual quality*, is part and parcel of its adaptive organization. To depict societies as falling into categories defined by multiple sets of fixed attributes is to depict societies that could not exist. Societies exist because of the possibility of including attributes and their opposites in the same organization, and because it is not necessary to make discrete jumps from one attribute to another. Constant incremental changes here and there maintain the adaptation of society.

To illustrate this rather abstract point, typological reification is behind the common trap of viewing tradition and modernity as mutually exclusive. A number of scholars are beginning to see that such an assumption is both empirically false and functionally impossible. A society can incorporate technological changes

---

[27] Buckley, *Sociology and Modern Systems Theory.*

without immediately transforming the entire panoply of tradition. Some tradition can be (and is) incorporated into the modern order.[28] In the case of the Japanese factory, traditional feudal social relations are adapted to the industrial context.[29] Caste associations have become units in a modernized political order of India.[30] Were such phenomena impossible, modernization would be either impossible or disruptive to an almost inconceivable degree. If there were literally two types of society, traditional and modern, then the process of modernization would compel each actor to make a forced choice between being completely immobile or utterly disregarding all of his prior investments.

Because so-called modern societies incorporate nonmodern features, to designate a society as modern and let it go at that is profoundly misleading. It blinds us to the actual structure and functioning of contemporary societies. We cannot view contemporary society as a mere opposite of traditional society. Nor can we see the traditional elements of modern societies as mere nonfunctional vestiges of an earlier past. They remain an integral component of modern social structure; their meaning may change, and their mode of integration with the larger society may take on new forms, but their social significance remains.

The foregoing discussion allows another opportunity to make a summary statement of the weakness of the concept of society as a self-sufficient social system: The self-sufficient society, unified by common values, protecting its internal structure by regulating its boundaries, differentiated along functional lines, and integrated by institutionalized exchanges between subsystems, *is a proposed ideal-typical model of the most highly evolved possible social system.* As such, it can provide insight into some of the processes, forces, and problems of modernization; it can provide models of some of the subtle processes that occur in relatively differentiated societies. But, as an ideal type, it describes a society that does not and cannot literally exist. Accordingly, the study of ongoing societies, even the most advanced ones, requires additional tools of analysis.

---

[28] Joseph Gusfield, "Tradition and Modernity: Misplaced Polarities in the Study of Social Change," *American Journal of Sociology* 72 (January 1967), pp. 351–362; Reinhard Bendix, "Tradition and Modernity Reconsidered," *Comparative Studies in Society and History* 9 (April 1967), pp. 292–346; Stinchcombe, "Social Structure and Organization"; Mayhew, "Ascription in Modern Society."

[29] James C. Abegglen, *The Japanese Factory* (Glencoe, Ill.: The Free Press, 1958).

[30] See Footnote 7, above.

Evolution, Development, and Modernization

Much of our previous discussion assumes, explicitly or implicitly, that societies undergo a process of evolution or development. In chapter two, evolution was described as a process of technological advancement, differentiation, and the centralization of control. In chapter three, societal populations were described as becoming larger and more mobile. These themes played an important part in the description of the institutional spheres of society in chapters four through seven.

Adequate treatment of the full range of problems involved in the study of development would raise issues well beyond the scope of the present volume, as would exposition of the various evolutionary schemes that have been proposed. The overlap and differences between the diverse concepts of evolution, development, modernization, industrialization, urbanization, Westernization, and mobilization, present numerous problems and difficulties. As in the case of problems of comparative method, only a few of the most important implications of previous chapters will be discussed. In order to make discourse possible, a few simple and imprecise definitions of the relevant terms will be necessary. Evolution and development will be taken as equivalent terms referring to the gradual movement in human history toward more and more control of energy through the social organization of technological advancement. Modernity refers to current conceptions of the most "advanced" stage of evolution, a stage characterized by the institutionalization of science, mass education, the bureaucratic state, the industrial economy, extended national loyalties, and a mobile population. Westernization, industrialization, and urbanization are specific sources of the thrust toward modernity. Mobilization is the process by which a population is brought within the purview of the economic, political, cultural, and solidary forces, and the institutions and markets of modern society.

Evolution and History

In broaching the subject of evolution in chapter two, it was remarked that any evolutionary scheme can be correct only in broad general terms. A precise sequence of evolutionary changes common to all societies and continuously manifesting itself in the sweep of human history does not exist. Concrete societies and groups of societies rise and fall; new levels of societal development emerge and then fall away. This is particularly evident in the political arena, where there is a rhythm of periods of centralization of power in the hands of the state and periods of feudal decentralization. Subsequent chapters added additional evidence of the difficulties facing anyone who would make evolutionary generalizations. This is particularly true in the face of the expansion of Western civilization and the diffusion of its ideas. Which of the features of Western modernity are generically modern, and which represent peculiarly Western (indeed Anglo-American) responses to problems of modernity?

Be that as it may, it is nevertheless legitimate to speak of "evolutionary history." The task of evolutionary history is to specify the organizational mechanisms by which new levels of social integration are achieved. Are there common features to the organizational devices by which the process systems of society achieve integration across larger populations? Conversely, are there common features to evolutionary failures, to the organizational attributes of systems that fail to respond to the challenge of integrating larger populations?

Evolution and Relations Between Groups

Social evolution, as defined here, is quite different from biological evolution. Biological evolution occurs over very long time periods within populations of very large numbers of reproducing organisms. It is clear that social evolution cannot consist in the "survival-of-the-fittest" social organization. There are neither enough units, a long enough period of time, nor comparable genetic devices to make the analogy viable.[31] Social change occurs quite rapidly, and, more important, it occurs in systems that cross-cut fixed aggregates of people. The struggle for life does not occur in a large number of separate societies, each one trying out new adaptive techniques and surviving or dying out according to the adaptive capacity of their social organization. Development takes place in cross-societal systems; its impetus is in large-scale population movements, the intensification of the intersocietal division of labor, the extension of political power,

---

[31] See Arthur Stinchcombe, *Constructing Social Theories* (New York: Harcourt Brace Jovanovich, Inc., 1968), pp. 92–93; and Anatol Rapoport, "Mathematical, Evolutionary, and Psychological Approaches to the Study of Total Societies," in *Total Societies*, ed. Klausner, pp. 131–135.

and the intersocietal diffusion of cultural innovation. Behind these intersocietal changes lie technological innovations that permit more energy to be harnessed, new weapons, and population growth.

These kinds of changes intensify the problems of social integration. Such changes increase the *de facto* interdependence of aggregates of people. Solidary groups, sovereign groups, and cultural groups are brought into closer contact and the problem of consolidating the relations between previously more-separate aggregates becomes crucial. Moreover, such changes alter the established relations between the component groups within the old societies. From this perspective, the study of social evolution is not the study of a set of parallel changes within separate unit-societies, but *the study of new levels of consolidation of the relations between aggregates*. It is important to recognize that this view does not imply that systems as such are teleological actors. The motivation to change and to integrate change comes from concrete groups of actors with concrete interests, particularly from elites with an interest in consolidating the integration of systems, the better to establish their own position.

Evolution and Types of Society

The concept of evolution as the achievement of greater and greater levels of integration provides a clue to the misstep that evolutionary schemes commonly take. Having defined the problem as one of achieving new means of integration, it becomes quite natural to then present evolutionary history as a series of stages, with each stage defined in terms of a set of organizational devices with a given degree of integrative power. The analyst is then trapped by all of the difficulties of typological analysis. In particular, the evolutionary scheme fails to ground its presentation of human history in the concrete historic events that make new levels of integration problematic—wars, the movements of peoples, technological innovations, alterations in the balance of power between elites, and expansions in intersocietal systems.

This problem can be illustrated by comparing two brief schematic overviews of the civilization of the ancient Middle East, one sociological and evolutionary, the other historical. Talcott Parsons, in *Societies: Evolutionary and Comparative Perspectives*, treats the various societies of the area, Egypt and the Mesopotamian Empires, as examples of "archaic societies."[32] Archaic societies are intermediate between primitive societies and "historic empires." They are characterized by "craft literacy," that is, literacy among some persons performing specialized priestly and administrative roles, but not extending to an entire elite, let alone the total society. Such societies lack an elite class with generalized administrative capacities and generalized prestige.

The "historic" society differs from the earlier archaic society primarily in the degree to which the culture penetrates the societal structure.[33] In historic societies, culture penetrates an entire elite but does not fully penetrate the entire society. This leads to a "two-class system," and the characteristic weakness of historic societies is their failure to incorporate the new populations outside of the original center of the civilization. No idea as inclusive as the modern concept of citizenship in a national state is institutionalized as an incorporative device with the capacity to cut across and through traditional affiliations. Archaic society is *even weaker* in this regard. A differentiated culture arises, but its penetration of the social structure is so tenuous as to make integration of the society very weak. The archaic society has a three-class system—a charismatic monarch, set apart from ordinary society, a very small group of literate priestly and political functionaries, and everyone else.

These are very interesting ideas about the relative integrative and incorporative capacity of various types of cultural systems. However, Parsons treats Near Eastern archaic societies as mere examples of a stage; we are given no sense of the concrete integrative problems that they faced, of their relations with other societies, or of the expansions and contractions of their constituent systems in the face of historic confrontations and challenges. We have evolution without history.

By contrast, in *The Face of the Ancient Orient*, Sabatino Moscati presents the ancient Near East as an arena within which societies rose and fell, met or succumbed to challenges, dynamically interacted with each other and, finally, were incorporated into the Persian Empire, the first pan-Oriental administrative system.[34] First, by a process of periodic expansion and contraction,

---

[32] Parsons, *Societies*, pp. 51–68.

[33] Ibid., p. 93.

[34] Sabatino Moscati, *The Face of the Ancient Orient* (London: Routledge and Kegan Paul, Ltd., 1960).

the foundation societies of Egypt, Babylonia, and Assyria were created. Then, with the perfection of chariot warfare in about 1500 B.C., bands of nomadic barbarians began to break up the old empires. Hittites, Hurrians, and Kassites came down from the hills and challenged the ancient centers of civilization. Desert peoples established themselves in the buffer region between the two ancient centers. In consequence, the entire Oriental arena was internationalized. The forms of international relations were established, and cultural interchanges and influences spread. Eventually, the ancient centers reestablished their dominance but in a changed, less isolated, international context. Finally, the Persian Empire established hegemony throughout the region.

Moscati gives a sense of the dynamic forces in the history of the area. But we are not provided with a functional account of the organizational devices involved in the ebb and flow of archaic societies. By what means did Persia establish the superiority of her incorporative apparatus? Beyond hinting that the religious tolerance of the Persian conquerors may have been an advantage, Moscati does not help us to understand the passing of archaic society and the functional superiority of Persian institutions. We have history without evolution.

Perhaps both authors achieved what they set out to do within the limitations of time and space, but that should not alter the aspirations of history and sociology. If evolutionary schemes are to remain true to the fundamental character of human society, they must be grounded not on typological classification, but on study of the historic challenges presented by the dynamic expansion of social *activity* and the integrative devices embodied in social *institutions*. It will not do to describe these challenges in a purely abstract way as general problems present in all societies. It is necessary to examine dynamic forces as they impinge upon historic forms of organization. To ignore this task is to fall back upon the sterile evolutionary typologies — traditional-modern, sacred-secular, folk-urban, etc. — with all the dangers and fallacies inherent in such typifications.

In the contemporary context, this clearly means that the study of development must be founded on a series of studies of the impact of growth and the expansion of social systems. How has the expansion of the economic and political systems of Western nations impinged upon the social order in both Western and non-Western societies? To what extent has the response to expansion involved the attempt to mobilize populations? (Note that by the definitions of integration proposed in chapters four through seven, integration always implies social mobilization.) What are the institutional forms of mobilization, and do they have a least common denominator across all societies? For the reasons suggested above, this type of question cannot be answered on the assumption that the various nations of the world constitute just so many independent examples of traditional, modern, or transitional societies. This is the case precisely because the forces of change, the forces of expansion and modernization, open systems to external influences. When systems with opened boundaries respond to integrative problems, they draw on the resources of other societies and intersocietal systems. By implication, modernizing societies are precisely the societies that are not independent.

Values, Elites, and Modernization

One element of Parsons' theory of evolution deserves explicit recognition at this point. The integrative capacity of a society depends upon its capacity to fully incorporate all of its *de facto* population. Primitive societies incorporate their members, but they do so in the absence of differentiated authority, with limited technology, and only within relatively small groups. Archaic and historic societies develop differentiated institutions and, in a political and economic sense, incorporate large numbers of people. Their relative weakness is a product of their failure to achieve solidary and cultural incorporation of all their members. The elite culture does not penetrate the rest of the society. This insight tends to undermine some other aspects of Parsons' theory of the social system.

In Parsonian theory, a social system is a plurality of actors who share a set of common values and who interact in the context of a set of social institutions that embody these values. But in archaic and historic societies, elite values fail to penetrate the society. It follows that archaic and historic societies are not social systems. Apparently, societies can only *become* social systems as they achieve total modernity. Since even very modern societies face serious problems of incorporation, very few, if any, societies have fully attained the status of social systems.

This fact suggests an important modification of any theory of social change that emphasizes the constraints of an established moral order. New dimensions are added to the constraints theory once one drops the assumption that an entire society shares values and instead locates consensus on values within an elite.

When a society confronts problems of coordination and conflict, its members draw upon a store of cultural symbols and values in the search for a solution. If the solutions they find are successful, they become institutionalized. This process of institutionalization leads to a downward penetration of cultural values into the norms and institutions of the society. But the relevant values are elite values; they are the values of the dominant, active groups that are in a position to guide social change so as to maintain the supremacy of their own values and their own established position within the institutional order. From this point of view, what is sometimes seen as a *downward specification* of the normative meanings of value premises is also an *outward extension* of cultural values, an attempt to include more of the population within a culturally unified system of institutions.[35] When integrative problems and conflicts challenge the position of an elite, the elite seeks to maintain the social order by extending and broadening the established institutional apparatus and the elite values on which it is founded.

This process is closely related to modernization. Modernization involves mobilization, that is, the emancipation of human energy from ties to traditional enclaves, the application of mobile energy within the economic and political units of the larger society, and the harnessing of these energies in the pursuit of further social development. Mobilization implies the inclusion of the population within the various systems of society, in our terms, the integration of the constituent systems of society rather than their fragmentation into segmentary divisions. Inclusion is problematic if the groups to be included do not share the values of the elite. Elites hope that inclusion can be accomplished through relatively minor adjustments and extensions of the institutional order as it stands—such reforms as the gradual increase of suffrage within an established quasi-democratic system, increased professional representation for new interests within an established system of courts, laws purporting to guarantee equal opportunity in employment, etc. Such reforms are designed to increase the number of people and segments within the community who enjoy the legal rights and benefits bestowed by the *established* institutional system.

As earlier comments on the inclusion of the American Negro suggest, inclusion in some systems accelerates the demand for

---

[35] Cf. Talcott Parsons, "Some Considerations in the Theory of Social Change," *Rural Sociology* 26 (September, 1961), pp. 219–239. See also Shils, "Centre and Periphery."

inclusion within all systems. When the demand for immediate inclusion becomes strong, there are great strains on the integrative facilities of the society. Mere formal extension of the rights of the institutional system does not produce rapid change in the substantive structure of participation in the society. For example, the passage of fair-employment laws forbidding discrimination does not produce immediate substantive changes in the patterns of participation in the labor force. The structural sources of unequal participation are too deeply rooted in structural exclusions within the various systems of society, systems bound together in the firm and complex ways suggested in this book. The demand for more rapid substantive inclusion is, in effect, a demand for increased participation *on the disadvantaged group's own terms*, not on terms established by elites who wish to preserve the integrity of established values. Conflict moves up several levels. Groups demand not extension of rights under an established institutional system, but the radical reconstruction of the system.

Hence, paradoxically, the process of rapid inclusion can lead to revolutionary demands. Just when the lot of a disadvantaged group is becoming better, its remaining exclusions become more salient, and it demands a "fair share" now, even if that means dismantling the institutional apparatus founded on the dominant values of the elite. Moreover, modernization is an inherently unstabilizing process, for it creates new groups whose inclusion is problematic and it increases the importance of the inclusion of traditional groups. Modernization creates its own difficulties.[36]

Beyond the Nation-State

Several of the themes of this volume suggest that the nation-state may not be the end product of the process of evolution, the most inclusive, self-sufficient, and well-bounded collectivity. Although the modern nation-state exercises more intensive jurisdiction over its boundaries than other political units, intersocietal systems continue to emerge, and national citizens are partici-

---

[36] Cf. S. N. Eisenstadt, *Modernization: Protest and Change* (Englewood Cliffs, N. J.: Prentice-Hall, Inc., 1966).

pating in transnational systems at an increasing rate.[37] Parsons has noted that to some extent the whole world approximates a society.[38] Even though there is not unified control over the means of compulsion, neither is there a constant war of all against all. Apart from the obviously international economy with the cross-cutting interests it creates, there is international economic law, international cultural organization, international alliances, regional economic and political organizations and communities of interest, agencies of international cooperation, cross-national solidarities, and perhaps even a nascent international value system focusing on the valuation of modernization itself.

Our definition of society insists that unified sovereignty is not a criterion. Some societal populations are clearly characterized by divided sovereignty, just as others are cloven by reinforced divisions in the solidary system. Germany was a society before the political unification of 1870. There had long been a pan-German cultural system, a cross-state unity movement, a customs union, and a series of loose political confederations. The treaty signed at Versailles at the end of the Franco-Prussian war by representatives of twenty-odd kingdoms, principalities, duchies, and free cities did not create German society out of whole cloth; it merely transformed the character of the German polity.[39]

Similarly, many regions in the world today can be taken to be at least emergent societies despite divided sovereignty. Perhaps the future will bring political unification to these units. The evidence is that such unifications are difficult to achieve but that they occur more easily when the nations involved are *modern* rather than underdeveloped,[40] an indication that modernity does not permanently tighten the boundaries of sovereign units. The Nordic Council (Denmark, Finland, Iceland, Norway, and Sweden),[41] the European Economic Community (Common Market),

---

[37] See footnote 4, above.

[38] Talcott Parsons, "The Problem of International Community," in *International Politics and Foreign Policy* ed. James N. Rosenau (New York: The Free Press, 1961), pp. 120–129.

[39] William Harbutt Dawson, *The German Empire: 1867–1914 and the Unity Movemen* (London: George Allen and Unwin, Ltd., 1919), pp. 1–370.

[40] Amitai Etzioni, *Political Unification* (New York: Holt, Rinehart and Winston, Inc., 1965), pp. 318–321.

[41] Ibid., pp. 184–228.

and the Council of Mutual Economic Assistance[42] (primarily the Soviet Union and her East-European satellites) may presage new levels of political integration in regional societies. Whether it does or does not, the trend to international organization of one form or another is unmistakeable. The number of intergovernmental organizations and international nongovernmental associations is constantly growing. *The Yearbook of International Organizations* for 1966–1967 lists 2,134 such organizations,[43] of which about 200 were governmental and the remainder private. This represents a growth of nearly 100 percent in a decade. In view of the continuing development of transportation and communication, the broadening of horizons associated with modernization, and the progressive intensification of international trade, we cannot expect this trend to reverse. Intersocietal systems will become more important, and the boundaries between societies will become even more difficult to draw. Students of social evolution will turn their attention to the emergent organizational devices by which men seek to cope with their increased level of world contact and interdependence. If the past history of social thought gives any clue as to its future direction, we can expect to see social theorists turn their attention to the depiction of world society as an external and constraining reality and as a source for standards for international unity.

[42] Andrzej Korbonski, "COMECON: The Evolution of COMECON," in *International Political Communities* (New York: Doubleday and Company, Inc., Anchor Books, 1966), pp. 351–403.

[43] Union of International Organizations, *Yearbook of International Organizations*, 11th ed. (Brussels, 1966), p. 9.

SELECTED READINGS

[Books available in paperbound editions are indicated by an asterisk.]

The student interested in structure and process in total societies would do well to start with the two most important products of the formative era of sociological thought. These are Emile Durkheim's *The Division of Labor in Society** (hardbound: The Macmillan Company, 1933; softbound: The Free Press) and Max Weber's *Economy and Society* (The Bedminster Press, Inc., 1968). More recent general contributions to the analysis of total societies as units include Talcott Parsons *Societies: Comparative and Evolutionary Perspectives** (Prentice-Hall, Inc., 1966), and Samuel Klausner, ed., *The Study of Total Societies** (Praeger Publishers, Inc., 1967).

On social morphology, two articles by Norman Ryder stand out as exemplary work on the implications of the concepts of population studies. They are "Notes on the Concept of a Population," *American Journal of Sociology* 69 (March 1964), 451–455, and "The Cohort as a Concept in the Study of Social Change," *American Sociological Review* 30 (December 1965), 843–861. *Population: The Vital Revolution** (Doubleday & Company, Inc.,

Anchor Books, 1965), edited by Ronald Freedman, and *Population and Society* (Houghton Mifflin Company, 1968), edited by Charles B. Nam, are useful collections of papers on current population problems and trends. The foundations for human ecology are laid in Amos Hawley, *Human Ecology* (The Ronald Press Company, 1950). More recently, Hawley has summarized his views in the article on human ecology in the *International Encyclopedia of the Social Sciences* (Vol. 4, 328–337).

On the various process systems of society, the following works are recommended:

Solidarity: The foundations of current discussions of solidarity were established in the late nineteenth century in Ferdinand Toennies' "Community and Society, translated as *Fundamental Concepts of Sociology* (American Book Company, 1940), in Durkheim's *Division of Labor* (op. cit.), and a bit later in Charles Horton Cooley's *Social Organization** (Schocken Books, Inc., 1962). More recently, the sociological imagination has been stimulated by the thought of Edward Shils, especially as it is expressed in "Primordial, Personal, Sacred, and Civil Ties," *British Journal of Sociology* 8 (June 1957). Kinship is the primary institution of solidarity, and the pathbreaking and still-useful comparative study of kinship is George Murdock's *Social Structure** (hardbound: The Macmillan Company, 1949; softbound, The Free Press). Impressive recent studies on the solidarity of communities and societies include Frank Young, *Initiation Ceremonies** (The Bobbs-Merrill Co., Inc., 1965), Guy E. Swanson, *Religion and Regime* (The University of Michigan Press, 1967), and Rosabeth Kanter, "Commitment and Social Organization," *American Sociological Review* 33 (August 1968), 499–517.

Economic Systems: The most systematic attempt to integrate economic theory with the theory of society is found in Talcott Parsons and Neil Smelser's *Economy and Society** (The Free Press, 1956). Gerald Meier's *Leading Issues in Economic Development* (Oxford University Press, 1964) and Gayl Ness' *The Sociology of Economic Development* (Harper & Row, Publishers, 1970) are excellent readers on development; the former is oriented primarily to economic issues, and the latter to sociological issues. The approach to economic integration taken in the present volume is clearly influenced by traditions of thought illustrated by Julius Boeke, in *Economics and Economic Policy of Dual Societies* (Institute of Pacific Relations, 1953), and Gunnar Myrdal, in *Economic Theory and Underdeveloped Regions* (Gerald Duckworth, 1957). On the economic institutions of industrial society, the work by Clark Kerr and his associates, *Industrialism and Industrial Man** (Oxford University Press, 1964), is the basic document.

Political Systems: Students interested in the basic sociological issues in political theory will profit from Leslie Lipson, *The Great Issues of Politics* (Prentice-Hall, Inc., 1965). The functional approach to politics is well stated in Gabriel Almond and G. Bingham Powell, Jr., *Comparative Politics** (Little, Brown and Company, 1966), and the historical approach in an excellent reader edited by Reinhard Bendix, *State and Society* (Little, Brown and Company, 1968). A number of recent collections provide valuable introductions to problems in the institutional organization of politics, most notably Seymour Lipset and Stein Rokkan, *Party Systems and Voter Alignments** (The Free Press, 1967); Joseph La Palombara, *Bureaucracy and Political Development** (Princeton University Press, 1963); and Gabriel Almond and James Coleman, *The Politics of the Developing Areas* (Princeton University Press, 1960). William Kornhauser's *The Politics of Mass Society* (The Free Press, 1959) and Seymour Lipset's *Political Man** (Doubleday & Company, Inc., Anchor Books, 1959) are classics of analysis of the dynamics of politics according to pluralistic theories. The foremost exposition of the monolithic theory of American politics remains *The Power Elite,** by C. Wright Mills (Oxford University Press, 1956).

Cultural Systems: The concept of culture used in this book owes much to Gertrude Jaeger and Philip Selznick, "A Normative Theory of Culture," *American Sociological Review* 21 (October 1964), 653–669. Several older sociological works have informed our understanding of cultural phenomena, most notably Max Weber's *The Sociology of Religion** (Beacon Press, 1964), Pitirim Sorokin's *Social and Cultural Dynamics* (The Bedminster Press Inc., 1941), and Emile Durkheim's *Elementary Forms of the Religious Life** (hardbound: Allen and Unwin, 1915; softbound: The Free Press). Contemporary sociologists have been less interested in cultural phenomena, or at least have been unwilling to treat culture as a generic entity. Notable exceptions can be found; and Guy E. Swanson, *The Birth of the Gods** (The University of Michigan Press, 1960) and *Religion and Regime* (op. cit.), and Robert Bellah, *Tokugawa Religion** (hardbound: The Free Press, 1957; softbound: Beacon Press), are particularly recommended.

On the relations between the subsystems of society, see Talcott Parsons' essays in *Sociological Theory and Modern Society* (The Free Press, 1967). His approach, though criticized in the present volume, still represents the most sophisticated general theory of intersectorial relations. The criticisms of his approach are ultimately founded in the lessons and implications of those accounts of total societies that stress the embedding of all social institutions in one or another unitary process or structure, e.g., Karl Deutsch, *Nationalism and Social Communication** (The M.I.T. Press, 1953), or C. Wright Mills, *The Power Elite* (op. cit.).

On comparative and evolutionary problems, Talcott Parsons, *Societies* (op. cit.), Robert Marsh, *Comparative Sociology* (Harcourt Brace Jovanovich, 1967), and Frank Moore, *Readings in Cross-Cultural Methodology* (Human Relations Area Files, 1961), are recommended general statements. Students interested in exemplary comparative studies of the institutions of large-scale societies will profit from S. N. Eisenstadt, *Political Systems of Empires* (The Free Press, 1962), and Barrington Moore, Jr., *Social Origins of Dictatorship and Democracy** (Beacon Press, 1966).

Index